On Bearing Unbearable States of Mind

Dealing with difficult patients is a problem almost all practising psychoanalysts will face at some time in their career, yet there is little in the existing literature which offers guidance in this important area.

On Bearing Unbearable States of Mind provides clear guidance on how the analyst can encourage a patient to communicate the quality of their often intolerably painful states of mind, and how he/she can interpret these states, using them as a basis for insight and psychic change in the patient. Employing extensive and detailed clinical examples, and addressing important areas of Kleinian theory, the author examines the problems that underlie severe pathology, and shows how meaningful analytic work can take place, even with very disturbed patients.

On Bearing Unbearable States of Mind should be a useful and practical guide for psychoanalysts and psychotherapists, and all those working in psychological settings with severely disturbed patients.

Ruth Riesenberg-Malcolm is a psychoanalyst working in private practice in London.

THE NEW LIBRARY OF PSYCHOANALYSIS
General Editor   Dana Birksted-Breen

The New Library of Psychoanalysis was launched in 1987 in association with the Institute of Psychoanalysis, London. It took over from the International Psychoanalytical Library which published many of the early translations of the works of Freud and the writings of most of the leading British and Continental psychoanalysts.

The purpose of the New Library of Psychoanalysis is to facilitate a greater and more widespread appreciation of psychoanalysis and to provide a forum for increasing mutual understanding between psychoanalysts and those working in other disciplines such as the social sciences, medicine, philosophy, history, linguistics, literature and the arts. It aims to represent different trends both in British psychoanalysis and in psychoanalysis generally. The New Library of Psychoanalysis is well placed to make available to the English-speaking world psychoanalytic writings from other European countries and to increase the interchange of ideas between British and American psychoanalysts.

The Institute, together with the British Psychoanalytical Society, runs a low-fee psychoanalytic clinic, organises lectures and scientific events concerned with psychoanalysis and publishes the *International Journal of Psychoanalysis*. It also runs the only UK training course in psychoanalysis which leads to membership of the International Psychoanalytical Association – the body which preserves internationally agreed standards of training, of professional entry, and of professional ethics and practice for psychoanalysis as initiated and developed by Sigmund Freud. Distinguished members of the Institute have included Michael Balint, Wilfred Bion, Ronald Fairbairn, Anna Freud, Ernest Jones, Melanie Klein, John Rickman and Donald Winnicott.

Previous General Editors include David Tuckett, Elizabeth Spillius and Susan Budd. Previous and current Members of the Advisory Board include Christopher Bollas, Ronald Britton, Catalina Bronstein, Donald Campbell, Sara Flanders, Stephen Grosz, John Keene, Eglé Laufer, Juliet Mitchell, Michael Parsons, Rosine Jozef Perelberg, Richard Rusbridger, David Taylor and Mary Target.

ALSO IN THIS SERIES

Impasse and Interpretation Herbert Rosenfeld
Psychoanalysis and Discourse Patrick Mahony
The Suppressed Madness of Sane Men Marion Milner
The Riddle of Freud Estelle Roith
Thinking, Feeling, and Being Ignacio Matte-Blanco
The Theatre of the Dream Salomon Resnik
Melanie Klein Today: Volume 1, Mainly Theory Edited by Elizabeth Bott Spillius
Melanie Klein Today: Volume 2, Mainly Practice Edited by Elizabeth Bott Spillius
Psychic Equilibrium and Psychic Change: Selected Papers of Betty Joseph Edited by Michael Feldman and Elizabeth Bott Spillius
About Children and Children-No-Longer: Collected Papers 1942–80 Paula Heimann. Edited by Margret Tonnesmann
The Freud–Klein Controversies 1941–45 Edited by Pearl King and Riccardo Steiner
Dream, Phantasy and Art Hanna Segal
Psychic Experience and Problems of Technique Harold Stewart
Clinical Lectures on Klein and Bion Edited by Robin Anderson
From Fetus to Child Alessandra Piontelli
A Psychoanalytic Theory of Infantile Experience: Conceptual and Clinical Reflections E. Gaddini. Edited by Adam Limentani
The Dream Discourse Today Edited and introduced by Sara Flanders
The Gender Conundrum: Contemporary Psychoanalytic Perspectives on Femininity and Masculinity Edited and introduced by Dana Breen
Psychic Retreats John Steiner
The Taming of Solitude: Separation Anxiety in Psychoanalysis Jean-Michel Quinodoz
Unconscious Logic: An Introduction to Matte-Blanco's Bi-logic and Its Uses Eric Rayner
Understanding Mental Objects Meir Perlow
Life, Sex and Death: Selected Writings of William Gillespie Edited and introduced by Michael Sinason
What Do Psychoanalysts Want? The Problem of Aims in Psychoanalytic Therapy Joseph Sandler and Anna Ursula Dreher
Michael Balint: Object Relations, Pure and Applied Harold Stewart
Hope: A Shield in the Economy of Borderline States Anna Potamianou

NEW LIBRARY OF PSYCHOANALYSIS

General editor: Elizabeth Bott Spillius

On Bearing Unbearable States of Mind

Ruth Riesenberg-Malcolm
Edited and introduced by Priscilla Roth

Routledge
Taylor & Francis Group
LONDON AND NEW YORK

First published 1999
by Routledge
27 Church Road, Hove, East Sussex BN3 2FA

Simultaneously published in the USA and Canada
by Routledge
270 Madison Avenue, New York NY 10016

Reprinted in 2000 and 2008

Routledge is an imprint of the Taylor & Francis Group, an Informa business

© 1999 Ruth Riesenberg-Malcolm

Typeset in Bembo by Routledge
Printed and bound in Great Britain by
TJ International, Padstow, Cornwall

All rights reserved. No part of this book may be reprinted or reproduced or utilised in any form or by any electronic, mechanical, or other means, now known or hereafter invented, including photocopying and recording, or in any information storage or retrieval system, without permission in writing from the publishers.

British Library Cataloguing in Publication Data
A catalogue record for this book is available from the
British Library

Library of Congress Cataloging in Publication Data
Riesenberg-Malcolm, Ruth, 1929–
On bearing unbearable states of mind / Ruth Riesenberg-Malcolm
p. cm. (New library of psychoanalysis; 34)
Includes bibliographical references and index
1. Object relations (Psychoanalysis) 2. Holding
(Psychoanalysis) 3. Psychodynamic psychotherapy. I. Title
II. Series
RC489.O25R54 1999
616.89′17–dc21
98–39629
CIP

ISBN 978-0-415-20519-1 (pbk)

Contents

Acknowledgements ix

General introduction 1
PRISCILLA ROTH

Part I: The internal world in the transference

Introduction 11
PRISCILLA ROTH

1 The Mirror: a perverse sexual phantasy in a woman seen as a defence against psychotic breakdown 15

2 Interpretation: the past in the present 38

3 The constitution and operation of the superego 53

4 Construction as reliving history 71

Part II: Defences against anxieties of the depressive position

Introduction 87
PRISCILLA ROTH

5 Self-punishment as defence 93

6 Technical problems in the analysis of a pseudo-compliant patient 113

7 As-if: the phenomenon of not learning 125

8 Hyperbole in hysteria: 'How can we know the dancer from the dance?'	137
9 Pain, sorrow and resolution	150

Part III: Theoretical refinements

Introduction PRISCILLA ROTH	165
10 The three Ws: what, where and when: the rationale of interpretation	168
11 Conceptualisation of clinical facts in the analytic process	181
Notes	194
Bibliography	196
Index	199

Acknowledgements

I want to offer my gratitude to my patients whose material appears in this book and the others who helped me to understand better and to clarify my ideas.

I wish to express my deep gratitude to Priscilla Roth, who has not only edited and introduced this book, but whose discussions and suggestions for several readings of different chapters, and her unconditional support, were invaluable.

I wish to thank Betty Joseph and Hanna Segal, who have read early versions of some papers and made helpful remarks. Also my thanks to Patricia Daniel and Ignes Sodre.

Elizabeth Spillius played a vital role in reading the earliest versions of most of my papers and making very helpful observations. Her friendship and help in editing the book have been of immense value.

I wish to thank my niece Nathalie Malinarich for her invaluable help in keying the manuscript into the computer, adding my continuous corrections and in the final editing of last bits and pieces.

I would also like to thank the following for their permission to reproduce copyright material: *The International Journal of Psycho-Analysis* for 'Technical problems in the analysis of a pseudo-compliant patient' (1981), ' As-if: the phenomenon of not learning' (1981), 'Conceptualisation of clinical facts in the analytic process,' (1994), 'The three Ws: what, where and when: the rationale of interpretation' (1995) and 'How can you know the dancer from the dance: hyperbole in hysteria' (1996); *The International Review of Psycho-Analysis* for 'Interpretation: the past in the present' (1986); the *International Journal of Psychoanalytic Psychotherapy* for 'Expiation as a Defense' (1980–1981); *Psychoanalytic Psychotherapy* for 'The constitution and operation of the super-ego'; *Revista de Psicoanálisis* for 'El espejo: una fantasia perversa en una mujer vista como defensa contra un derrumbe psićotico' (Chapter 1 this volume) (1970); and A.P. Watt Ltd on behalf of Michael B. Yeats for verse VIII of 'Among School Children' from the *Collected Poems of W.B. Yeats*.

To Norman

General introduction
Priscilla Roth

Ruth Riesenberg-Malcolm's work holds an important place among British Kleinian analysts and in several European countries, as well as in her native South America (Chile). She is recognised as an outstanding clinician and teacher. The quality that makes her way of working so special is her extraordinary sensitivity to her patients' feelings and her capacity to find words to describe accurately what they were only just beginning to become aware of. I think this capacity is based on her ability to take into her own mind feelings and thoughts that her patients cannot stand, and to transform them into something more tolerable which the patient can then bear to think about. This is the process which Wilfred Bion describes as 'containment' and which requires what he calls 'reverie', and which, using the model of mother and infant, he defines as 'that state of mind which is open to the reception of any "objects" from the loved object and is therefore capable of reception of the infant's [or patient's] projective identifications whether they are felt by the infant to be good or bad' (1962: 62).

Although well known to her students and colleagues, Riesenberg-Malcolm's published work, which has appeared in a variety of books and journals, is not readily available to all psychoanalysts. This book gathers together most of her published papers in order to make them available to a larger audience. The papers have been updated and in some cases rewritten for this book. They have been grouped by subject rather than chronologically; each of the three resulting parts is preceded by an introduction which discusses the papers in the light of their relevance to the subject and to current Kleinian theory and practice. Part I, 'The internal world in the transference', contains papers which demonstrate particularly well Riesenberg-Malcolm's ability to follow the rapidly changing projections and introjections of her patients from one moment to the next in the analysis. The papers in Part II, 'Defences against anxieties of the depressive position', focus on a number of defensive structures, and Part III, 'Theoretical refinements', contains papers whose focus is the development and use of theory.

Riesenberg-Malcolm's work is firmly within the Freudian-Kleinian tradition. It has as its foundation Klein's particular outlook on 'unconscious phantasy', on 'internal objects', the 'inner world' and on our inherent capacity to relate to objects in external reality and in phantasy. These concepts are interrelated: they refer to Klein's view that from the beginning of life we take our experiences of important figures into our minds, where they are felt to have a forceful reality of their own. They may be experienced as benign, in which case they are felt to support and comfort us, or they may, for example, be felt to be hostile, disappointed or accusing; they then are felt to persecute us. These objects also relate to each other. They may be felt to join together, or to be attacking each other, as, for example if my mother *in my mind* is felt to be jealous of my love for my father *in my mind*. Or they may be felt to be in harmony. This picture of *internal objects*, making up an internal world, grows out of and extends Ferenczi's (1909) description of introjection and Freud's (1916, 1923) and Abraham's (1924) descriptions of the incorporation and internalisation of objects. In Klein's view these internal objects are affected by our relationship with our external objects, but they are not identical to external objects. My picture of someone in my mind can alter, even radically, depending on my state of mind without reference to any actual change in the person in the real world. The character of one's internal objects is therefore assumed to be dependent only partly on the nature of one's external objects: it also depends on the way one projects one's own impulses and qualities into the objects. Klein further assumed that the infant is born with impulses of love, which propel him towards objects and towards internalising good experiences, and of hate, which propel him to attempt to destroy his perception of his own experiences and, particularly, his links with his objects.

It is these *internal objects*, relating to each other and to various aspects of the self, which make up *the inner world* of a person. The quality of these internal relationships is thought to be determined by a variety of factors, including the person's own impulses, his experiences with important external figures, and his varying capacity to feel identified with or supported by benign, loving objects, or at the mercy of internally persecuting experiences.

This *inner world*, consisting of internal objects and different representations of the self in interaction with one another, exists, in Klein's view, in the form of *unconscious phantasies*, which she assumed to be ubiquitous and constantly active in everyone. Unconscious phantasies are the life of the unconscious mind, accompanying and representing experiences. They are primitive and in some cases permanent phantasies which the ego has about itself and its relation to its internal objects, and they become the basis of the structure of the personality. It is these unconscious phantasies, as they manifest themselves in the analytic relationship, that are the focus of Ruth Riesenberg-Malcolm's attention in the papers in this book.

Melanie Klein formulated her theories of mental functioning in terms of infant development; she wrote about the infant's attempts to use the rudimentary capacities of his ego to structure his perceptions of his world, particularly the important figures in his world, first his mother as a part-object, the breast, then his mother as a whole object, but very quickly including his father and siblings. As these ego capacities develop, so, Klein believes, does his way of perceiving, defending against, and understanding reality.

Most contemporary Kleinians tend not to conceptualise their ideas about their patients in terms of actual infant development so closely as Klein did; instead they tend to think about the theories Klein developed as being essential for the understanding of mental functioning in children and adults. What was formulated first as a theory of mental development has become a theory of mind. As the papers in this book show, Riesenberg-Malcolm is always interested in the way her patients use their minds to negate, deny, alter or, sometimes, confront and think about reality. Thus, for example, in her paper 'As-if: the phenomenon of not learning' (Chapter 7), she describes the way her patient denudes analytic interpretations of meaning; the patient hears the interpretations and seems to agree with them, but subtly 'slices' them into such thin 'slivers' of meaning that they are rendered innocuous. Riesenberg-Malcolm speculates about the possible developmental antecedents of her patient's mental manoeuvres, but she is always aware, as she makes clear especially in 'Interpretation: the past in the present' (Chapter 2), and in 'Construction as reliving history' (Chapter 4), that reconstructions of the actual early history of her patients must remain speculative.

Beginning in 1935 with her paper 'Notes on the psycho-genesis of manic-depressive states', Klein progressively outlined two different 'positions': the paranoid-schizoid position, first described in 1946, and the depressive position, first described in 1935 and 1940. The notion of 'position' is important. Though Klein described the process developmentally, her 'positions' can actually be thought of as two different states of mind, each of which is composed of a constellation of anxieties and other feelings, defences, and ways of relating to objects.

The paranoid-schizoid position is, as described by Klein, the infant's first means of structuring his experiences. From birth onwards he is assumed to be capable of and to be pushed by his impulses to relate to objects in reality and in phantasy. He does this from the beginning in order to have and hold on to good experiences and feelings inside himself, and to protect himself and his internal world from bad experiences, internal and external. To this end the small infant is thought to structure his perception of his inner and outer worlds in such a way as to minimise his anxiety: he divides his world into 'good', which he attempts to possess and to be, and 'bad', which he ejects and locates outside himself, in his object. 'Good', for the infant, therefore equals 'me', and is made up of good object/good me; 'bad' equals 'not me' and consists of bad object/bad me. In severely pathological, especially psychotic, states of mind, such bipolar structuring does not take place so clearly; instead one encounters minute fragmentation of both the object and the self.

Such a failure to establish clearly differentiated internal bad and good objects prevents the eventual and gradual integration of good and bad aspects of the self and the object into an object and a self each perceived as more whole, more real and more clearly separate from each other. A number of Kleinian analysts including Bion (1967), Rosenfeld (1965) and Segal (1973), as well as Klein herself (1946, 1957), have explored states of mind in patients in which fragmentation of self and object is a major disturbing factor. Riesenberg-Malcolm's work has added to our understanding of these processes as they appear and can be addressed in analysis. In the papers, 'The Mirror', 'Self-punishment as a defence' and 'Hyperbole in hysteria', among others in this book, she examines the way a patient's mind can become fragmented, how this manifests itself in different ways in analysis, and how the analyst's sensitive understanding and interpretation of the anxieties behind the fragmentation can allow the patient's ego to become more cohesive.

Klein's discovery of the paranoid-schizoid position enabled us to understand the mechanisms of splitting and projection, whereby undesirable aspects of the self are split off and projected into the object. It also began the exploration of the phenomenon of projective identification, although Klein herself never developed this concept beyond her first formulation of it (1946). Its further development came mainly with the work of Wilfred Bion.

Projective identification is a concept which is used to describe a variety of phenomena, but basic to all of them is some confusion of the boundaries between self and object. There are many motives for projective identification, in which split off parts of the self are disowned, projected and attributed to someone else *who is then felt to be characterised or affected by these attributes* ('attributive' projective identification [Britton 1998]); or, and often simultaneously, aspects of the object are experienced as actually belonging to the self ('acquisitive' projective identification [Britton 1998]). Among these motives are to control the object, to acquire its attributes, to protect a good quality, to get rid of a bad quality, to avoid separation. The concept 'projective identification' includes the possibility of a range of responses in the object: Kleinians now use the term not only to describe the process when the projection actually evokes the projected response in the object ('evocatory' or 'realistic' projective identification) but also to describe the process in which the subject's perception of the object is influenced by the projection but the object's thinking and behaviour are not very much affected by the projection.

Following the work of Bion, Kleinians have understood that whatever its motive, projective identification, particularly the splitting off and projection of parts of the self into an object, has the essential function early in life of being the infant's primary means of communication. It is profoundly important for the growth of the individual that these communications are received by an object who contains them well enough for them eventually to be taken back into the subject's personality. If they are not contained by the object they cannot be thought about; they remain not bearable, not comprehensible; they cannot then be taken back and integrated into the subject's ego. This process of projection, containment by the object and re-introjection by the subject is mirrored within the transference–counter-transference relationship in analysis.

Ruth Riesenberg-Malcolm's special capacities in this area are clearly manifested in the work collected in this volume. Each of the papers, whatever its particular theoretical or clinical argument, demonstrates her extraordinary capacity to tolerate and think about extremely painful mental states, particularly the rapidly changing projection of part-objects and parts or fragments of the self. She also demonstrates how she is particularly alert to movement and fluctuation between positions; she describes the way she uses her counter-transference experiences to enable her to understand the quality of the patient's internal object relations. This allows her to be in touch with the nature of her patients' anxieties, particularly when these anxieties are largely paranoid in nature so that they are concerned with protecting the patient's self, or when the patient is disturbed and frightened by anxieties on behalf of his objects, internal and external. In other words, she watches for the patient's fluctuations within the transference between the paranoid-schizoid and the depressive positions.

What is the depressive position? Melanie Klein described the way in which, if the infant has been able to establish a primal differentiation early in life between bad and good experiences, the gradual strengthening of his ego, and of his capacities of perception, plus the good experiences he has, will bring him towards what she called the depressive position. In the depressive position, objects are no longer purely good or purely bad, as they are in the paranoid-schizoid position, but are perceived as containing a more realistic mixture of qualities and functions. The person therefore has more ambivalent feelings towards his objects; someone with whom the person feels angry, even hates, is the same someone whom he loves. Thus in the depressive position feelings of concern and remorse about the loved one begin to arise, because the person comes to realise that the object he hates and wants to attack is also the object he loves. Accepting responsibility for the bad parts of himself, for his aggression, jealousy and envy for example, and accepting the guilt feelings and need to make reparation which follow, are major struggles for the individual as he encounters what Klein describes as depressive anxieties. Equally, the relinquishment of the object, the acceptance that there is a separation between himself and his object, is a primary task in this state of mind.

Klein describes how the fear that, in his frustration or hatred or rage, he has attacked and destroyed his good internal object confronts the infant and later the adult with what can feel like unbearable pain and sadness, and he often fears that his objects have been damaged beyond repair. Against this pain he erects new defences, particularly the manic defences of denial, contempt and triumph. These defences protect him from anxiety and remorse, but, if used excessively, they prevent the integration and deepening of his personality. Part II of this present volume is particularly concerned with Riesenberg-Malcolm's study of the various defences which patients mobilise to protect themselves against the anxieties of the depressive position. Here her work is very much in the tradition of both Betty Joseph (1989), with her emphasis on being in touch with the 'total transference' situation, and John Steiner (1993), with his description of pathological organisations which hold the individual in a 'psychic retreat', defensive against both paranoid-schizoid and depressive anxieties.

It is important to remember that all these processes are assumed to be unconscious; they exist in the form of unconscious phantasies. These unconscious phantasies constantly influence and alter the perception or interpretation of reality, and the converse also holds true: reality impinges on and has an effect on unconscious phantasies. These phantasies express themselves in dreams, in conscious fantasies or daydreams, in behaviour and character, and they powerfully manifest themselves within the transference relationship. In analysis this is our primary way of understanding the nature of the unconscious phantasies which underlie character, behaviour and symptomatology. Containing projections, monitoring minute changes in mood and atmosphere, Riesenberg-Malcolm attends carefully and painstakingly to the movements in the transference and the counter-transference. This allows her to begin to build up a picture of the particular unconscious phantasies, the unique inner world, of her patients.

Riesenberg-Malcolm's technique is also, of course, Kleinian, most of the basic features of which, as Hanna Segal has noted (Spillius 1988: 5), derive closely from Freud: these include a rigorous maintenance of the psychoanalytic setting, an emphasis on the transference as the central focus of analytic interaction along with a belief that the transference situation is active from the beginning of the analysis, an emphasis on transference interpretations as the agent of therapeutic change. She sees all her patients five times a week; all patients use the analytic couch except for periods when they feel unable to do so. But more important than these formal characteristics is the focus on taking in the patients' feelings and moods emotionally, and using analytic understanding to give them new meaning.

The papers which follow have an extraordinary clinical vividness. They demonstrate Ruth Riesenberg-Malcolm's engagement in an active dialogue with her patients, a dialogue which is consistently psychoanalytic and at the same time marked by close emotional contact.

PART I

The internal world in the transference

Introduction
Priscilla Roth

The papers grouped in this section highlight particularly well Riesenberg-Malcolm's sensitive and sophisticated analytic attention to the movements of internal objects, and, along with these, the different parts of the self, within the transference. They are, thus, about splitting and projection. They demonstrate the way she receives and contains confusing projections without either projecting them back at the patient or, equally disturbing for the patient, ignoring them by refusing to recognise their intensity and their disturbing quality.

This is beautifully illustrated by 'The Mirror' paper, the earliest of her papers to be published here. The patient's material is disturbing; it is disconnected, strange and uncomfortable to listen to, both in its content and in its emotional tone. This is an experience familiar to all analysts – when what we listen to seems like undigested, unformulatable bits of experience. We deal with this in various, often defensive ways: we try to ignore our mildly uncomfortable feelings, we try to decode the manifest content of the material, or we assign meaning to one or another of its elements. What Riesenberg-Malcolm did here was, first of all, to trust her own experience of the bitty-ness of the material, her sense of unease, discomfort, however subtle and evanescent it seemed, and to use it to help her understand what the patient has done with her own ego and internal objects. In this way Riesenberg-Malcolm began to understand the patient's anxiety (in this case a fear of curiosity) and the defences the patient used against the anxiety. In Kleinian terms, she split her ego into curious and not curious parts. She herself did not feel curious, but her analyst became intensely curious. The patient had an unconscious phantasy of projecting curiosity into her analyst, and she acted in a way that evoked curiosity in Riesenberg-Malcolm.

This is a basic piece of analytic work, remarkable for its economy, simplicity and effectiveness. It is an example of Bion's description of the maternal conversion of 'beta' to 'alpha' elements: the analyst, as container of disturbing, unthinkable beta elements of experience, transforms them and renders them, modified by thought, into bearable experience (Bion 1967: 90–4). One expects that the effect on the patient would be one of relief; and in fact this patient responded by agreeing with the interpretation and, much more importantly, by being more able to describe her difficulties in a coherent, more direct manner – her own ego functions were now more available to her. She was able to tell her analyst about her dream, which had disturbed her to such an extent that when she woke from it she felt compelled to masturbate while filling her mind with an habitual perverse sexual phantasy.

The analytic work that followed demonstrated the relationship between the acute anxiety which had led to and was manifest in both the dream of the previous night and the state of her mind early in the session, and the way the masturbation phantasy worked to 'cure' the patient temporarily of this anxiety. Throughout the work, the analyst's attitude to her patient is sympathetic. In stark contrast to The Mirror in the patient's phantasy, which represents a non-containing object whose only capacity is a remorseless reflecting back of the self, the analyst becomes a person able to carry out the functions of holding, metabolising, and understanding what her patient has offered her.

The way Riesenberg-Malcolm handles such situations of intense projection can also be seen clearly in an example from 'Interpretation: the past in the present', the second paper in this section. Early in this patient's analysis, Riesenberg-Malcolm had noticed a peculiar 'verbal mannerism' – the patient punctuated her comments to him, and even his own, with a mechanical, seemingly unconscious 'yes'. Riesenberg-Malcolm's interest in the symptom grew as she recognised its persistence and ubiquitousness, and she explored its meaning within the analysis, until she began to understand the relationship between the symptom and important aspects of the patient's object relations. This process of experiencing the patient's projections – however subtle, confusing or disturbing they might be – and understanding them as a communication from the patient of the most pressing aspects of his object relationships, is the cornerstone of her work.

Later in the same paper Riesenberg-Malcolm interpreted the precise way the patient's hurt and angry feelings about being left alone over the weekend transformed his picture of her in his mind, so that he felt her to be an unreliable, untrustworthy person. He felt he had muddled, attacked, and so subjected her to abuse that she would turn her back on him by not understanding him; he believed his attack on her had destroyed his analyst as receptive, containing and thinking and that she would forget how much he needed his analysis. This is an omnipotent belief; the patient could not consider whether or not it was true, he simply 'knew' it to be true. 'The object's separate existence', as Riesenberg-Malcolm says, 'is felt as tantalising. And because of his reaction to this, he feels threatened by the total loss of the good object.'

It should be noticed that Riesenberg-Malcolm's comments to her patient were not limited to here-and-now transference interpretations. Following the patient's material, she made links with his current life situation (for instance his plans and worries about university) and with his past history. But her understanding of these external and historical events came from her understanding of the patient's unconscious phantasies and conflicts which were manifested within the transference relationship.

The two vignettes from this patient's material illuminate each other: what in the earlier session is perceived as a relationship with an emotionally absent mother becomes elaborated and clarified in the later material. The emotionally absent mother is seen to be experienced as tantalising; she offers hope which is itself tantalising, and therefore feels cruel. Riesenberg-Malcolm returns to this theme, the way in which hope can itself seem tantalisingly cruel, in 'Conceptualisation of clinical facts in the analytic process', in Part III of this book.

The third paper in Part I is 'The constitution and operation of the superego'. While the clinical material in this paper illustrates the type of work I have been describing, the paper has been elaborated since its first publication so that its theoretical section is particularly important to note. In this first, theoretical, section Malcolm tackles two important differentiations. In the first place, she discusses ego and superego development, differentiating the one from the other as regards the process of the internalisation of objects in each: here she is describing the earliest internalisations and identifications, and how they affect on the one hand ego development and on the other the development of the superego. Second, Riesenberg-Malcolm addresses the question of the superego's capacity to change: what elements of the superego are fixed and unchangeable, and which elements are responsive to developmental and analytic modification. She discusses Freud's views on ego and superego development, and considers them in relation to Melanie Klein's views. She points out that Klein, like Freud, appeared to contradict herself about the development of these structures, and she (Riesenberg-Malcolm) presents her own view.

The material she describes in this paper illustrates the points she is making and demonstrates again her view of her analytic function as receiving, containing and understanding the projections of the patient, a function she can only fulfil so long as she can differentiate herself from her patient's projections into her. It is particularly interesting to notice that the careful work that she is able to do with the second patient she describes here, work which clearly seems to strengthen his ego functioning and render his superego less harsh, rests on her own conviction about the value of the analysis. She believes her patient felt helped by the first session she describes; she holds onto that belief in the face of the patient's attacks on it and on her. This sturdiness in the face of emotional attack, which includes holding on to or recovering the capacity to think about what is going on, beautifully illustrated by the material, is an essential part of the analyst's function for the patient.

In 'Construction as reliving history', the fourth and last paper of this section, Riesenberg-Malcolm describes her own way of approaching the problem of reconstruction in analysis, and suggests that Klein's theories of infantile development may do away with need for the patient's recollections of his earliest history. If the earliest internalised experiences which colour the personality take place at a pre-verbal stage, then the patient cannot remember in words, but can have what Klein called 'memories in feeling' (Klein 1957: 5) which the patient conveys to the analyst by means of projective identification in the transference. It is these pre-verbal experiences, these 'memories in feeling', that the analyst perceives, and it is then the analyst's task gradually to find ways to describe them verbally to the patient. 'The analyst's sensing of the patient's projective identification is similar to maternal reverie', writes Riesenberg-Malcolm, 'but differs from it insofar as the analyst always requires a *conscious perception and further elaboration of what he has felt*' (my emphasis) to be able to understand it as a communication. This is the use of the counter-transference as a tool to help the analyst perceive and understand the patient's material, but Riesenberg-Malcolm is also emphasising the importance of the conscious work the analyst does to make sense of the patient's communications and to use them to understand the patient's history as it is being re-experienced within the transference. She describes 'an interweaving of threads of history as they are experienced in the analysis, and threads of remembered history' creating 'a new autobiography'.

1
The Mirror
A perverse sexual phantasy in a woman seen as a defence against psychotic breakdown

In this paper I intend to discuss the use of a perversion as a defence against psychosis. I have come to recognise in the material of the patient I shall discuss that her personality could be divided into psychotic and non-psychotic parts in the manner described by Bion (1957). The psychotic parts are encapsulated within a perverse syndrome which allows the rest of the personality to establish some contact with reality and to maintain at least a modicum of normal functioning.

The psychotic state I shall describe consists of a condition in which the internal objects are destroyed and fragmented; the main anxieties are of disintegration. To cope with this situation the perversion has been erected as a protection against breaking into pieces.

History

The patient was forty-two at the beginning of treatment. She is the eldest of three children. The family used to own a shop in a small village in Northern Ireland. The mother attended to the customers while the father manufactured the products which were sold in the shop. When very young the children were expected to help either in the shop or with the housework. The patient describes the mother as weak, very much dominated by her husband and afraid of him. She was concerned about her children's well-being and education but was not very sensitive. The father is said to

---

This paper was first read to a scientific meeting of the British Psycho-Analytical Society in 1970. It was published as 'El espejo: una fantasia sexual perversa en una mujer, vista como defensa contra un derrumbe psicotico', *Revista Psicoanalisis*, 27 (1970): 793–826. It was published in English for the first time in *Melanie Klein Today*, volume 2, edited by Elizabeth Bott Spillius (1988).

have been tyrannical, ill-tempered and rigid. The mother was felt to abandon the children because of the father's demands on her. Father had suffered a mental breakdown in his youth. Life at home was described as gloomy, restricted and isolated. The patient's relationship with her next younger sister, four years younger than the patient, was characterised by intense jealousy and rivalry. With this sister the patient had a homosexual relationship for five years, from when the patient was ten until she was fifteen. The next sister, seven years her junior, has always been her favourite. She is the person she loves most in life, but this is because she feels it to be an exclusive relationship. This sister is unmarried and it sounds as if she is a very isolated person. At school there were innumerable behaviour problems, mainly stealing and lying. The patient had very few friends and remembers it as a very unhappy time. She left school at sixteen against her mother's wishes, got a secretarial training and started work at seventeen. She lasted in the job only for a few weeks and had to leave it because of what appears to have been a paranoid breakdown. Following this she had several jobs, and after the war went overseas to work for an international corporation. During this time she was very promiscuous and eventually had to be brought home after some eighteen months because of a mental breakdown requiring hospitalisation.

On leaving hospital she enrolled at a university to read science. In spite of great difficulties, and having to go to hospital for a short time from university, she managed to get a good degree. After leaving the university she joined a convent as a postulant, remaining there for some months.

She has been unable to work in her own field and has been working as a secretary in a research laboratory for some years, where she seems to be efficient and capable. During the past twenty years her sexual life has consisted exclusively of masturbation with perverse phantasies which have a compulsive character. They take up a large part of the patient's time, during which she either practises them directly or is preoccupied by thoughts about them. 'The Fantasy' (she refers to it by this name) consists of a 'mirror with one-way vision' inside which a number of sexual activities take place. These activities are generally violent, including openly sadistic actions. The experiencing of humiliation is fundamental and must be felt by every participant in the action. The participants often form incestuous couples. They are described as 'a man', 'a mother', 'a father', etc., with no individual or personal characteristics. There are often openly grotesque or bizarre couples. The duration of the intercourse is usually extremely long; the couples are prevented from reaching a state of satisfaction by frequent interruptions. In general the satisfaction that is allowed to them is very meagre, and cruelty is a prevailing factor throughout. In The Fantasy, homosexual activities occur frequently, sometimes parallel with, sometimes simultaneous with, and sometimes consecutive to the heterosexual ones. During The

Fantasy the patient feels that she 'is' or she 'is in' each one of the participating characters.

While these events take place inside The Mirror, outside The Mirror are several onlookers. These onlookers can be 'just people', but more often they are specified as photographers, cameramen, or reporters. The presence of the onlookers outside The Mirror is an essential part of The Fantasy. These spectators are often excited by what they are witnessing inside The Mirror, and they have to put up a struggle against this excitement. If they succumb to it, they become drawn inside The Mirror. Once inside, a partner has to be provided, as unaccompanied persons are not allowed in The Mirror. The number of people from outside The Mirror who are attracted and drawn into it varies. The temptation to succumb to the excitement is always made great for them.

The thesis of this paper is that The Fantasy represents an attempt to reconstruct the parental couple as a means of reconstructing the patient's ego which is otherwise felt to be in bits, like the destroyed parental intercourse contained by her.

The Fantasy and promiscuity

As I have mentioned, The Fantasy 'settled in' in the patient's life some time after a period of intense promiscuity which ended in her first admission to hospital with a breakdown in which she felt unable to cope and had feelings of 'falling to pieces'.

During this promiscuous episode she had drifted from man to man for sexual relations, occasionally perverse, characterised by lack of personal contact with her partners and by an excited childish attitude, tinged with cruelty, and followed by a masochistic reaction. The sadism was often expressed in her thoughts towards the men but was sometimes also expressed directly in her behaviour in an intense and uncontrollable way. For instance on one occasion when asked by a man to masturbate him manually, she got hold of his penis and started banging it up and down and pulling at it with extreme violence, unable to let go in spite of the man's screams of horror and pain.

The breakdown after this episode could, in my view, be explained as the result of the intense projective identification which went on with her different partners. They always contained 'the desire and the wish'. The patient felt sexually cold and had an intense contempt for her partner's excitement. During the sexual relation she felt how humiliating it was for her partner to be prey to such intense desire. Immediately after intercourse she felt humiliated and tried to rationalise this humiliation by the thought that things never worked or developed, or that the man did not love or respect her. The continuous change and drifting from man to man seemed to have been accomplished by intense splitting of herself such that each man came to contain a different part of herself with which she was unable to establish any proper contact, so that in the end she was left in bits, as represented by the different men going off in different directions. Once she had split herself and projected these split-off parts, they seemed to be lost for her, thus leaving her feeling impoverished and unable to re-introject or to bring these parts together, feeling that there was not sufficient core in her with which to do this, and she broke down. Later on she tried to deal with the consequences of this fragmentation by encapsulating the fragments in The Mirror fantasy.

This tendency to disintegrate, as seen in the promiscuous episodes, often seemed to overwhelm the patient. She used various devices to try to cope with it. When things appeared about to overpower her, particularly when at home by herself, she would lock herself into a cupboard as a means of getting inside a concrete container where she could feel a little safer. For a time she entered a convent. By entering the convent she tried to cope with her anxieties not only by finding a safe, restricted container, but also by cutting out sexuality altogether, trying to become part of an idealised asexual world. It is worth noting that her description of her stay at the convent made it clear that the characteristics of that institution did not differ very much in her mind from the cupboard. Both were expected to be solid, with unchangeable borders, but lifeless.

None of these methods of defending herself from madness seemed to work for any length of time; each just helped her out of the immediate situation for a short time. Only the masturbation phantasy has had more lasting effects, and when she has felt that she is falling to bits it has helped her for a longer period of time.

Work situation and The Fantasy

In spite of having a good training in science the patient has never been able to use it directly in her work. Work is the central aspect of her life, but she is completely unable to take any part in the real scientific life of the laboratory where she works; she cannot participate in discussions or use her knowledge in the creative aspects of the work. In her post as laboratory secretary she is constantly witnessing, listening to, and observing the discussions and experimental work being carried on by others. She projects parts of herself in phantasy into the different members of the staff, with whom she then feels identified, managing in this way to believe that she is part of the work being done and at same time that she is not. Thus there is the endless repetition of being an onlooker, the secretary who is only on the periphery of the practical aspects, recording them, reporting about them, while secretly feeling she is the one who has the ideas and does the scientific work, but really being powerless to contribute and to be creative.

In this sense she seems to feed on the excitement of what is going on like the onlookers do in The Fantasy. This excitement, as I have said before, is created not only by her being a permanent outside witness, but mainly by getting, in her mind, into the inside of each member and feeling that she makes them act. This excitement is a substitute for the real thing, as she never participates in the real scientific life of the laboratory, and it is excitement like that of the perversion which is substituted for real life. I should like to emphasise the difference between the patient's work as a secretary, in which she is efficient, doing real work for which she is evidently highly assessed by the people with whom she works, and the scientific work of the laboratory which is much more valued by her than her actual tasks.

The role of the eyes and looking

Long before the patient admitted the existence of The Fantasy in the analysis, the role of the eyes for her had caught my attention. The following material is from a session that took place in about the third month of the analysis, on a Friday.

The patient came into the room giving me an unusually prolonged, penetrating and sustained look; then she lay down. She said she thought that everything would now be all right, because she had it all under control. She proceeded to tell me that while she was trying on a hat in front of a mirror, a hat that was too big for her and kept falling over one eye, she remembered that she had dreamed about putting on a ski hat which was too small for her. The hat had a dark blue and white pattern.

She associated that the colours reminded her of the blue pullover and white skirt that I had been wearing the previous day. She commented that it was funny that the hat in the dream was too small while hers is in fact too big. It actually reminds her of her sister Maria's hat, which *is* too small for her. She recalled a skiing holiday that she had had with Maria. While they were abroad Maria met a man she liked. When they came back home Maria and the man started going out together. She spoke here about her feelings about it: how she could not stand seeing them together, or stand her sister touching her while this friendship lasted, not even touching her by chance, as for instance when sitting in a cinema. She had had to go away from Maria with whom she was living at that time, and shortly afterwards she had had a breakdown. (These last events were already known in the analysis.)

I thought she was telling me about how unbearable jealousy is for her and how she deals with jealous feelings to make them bearable. I interpreted this way of looking at and watching me when she came into the room as her getting into me and then being able to control me, hence her reference that now everything was under control. In this way things are felt to be all right; my weekend, my going out, my relationships with men became controlled by her in her mind. I linked it with the hats, their sizes, and how in the dream she ends by wearing a combination of Maria's hat and my clothes so that she does not have to see her phantasies about my weekend. Through this projective identification she was avoiding being aware of having any phantasies about my weekend. If she had become aware of having such phantasies, she would not have been able to avoid attacking and breaking me up inside herself, which would have resulted in her being unable to stay in touch with a more helpful me in her mind.

The patient remembered that the previous day one of the heads of the research department came late to the laboratory and had brought his girlfriend with him. The patient felt anxious, agitated, and thought that the lateness was due to their having been in bed. She felt that she could not stand having to look at them, and proceeded to lock them out of his laboratory. After doing this she felt much better. My first interpretation had referred mainly to her use of her eyes in the session to get into me and control me, but here she was also letting me know that if she feels she cannot bear to look at an interpretation about my relationships over the weekend, she will stop watching, lock me out, expel me from her mind as she expelled the couple from the man's laboratory. While we were working over this, the patient brought two memories.

The first was that when she was around ten years old, she and her sister Anna (the sister who was four years younger than the patient) witnessed through the window a couple having intercourse in the house next door. A day or two later the two sisters started a homosexual relationship which went on until the patient was fifteen. It consisted of mutual masturbation imitating intercourse. The other memory referred to a period when she was about four years old. She was suffering from eczema. For some days she could not open her eyes on waking. She remembered this with intense horror and acute anxiety.

It appears to me that these two memories help our understanding and illustrate the use the patient made of her eyes as organs of projection and re-introjection. In the first, as she watched the couple she felt that she got into the intercourse, and by projective identification she 'became' one of the partners of the intercourse; she did the same thing in the dream by projecting herself into Maria via her hat and in the session by projecting herself into me. The second example shows what would happen should she be deprived of this means of projection; she would be exposed to the terror of being blind, trapped in an insane world with no way out.

It is the eyes that create the visual image in The Mirror, into which she projects herself and becomes identified with (she 'is' or 'is in') each one of the participants. In The Fantasy the eyes play a similarly central role by 'putting' into The Mirror the participants and their activities. If she cannot use her eyes to be someone else, she is trapped with her own terrifying phantasies in her own mind. It seems that the eyes, as well as having an expelling function, play a unifying part in an attempt to keep things together. What the onlookers see they report and warn about.

Aspects of acting out in the transference, leading to the patient describing the fantasy of 'The Mirror'

At the beginning of her treatment I knew very little about the patient's history and it was very difficult to obtain information from her. Most of the data that slowly emerged in the course of the analysis was obtained through interpretations in the transference of the feelings that she provoked in me and was only later confirmed by her associations. For months I had no knowledge of The Fantasy or any perverse activities of the patient, and I should like to describe how the gradual understanding of her behaviour towards me within the analysis finally brought this central problem to light.

During the first six months of the treatment there evolved very slowly in the sessions a situation in which I was continually submitted to material which was enacted in the transference rather than communicated by words. Often the relation between what she was saying verbally and her actions was very slight and her greatest aim seemed to be to make me curious and excited. Her communications often seemed to invite me to witness something very fascinating, something which she did not express verbally. She spoke about work and details of everyday events. Sometimes she would start something and then break off as if she had never mentioned it. If I questioned her my words were felt as very concrete, and she reacted with excitement and anxiety, sounding confused.

My questions were taken as an indication that I was very curious and that she had succeeded in involving me in whichever situation she seemed to want. For instance, she would announce that she had seen Peter (a physicist in the laboratory): he came into her office – already her way of saying this was such that I found myself wondering about his reason for coming. My curiosity seemed unrelated to what she was saying and to the fact that it was absolutely natural for him to go into the secretary's room. After saying that he came into her room, her voice changed; she started to say something else, interrupted herself and started something different yet again. The feeling it gave me was that something was going on and that I was missing important links. I was getting intrigued and confused. The more she said the more confusing it felt to me, but it did not appear that the patient was confused; on the contrary she seemed to be following a clear line of thought. If I made an attempt to question her (which I quickly learned to avoid) on any aspect she was speaking about, her reaction was very excited both in posture and in voice.

Gradually it began to emerge with more clarity in my mind that I was supposed to be very curious about and excited by *something* that was happening in her. Something in the situation which I was supposed to be witnessing was presented as having fascinating qualities which were meant to act as a temptation to me and to compel me to join in.

This I interpreted in a rather blind way, since I did not know what the situation was or the meaning of the fascination that it was meant to excite in me. However, I was well aware that this was going on.

By the continual interpretation of this behaviour the patient gradually begun to perceive me as an analyst – as trustworthy, and as able to contain these problems without being reduced to acting them out but able to give her the hope of getting some understanding about them. In this sense I had been, without realising it, and without any direct information about The Fantasy, one of the onlookers outside The Mirror. Thus she had tried, during all this time, to drag me inside The Mirror, as she did the onlookers. I was supposed to struggle against this, in spite of the excitement I was meant to feel, but I was unable to understand more than that.

To illustrate this I shall bring extracts from sessions that took place around two weekends immediately before she brought the narrative of The Fantasy into the analysis.

One Monday she arrived looking very strange, a mixture of withdrawn and excited. She started by saying, 'All right I tried to write dreams, it is no good...' Her language sounded very peculiar with prolonged pauses between syllables. She said, '...a dream, Reis-Violet, washed her head, no, it is no good.' My first interpretation, which I cannot recall exactly, referred to her behaviour. She answered it by wringing her hands in a highly theatrical way and saying, in a hoarse voice: 'Oh you! – you – what do you want? – why do you speak like that? – why do you make me suffer, it doesn't matter,' etc. Her way of speaking is very difficult to transcribe because any way of describing it appears to make more sense grammatically than it actually did. But it conveyed very strongly how excited she was. This excitement had a very cruel quality. I felt she was trying to tease me, to make me want to ask questions – and I strongly felt she was trying to provoke my curiosity. I interpreted how her way of speaking was meant to provoke me into questioning her, and that this would be a proof of my being excited by her. I explained that her attitude was meant to make me feel frustrated and curious and that she was getting intense satisfaction from this. I also linked it with feelings and fears she had in relation to the meaning she attached to the weekend and the reversal of roles by projective identification which made me into the curious child. After a while she quietened down and started a repetitive complaining. 'Well...I can do nothing about it, you say I want to make you curious, I can see that, I feel excited, I see what you mean, but that is all that comes into my mind. I cannot do anything about it.' A bit puzzled, I interpreted that she could not allow me to do anything more than describe her behaviour. That was all she took in from my interpretation; she did not take any notice of the more dynamic elements of it (such as the projective identification with parents in intercourse, as related to my weekend, as a reaction to separation, etc.). Then slowly she started to speak in a coherent way.

During the week that followed we were able to continue to explore these themes. For instance, the following Friday she spoke about a Mr X whom she had met and whom she believed to be a friend of mine. She spoke in a kind of broken way, and, as usual on Fridays, it was more difficult to establish contact with her. She reported a dream in which she was carrying a folder from which bits of corpses were falling out. She associated to a previous dream about hiding corpses wrapped in a red skirt of hers, and her mother standing near and looking very sad. The cupboard was the one in which she used to hide her wet panties at home. In that dream her mother had looked like her piano teacher, her expression being the one she remembered the teacher having had once when the patient urinated on the chair during a piano lesson. In summary, my interpretations referred to her feelings when I came into her mind in connection with Mr X, what she did to me inside her with her urine, and how it seemed to drop out as faeces and water. I linked it with the attack on the parents and with masturbation activities, which I also connected with her behaviour in the session.

In the following session, Monday, for the first time, she brought The Fantasy. I think she could tell me about The Fantasy because by now I had been turned in her mind into a 'sane onlooker' in the sense that not only was I felt to have resisted the temptation to be drawn into The Fantasy and to be just a reporter of what was going on, but I had become different from The Fantasy onlookers in the sense that I appeared more capable of bringing modification into the situation, and hence I could be told about The Mirror, its copulating couples forever unsatisfied, and the onlookers threatened with being drawn in.

Fragmentation of the object as a result of the attack on sexuality

Gradually the meaning of The Mirror situation could be elaborated and clarified. The material my patient typically reported on Mondays, both verbally and in her behaviour, could be linked with her feelings that the weekends represented my sexuality; in her mind she made an intense attack on my sexuality and my relationships with others. Because of this attack I was often felt by her at the beginning of the week not only to be no good to her but to be unreal or non-existent. During such times her general way of speaking was very fragmented: it became cold, muttering, sounded distant, was delivered as somehow fluent but made very little sense. It was very difficult to follow her speech and it is difficult to reproduce it convincingly here. It was her tone, her general posture, and her way of pausing that felt more expressive than her actual words. I directed my interpretations mainly to this behaviour in the sessions, in an attempt to establish some contact with her.

In a Monday session immediately after a Christmas break (after approximately eight months of analysis), she began by saying how horrible she felt the holidays to have been, and then spoke about her sister Maria spending some days with her and that she had dreamt about her. (Maria had often stood in the analysis for an ideal asexual mother; when anything happened to contradict this view, as for instance the episode in the cinema, she got very disturbed. The other sister, Anna, was mainly connected with sexuality.)

In the dream she and Maria were in a garden. Through a fence they could see that preparations were being made for a wedding party in a neighbouring garden. She felt that one of them was not invited, although she was not sure about the other. She started walking towards the party, her sister disappeared, and she herself was at the wedding.

Her associations to this dream referred first to her grandmother's garden. She remembered weddings in her home town, events to which her parents often had to go as part of their business, where they did not take her. She usually felt very curious and intensely resentful at being left out. She then spoke about her Aunt V, whom she saw when she went home for the holidays. Maria's staying with her during the holidays went all right and she was helpful to the patient, but it was very bad when she left; she felt like running away and has been running away from herself ever since.

My interpretations of this dream referred first to the holidays and her 'running away' from contact with myself as with Maria on parting. I pointed out how the holidays were felt to be like the wedding in the dream, historically the parental intercourse; when this occurred she felt left out and resentful and rushed to get into it, to go to the wedding and attack it. This made her feel so destructive that the 'helpful' analyst, the asexual Maria in the dream, disappeared and ceased to exist.

At this point the patient remembered that when she was about five years old her family went to Aunt V's wedding, which did actually take place in the garden that she was reminded of by the one in the dream. Her mother was wearing her best dress. When trying to open a bottle of milk to give some to the child, she pushed the cardboard lid into the bottle, spilling the milk over her dress, particularly her blouse, spoiling it forever.

It could be seen from this dream and the associations to it how sex was felt by the patient to spoil the relationship with the mother, not only in the present but in any possible future. It was 'spoilt forever'. The envious attack on the parental union made her feel this union to be so damaging that it destroyed any hope for her. The blouse, the breast, the mother, all were put out of use.

This feeling, that the mother's sexuality spoiled the patient's relationship with her, was re-enacted continually in the transference, mainly in relation to holidays and other interruptions.

During periods in which this kind of conflict and its accompanying behaviour were prevalent, the information that I could gather from her about her life outside the analysis pointed to intense anxieties of falling to bits and a continuous state of terror which made her whole situation very precarious. In working on such material, mainly from her verbal expressions, it became clearer that this type of fragmentation corresponded for the most part to a urinary attack. The patient had suffered all her life from urinary incontinence both by night and by day, the urine being felt by her as very corrosive and used as a weapon. It appeared in her mind, both in memories and in dreams, as powerful and destructive, and one of the things she felt very badly about and had to hide; this was expressed in the dream in which she was hiding the skirt with the bits of corpses in the place where she used to hide her wet panties. Preoccupation with urine also indicates the intense fragmentation of her internal world. This was often felt by the patient to be in a mashed or liquid state. (The terms 'liquefied' and 'liquefying' appeared very often in her dreams.)

To illustrate this I should like to refer to a problem that the patient had for some months with her flat: the roof was in a very bad state with the rain coming through all the time. She felt despairing about this but at the same time could not get herself to have it surveyed for repairs. Analysing her reaction to separations, as described before, gradually allowed the material to evolve and be worked through so as to bring some modification. After some weeks of preoccupation with this flat situation, the patient brought the following dream: *she was in a room similar to the analytic room, but it was connected to another room. A man walked through it into the next room. Then she was alone, and at her side there was a bun of the kind that has cream inside and a top. She pulled the top off and all the contents spilled on to the floor, turning into a mess.* She woke up in a state of anxiety.

My interpretations referred to the man as my partner; when we came together she felt left out and alone. In her anger she tried to pull him out like the top of the bun, turning it into a mess. This partner's penis was confused in her mind with the nipple felt as joining the breast to make a joined couple; by pulling it out she spilled the contents and turned them into a mess. Having understood this, we could then work on her fears of being found out, and the links with the present situation of her difficulties with her flat. Only then could she communicate with the landlord and get the leaking roof mended.

Fragmented state of her internal object

The following dream is from a session some days before a holiday.

She was in Germany. She had to meet a man, Mr Y. Prior to meeting him she went into a big store where she got a 'funny looking' white cream in a glass jar, which she put in her carrier. She thought the cream could be shaving cream and it was presumably for Mr Y. When she came out of the shop she found herself taking a tram. Mr Y was in it, but he was neither sitting nor standing but levitating perpendicularly and she thought perhaps she could hold on to him; she thought he looked like a penis.

On waking up she felt the dream to be terribly funny, and even when reporting it she could not help but laugh. Nevertheless, she said that it also felt as if it had a sinister atmosphere about it.

On associating to the dream she referred to Mr Y as somebody known to have been a Nazi. She considered him good-looking and very attractive, with something in his facial expression that made her wonder how cruel he might be. The cream reminded her of a depilatory that belonged to an aunt of hers with whom she was staying when the news about the first atom bomb came. The cream also reminded her of soaps and other objects made of the remains of people killed in concentration camps. She felt horrified and she recalled that the previous night she had been looking at a book with illustrations of women and children walking into the gas chambers.

My interpretation dealt mainly with her feelings about my holidays, how my leaving her immediately gave rise to a deathly war in her which was directed to the extermination of the Jewish woman analyst. I pointed out to her that the attack was done via the penis, Mr Y, into whom her sadism and destructiveness were projected. By means of this projection, it is the penis in the intercourse, the Nazi man, who distorts the mother-analyst and atomises her into the mashed cream.

Work on the dream revealed how this atomised, destroyed analyst (the mother) was what the patient contained inside her, like the jar of shaving cream that she put into her bag. This destructiveness was felt to have to take place because of the mother's/analyst's sexuality. Although the penis was blamed for this, it was she who took hold of it and used it to attack the mother, because of her relationship with the father.

Secondary fragmentation

Progress in working through such material was very slow, and there was always an immediate setback because of the patient's horror at becoming aware of this situation. The realisation of her sadistic attacks on the analyst made her feel extremely persecuted by guilt and frightened of containing both a very destroyed and destroying internal analyst. She was continually terrified, and suffered from intense hypochondriacal symptoms. These consisted mainly of feeling her inside to be 'wrong'; abdominal pains made her believe that she had a very damaging cancer which had already affected most of her organs. The affected organs, though mainly in the abdomen, could also be her throat, lungs, or mouth, depending very much on the type of attack or introjection that had taken place. For instance, after a particularly ferocious verbal onslaught on me she developed overnight a severe pain in her throat and was convinced that the cancer was there. When her doctor saw her he could not find anything wrong with her, a fact that did not reassure her at all; her fear diminished only after days of interpretive work.

Any little insight achieved could only be held for a very short time, and she would then immediately resort to secondary fragmentation as a defence. During such times, with the increase of her anxieties, her urinary incontinence used to increase too, and she felt that she was 'dripping' all the time. This kind of fragmentation made her feel as if she was in bits and lost, feeling that everything was slipping away from her. The contact with her in the analysis was very tenuous and she felt harassed by anxieties about death.

While analysing this kind of material there occurred a series of dreams, or sensations while half-awake. They were described as looking at newspapers on which the black print felt like incoherent letters which she was completely unable to bring together so as to form a word, let alone sentences. They also often appeared like film newsreels running 'non-stop' in front of her eyes. During these periods it was difficult for her to differentiate between being asleep and being awake.

All dreams or sensations terrified her, and she remembered that this had occurred just before her various hospitalisations. They made her feel horrified and in a state of continuous panic because she could not stop them.

Sometimes the only way for her to deal with these experiences and the terror of them was by resorting to The Fantasy, which she felt helped her to come out of the terror and pull herself together a little. While we were working on this, the following dream occurred.

She was in the station in B. She felt that from there she had to go somewhere, possibly to her analytic session. B also appeared to be Hampstead Tube station (the analysis takes place just two blocks from Hampstead station). It was time for her analysis but she could not move from there. She wanted to communicate with me but she could not remember my name, only some letters came into her mind: 'r − s − c?' They were scattered letters and she felt desperate. Nor could she remember my telephone number; if she recalled some figures, then she could not remember the exchange. She felt she was going to faint and was in a panic. Some very frightening and bizarre-looking buses were there and she wondered whether she should take one. This possible action was regarded with horror.

From this dream it could be seen how trapped she was in this terrible state. To get out of it she had to get in touch with me, but this was prevented by my being turned into unrelated bits inside herself. Should she not be able to contact the analyst − standing for a good object, the breast − she felt she was left to madness, the bizarre bus which she thought she had to get into, and that horrified her. However, to get in touch with an object felt to be more whole, she would have to see what she had done to it.

On interpreting this we were reminded of a previous dream some time ago. In this dream she was at Euston station and had lost a child, then seen as a child part of herself. To find the child she had to go to Golders Green, but to get there she had to go through the Chamber of Horrors at Madame Tussaud's. (Between Euston and Golders Green she had to pass through Hampstead.) She was also reminded that some years ago she went on holiday to B. On the day of her arrival she went to a cinema. On going inside she was overtaken by uncontrollable vomiting which lasted for over twenty-four hours. The doctor who saw her could not find any physical reason for this and advised her to consult her psychiatrist, who had admitted her back into hospital.

The link between the dream, the scattered letters, and the above-mentioned episode could then be seen. In the dream she seemed to have fragmented the internal image of her analyst and expelled it in such a way that she could not remember my name. She was then left in a state of collapse, with nothing to support her and in danger of getting into complete madness, represented by the strange and frightening bus. The newsreels and newspapers represented the expelled fragments of her internal object, now persecuting her from outside, but which she could not bring herself to put together because of the dread of facing what she had done to them: this was the chamber of horrors that the newspapers or newsreels would reveal if the letters made any sense. She was left feeling that the only resource left to her was more fragmentation and bizarre combinations, such as the buses in the dream.

It is worth noting that over a period of time this dream was followed by a series of several dreams on the same lines, in which she became progressively more able to remember the analyst's first name and surname. In that sense it seemed that the pressure from the horror and persecution because of her unconscious attacks on her object must have diminished somewhat, bringing a lessening of this type of fragmentation.

Explanatory attempt

In my view the perverse Fantasy was established as an attempt to 'cure' a state of internal disintegration which arose mainly from the internalisation of a very destroyed intercourse leading to the destruction of the patient's ego. Before discussing these phenomena theoretically, I should like to bring some material which demonstrates the use the patient made of The Fantasy.

In the sessions immediately prior to the one I am going to present, the patient's sister Maria came very much into her thoughts. Maria, who lives out of London, had come to visit her and brought her some of her clothes, but in accepting them the patient had felt like a beggar.

On the previous day the central theme had been a dream in which the sea figured prominently, and by association it had come to represent an ideal relation to the mother.

She started the next session, which was on a Wednesday, by saying that she hated herself, and that on coming here she felt that she would not be able to talk, and that she did not wish to tell me anything. She appeared withdrawn and depressed. She went on to say that this was one of those days when anything she read, thought or did starting with 'ma' sounded immediately to her like masturbation. She sounded a bit dramatic and said 'it is terrible', checked herself and said, 'I am being daft'. Then she said that the picture in the waiting room says Chile but she had always read it as Cheile. She had had a dream which she could not get out of and had had to masturbate, she had started rubbing and this had started off The Fantasy.

She was saying all this in a rather bit-by-bit way, getting high-pitched as she went on, and speaking in a tone that partly suggested anxiety and partly that she was trying to make me curious.

I interpreted how curious she felt about my life, the Chile picture, and how she tried through her way of speaking to make me into the curious child. She said this was true; her tone changed and was more direct; she said that she found it difficult to speak, maybe it was better to start with the dream, as this is what she thought led to The Fantasy which felt so difficult to talk about.

In the dream she was with Maria, in a place like a cinema. There were empty seats at the back and also further forward. Maria walked to the centre of the cinema and chose seats; the patient resented her doing this without consulting her. At this point in the dream a story went through her head, which was 'Men make passes at women in places like this'. It felt exciting. Also, it went on, the passes were at women like herself who were likely to respond to them. At this point the scene changed and it looked more like a theatre with a frosted glass screen on stage. Maria had disappeared and she was sitting with John (a physicist who works at the laboratory) in the front row. Something was happening on the stage. She had no idea what it was but could vaguely see some figures. It also felt like something frightening and could be to do with the sea. Fog or smoke was coming from the back of the place. She felt like pushing with her feet against the screen, but here the whole thing felt very confused to her and the scene changed completely and she was in the school hall: it looked as if it was covered with green linoleum. Her family was there including Anna, but she is not sure about Maria. The headmistress was also present. The green floor covering everything grew. She knew in the dream it could not grow, but it continued to grow as if proliferating. At this point she woke up in a very anxious state; she felt that she couldn't pull herself out of the dream, especially the green growth, and had to masturbate in order to get out of it all.

The Fantasy in the masturbation consisted of The Mirror, inside which there was a man who was tied on to a bench. A girl came in to have intercourse with him. The man couldn't move and she had to lower herself to get his penis. It was all extremely unsatisfactory for the two of them and very humiliating. But they had to do it so as to make a baby, and the girl was going to stay until she made sure that she was pregnant. Then another man came in; the first one must have been homosexual because he started sucking his penis, but couldn't be left without a partner, so a girl was brought into it. Here it stopped. The patient thought she was in all of them but was not quite sure where by the end. During all the time the onlookers were watching but she did not think that they were drawn into the excitement. Associating to this material, she started by saying that the previous evening she went to the cinema and saw a film with Yul Brynner, whom she felt was very attractive because he looked cruel. In relation to Maria choosing the seats, she was reminded that she always wanted Maria to be the one who decided about things, but when she did the patient resented it bitterly. Sitting next to Maria reminded her also of the time when Maria was going out with her boyfriend and the patient had not been able to stand any contact or proximity to Maria as this made her feel unbearably anxious.

John, the man in the dream, is a very anti-establishment person. The school hall is a place she hated. It was there that the headmistress admonished her for stealing. It was in the hall that the school dramatic presentations were performed, but she was not allowed to go and watch them because of the stealing for which she had to be punished. The hall was not green, but the lavatory in her flat is, and, she added, the colour of envy is green. She also associated the thought of 'men making passes' to an event that happened when she was fifteen: a man made a pass at her in a cinema; she had let him do it.

In interpreting I started by pointing out how Maria (looked at in the light of previous material) represented the analyst in a very central position, and how this aroused intense resentment. When I, as Maria, came into her mind associated with a man, she hated it intensely and turned to stories of men making passes at her. At this point Maria-myself, standing for a feeding/caretaking mother, disappeared. She had the man, John, probably a masculine part of herself, based on a faecal phantasy. They joined together in an anti-parents, anti-establishment activity. These were very intense attacks of an anal nature, the fog from behind. She turned the scene on the stage into something very frightening, although it had started by being related to the sea — the expression of an ideal relation to the mother in the previous session — but ended by growing into a lavatory.

This attack in her own mind on the couple, Maria central and with a man, the parents together, made her feel trapped and she had to resort to The Fantasy, which seemed to have as its main aim on this occasion an attempt to reconstruct intercourse for the 'baby' to be made, and it was only when this was felt to be achieved that she could escape from the feeling of being trapped in horror.

This interpretation was given in parts, and with a bit of dialogue. At the end the patient was silent for a moment, looked depressed and spoke in a slow sad voice. She said that she saw what I meant about the dream, and the green was awful, like a cancerous growth. The Fantasy was so humiliating for everyone, with it she could somehow pull herself out of the green and into one piece. Then she said that now when she said the word 'green' what came into her mind was *Viridiana*, a film which she was not able to remember but for one scene. In it the beautiful girl and her cousin had gone out together, and a lot of beggars who had been kindly protected by her invaded the dining room. The beautiful table with its white tablecloth, shining silver, china, and food was assaulted; they made a ghastly mess, spilling and breaking everything, and finally when the girl came back they attempted to rape her. There was also a murder. She said it was awful. She was speaking in a rather anxious voice. She stopped, and said she felt frightened of getting excited.

I summarised the interpretations for her and said how this excitement was in my view an attempt to bypass the 'awfulness' she felt about what she does to me in her mind, as she had done to her parents when she was little.

Discussion

I believe that by establishing the division between the onlookers and The Mirror, it became possible for my patient to make a structuralisation by which the most disturbing aspects became encapsulated, contained in a firmly delineated area, and only then could an attempt to deal with them take place. The main task seemed to be an attempt to reconstruct her internal world as a way of reconstructing her ego by bringing her parents together. The parents, or aspects of them, were represented by the participants in the scenes inside The Mirror.

These couples, as illustrated by the last example, were only allowed to join under intense control and with no freedom whatsoever, because all this was done through mechanisms which allowed her either to be, or to be in, each of the participants in The Fantasy. Because of this she was identified with every participant and took part in each single action that took place, avoiding thus ever being excluded or feeling left out or stimulated by the parents. The parents were controlled or triumphed over by being made to do what she ordered, and also they were constantly humiliated and treated with the greatest contempt. They were robbed of any satisfaction or pleasure and were only allowed to come together just enough to keep the situation (herself, the baby in the example) going. It is of interest to note how in the different variations of The Fantasy no one was ever allowed pleasure of any kind, and the delaying, so much connected with prolonged masturbatory excitement, was used instead of satisfaction.

The central factor prevailing in all this was the cruelty under which these activities in The Fantasy took place. The whole structure, though intended to preserve the patient's ego, which is a minimum requirement for love, was created under such conditions of cruelty, hatred and humiliation that it appeared that her love impulses were suffused by her destructiveness, turning in this way into sadism, which then prevailed over all the activities. It was this sadism that was never properly modified by love; on the contrary, as can be seen, sadism was constantly gratified so that a true integration or an approach to integration never occurred. It seems to me that by this means the problem of having to deal with the diminution and sublimation of sadistic impulses was bypassed and kept static, which in its turn made for the continued repetitiveness of the symptom. Nevertheless, The Fantasy, I think, also constitutes a clear attempt to bring about a cure of the psychotic process, which was achieved to a certain degree by bringing a halt – or pause – to the more fragmenting processes.

I think that in this sense it could be understood in terms of Freud's observations about the relation between delusions and more severe psychotic expressions and the constructions which are built up in the course of an analysis (Freud 1911, 1937).

It is by means of attempting some kind of integration, although in such a bizarre and confined way, that this patient managed, not to be 'normal' or 'ordinary', but somehow not to disintegrate and not to be overtly mad. It would seem that whenever her ego collapsed completely, the feeling was a total loss of coherence – a falling to pieces – followed probably by a massive projection into her outside world, resulting in a paranoid state in which the patient was incapable of contact with reality. Historically this was the main element of her first breakdown.

Through this encapsulation in The Mirror she managed to keep the destruction within certain limits, preventing it from affecting the whole of her personality and allowing other parts of it to resort to less damaging means, permitting them some degree of development and function.

A real improvement would have required a modification of her sadism, which would have allowed some proper reparation to her objects. This had never been achieved prior to her analysis. The bringing together of the parents under the rigid control, lack of freedom, and continuous intrusion by the patient only allowed for a minimum of cohesion so as to prevent her from falling to pieces.

To be able to make real progress from there, she had to face intense pain and frustration in experiencing love for her objects and the consequence of the attacks to which she had submitted them. The horror that this situation produced in the patient tended to make her resort to further fragmentation, this time of a defensive nature, which made for an increase in her state of disintegration, and this could only be stopped by resorting to The Fantasy. The Mirror, as a concrete image within which the encapsulation took place, provided her with borders firmly delineated and stable. In the choice of the device to assist her it is interesting to note that a mirror is an object only capable of reflecting the subject's image and with no other characteristics. It was in this sense the ideal thing into which to project various internal objects, controlling them and allowing them to reflect only what she put into them. The Mirror also represented a breast, but a dead breast whose only function was to act as a concrete container, with solid borders but nothing more. This breast was felt to be hard, cold, and absolutely mechanical, lacking any life of its own to provide the baby with anything in a positive way.

I should like to differentiate this sort of 'containing' from the containing qualities of the breast described by Bion (1962), in that there was no feeling expressed by it or allowed to it; it was meant just to be there, to allow feelings to be put into it and to reflect them, but not to modify them at all, neither by furthering change nor by relieving the intensity of the anxieties.

This conception of the breast seems to contain only one positive aspect, the stability or firmness of its frame, which never seemed to be affected or threatened by change. This aspect seemed to be not only the basis of the breast's functioning but also the means of some development in the phantasy and in the work of the analysis.

Regarding the other aspect of The Fantasy, that is, the onlookers outside The Mirror, they represent the so-called saner parts of the patient. She felt also that she was all the time 'in them'.

It is interesting to note that the patient herself compared them to a 'Greek chorus', as the onlookers very much share their functions. As I had been felt to do at the beginning of the analysis, they appeared to know what had happened and its meaning, and its results, catastrophic or otherwise. But they were powerless to modify events; they could report them but their warning was unheard. When, as often happened, they felt threatened in their very existence as onlookers, the only thing they could do was to struggle against the excitement and curiosity which threatened to pull them into The Mirror.

The number of the onlookers outside The Mirror varied, and gave a measure of greater or lesser availability of the patient's sanity. Should they all be drawn into The Mirror, it would seem to me that the outcome could be an hallucinatory state. However, their existence outside could not be of any modifying help, as they were powerless to change anything at all.

It seems that the onlookers represented partly the patient's superego functions, the reporters of the moral implications of what was happening, and partly ego functions, in the attempt to report about reality which should be perceived and perhaps accepted. But the expression of both appeared to be merely formalistic, devoid of any life, just empty and opaque. In this sense both Mirror and onlookers were represented as dead or almost dead objects, being without life, which is then replaced by the perverse excitement of the events that take place in The Mirror and which are being witnessed by the onlookers.

The excitement was glorified and put above any other feeling. This kept the perversion in place and did not allow any other relationship with real people or objects to develop. In the analytic situation excitement had taken a central place in the patient's expressions; she felt it most of the time and tried to make the analyst feel it.

In this sense, excitement seems to have been a basic defensive response against the envy experienced at the breast and later on towards the parents' intercourse. It seems that for the patient it could be expressed in the following way: 'I am excited and I am alive. Provided they are excited – analyst, breast, parents – they want me, need me, and that's why they come to get it from me.' In the sessions, over and over again I was felt to want to know about her laboratory or flat because of my being excited. Here it can then easily be linked with her promiscuous experience; she felt nothing but arrogant superiority and contempt for her partners because they were the prey of such hot desire and excitement.

Through the exaltation of excitement, the repetitiveness of the situation and the total impoverishment of the patient's life can, I think, be explained.

I would like to add here the role I think intelligence plays. This patient was highly intelligent, but used her intelligence in the elaboration of sophisticated and complicated mechanisms to maintain a state of perverse equilibrium. The price for this equilibrium was that she was unable to use her intelligence in a more constructive way.

In speculating on the possible explanations for this state of affairs in which the anxieties were never modified to a degree which would have made greater integration possible, it seems to me that it can be traced to the relationship between internal factors, mainly primary envy, and a mother as she appeared in the transference who, although externally concerned about her children, lacked real empathy with them. I think the need for a breast to contain, hold, and modify the baby's anxieties was never fulfilled by the mother.

It is worth noting here that the patient had often mentioned the feeling of remembering her mother feeding her siblings and interrupting the sucking, putting the baby down for some moments to attend to customers coming into the shop and resuming the feeding only after she had finished with the customers. The patient felt that this was done under the orders of or intimidation by her father, who always played a dominating role at home. She believed that the same procedure must have taken place with her. This feeling only came into her mind after continuous interpretation in the transference of reactions to what she felt to be interruptions, either real or taken as such, such as my coughing and similar things; while working on such events and the subsequent excitement, the memories mentioned above came into her mind.

This impossible situation, together with the patient's intense envious impulses, seem to have played an important part in preventing the establishment of a relationship with the mother with any degree of security. The combination of these factors must have made the patient perceive the mother (breast) as an unreliable object, desirable, exciting, and tantalising.

With such a precarious relationship to the breast, and when faced with an early awareness of the parental relationship, her reaction of intense hatred led her to attack this relationship and also to the blame it for her deprivation and lack of satisfaction at the breast. It is this very early Oedipal situation and her response to it – the hatred and attack on the parental intercourse – in which she seemed mainly to have become fixated. In my view the father's domination of the mother confirmed and reinforced this pattern. It is interesting to note that this type of pattern has been carried into all the patient's relationships.

As previously mentioned, the attempt to enclose the most disturbing conditions inside The Mirror was made through projective identification.

This omnipotent phantasy was doomed to fail with the return of that which she tried to eliminate or 'imprison' in The Mirror. Projective identification or any other omnipotent mechanism cannot successfully be used to get rid of bits or part of the self, as these cannot be disposed of. The return of what has been projected in this way is felt as an invasion or an intrusion by the rest of the personality, which has then to resort again to violent splitting and projection to deal with the newly created situation, and thus perpetuates the vicious circle which undermines more and more the integration process and brings about such a considerable impoverishment.

The spectators, with their function of sanity, were felt as intruders and were resented by the more ill parts of the patient. These more ill parts then tried to get rid of the healthier spectators by tempting them and turning them into inside participants.

Bringing The Fantasy directly into the analysis was a turning point in this patient's analysis. From that point on we had the possibility of understanding the anxieties coming from her fragmented internal world and the ways she coped or failed to cope with them. The analysis of this helped the patient to gain a sense of integration, and the occurrence of the fantasy diminished, eventually to disappear completely.

Her improvement also brought changes in her external life. She got a greater satisfaction from work and became more able to take part in and enjoy social activities. She met a man with whom she established a lasting relationship. This relationship, though not easy by any means, turned out to be solid and allowed her for the first time in her life to experience emotional and physical closeness. This was a source of great pleasure and security for her. As I learnt years after her analysis, this improvement was sustained and she developed further, especially in the use of her intellectual capacities. In her last dream in the analysis she dreamt that she was going back to visit Northern Ireland, but this time it felt different to her – she had a proper warm coat and a solid pair of walking shoes. I think this dream was an accurate reflection of the improved state of her internal world.

Summary

In this paper I have described a perversion and its function as a defence against psychosis. The aim of this perversion was to encapsulate the most severely psychotic parts of the patient's personality, and once this had been done, to allow certain modifications to occur without any real alteration of sadism. There was no real reparation, and only with great cruelty were such modifications allowed to occur, intended only to prevent the ego from breaking completely into bits.

I have presented some material to illustrate the type of relationship to the breast, and how this has been carried as a basis into an early Oedipal situation, which, under the pressure of intense envious and jealous attack, was being destroyed, introjected in that state, and blamed for the difficulties of the breast relationship.

I have also brought material to show how these aspects were perceived by the patient, the anxieties which they aroused, and the defences used against them.

Finally, I have tried to provide an elaboration and explanation of the underlying meanings of The Fantasy, and have discussed the role of intrapsychic and possible external factors in contributing to the patient's state.

2

Interpretation
The past in the present

The analytic process is a process of communication. The patient communicates his psychic world to the analyst by experiencing it and reliving it in the transference. The analyst communicates to the patient his understanding of this relationship – that is, he interprets the relationship itself with the aim of bringing about psychic change. The transference is an emotional relationship of the patient with the analyst which is experienced in the present, in what is generally called 'the "here-and-now" of the analytic situation'. It is the expression of the patient's past in its multiple transformations.

In this paper I want to make the following points:

1. that by interpreting the transference the analyst is interpreting the patient's past and present simultaneously;
2. that the genesis and resolution of the patient's conflicts can only be reached and achieved by interpreting the patient's relationship to the analyst; and
3. that genetic interpretations, that is, interpretations that refer to the patient's past history, are not the aim of analytic work, but do have the function of providing the patient with a sense of continuity in his life.

This paper was one of four presented to the sixth conference of the European Psychoanalytic Federation on 'Interpretation of the past or the present?' in The Hague, 1985. It was first published in the *International Journal of Psycho-Analysis*, 13 (1986): 433–43, and in Spanish in the *Libro Anual de Psicoanálisis*, volume 2 (1986). It was also published in *Melanie Klein Today*, volume 2, edited by Elizabeth Bott Spillius (1988).

What transference is, its place in analysis and how to understand it, has concerned analysts continually (Sandler 1983). Isaacs (1939), Klein (1952) and Joseph (1985) emphasise that transference should be looked at as a total situation, encompassing all the patient's communications. Recently Gill (1982) argued for the centrality of the transference in the psychoanalytic process, and he also conceived of transference as an amalgam of past and present. His views have been discussed in great detail and argued for and against by writers such as Sandler and Sandler (1984), Steiner (1984), Wallerstein (1984) and others.

Let me first focus briefly on what is being 'transferred' in the transference. Strachey (1934) has described lucidly how 'the neurotic' tends to repeat with each person his old patterns of relating to objects and how the analytic situation, by virtue of the specific behaviour of the analyst, facilitates this repetition as well as the understanding of it. The patient brings into the analysis predominantly his relations to archaic objects which, for different reasons, have not developed. These archaic objects are objects into which, in infancy and childhood, the child has projected great parts of himself; combined with subsequent introjection of the objects plus parts of the child's self. Therefore these archaic internal objects do not necessarily correspond to or much resemble the original external objects; the internal objects are distorted by projection. The patient goes on relating to them in ways similar to those in infancy – that is, they are often perceived either as hostile or idealised. The patient experiences anxiety, against which he uses defensive patterns, and the analyst will be perceived by the patient in the very way he perceived his objects; the patient will react to the analyst accordingly.

Joseph (1985: 447) enlarges and refines our understanding of the transference. She wrote:

> Transference...by definition must include everything that the patient brings into the relationship. What he brings in can best be gauged by our focusing our attention on what is going on within the relationship, and how he is using the analyst, alongside and beyond what he is saying.

I have chosen this quotation from Joseph's paper because it expresses, in my opinion, what should be the centre of the interpretation – that is, the immediate relationship between analyst and patient, with its verbal and non-verbal expressions. This means that the recognition of projective identification is central to the understanding of the analytical material. 'Projective identification' is an unconscious phantasy through which a person projects parts of himself into his object, which is then perceived as affected by that which has been projected. The reasons for projective identification are multiple and beyond the scope of this paper. Whatever the reasons for using this mechanism, it usually contains some elements that the analyst can regard as communication, elements that often cannot be expressed in any other way, perhaps because the experiences and phantasies involved occurred before language had been established, or perhaps because the projection refers to nameless feelings, or perhaps because it repeats a very early infantile experience.

By focusing on what goes on in a relationship one is, of course, referring to both sides of this relationship. The analyst's reactions to the patient's communications play a part in his understanding of the patient. Bion's research (1962) on the impact on the mother of the baby's projections, and her capacity to transform those feelings projected into her by the process which he called 'reverie', opened great insight into the understanding of the counter-transference and the analyst's role of containing the patient – that is, being emotionally affected by the patient and transforming his own reactions into an understanding of the patient.

The patient does not only express himself through words. He also uses actions, and sometimes words and actions. The analyst listens, observes and feels the patient's communications. He scrutinises his own responses to the patient, trying to understand the effect the patient's behaviour has on himself, and he understands this as a communication from the patient (while being aware as much as possible of those responses which come from his own personality). It is this, comprehended in its totality, that is presented to the patient as an interpretation. This interpretation should be verbalised directly and concisely in terms of the present. We describe to the patient what is going on, and we explain why we think it is going on; we allow the relationship to evolve and we try to draw the patient into looking at the relationship.

Generally the patient perceives what we say in (at least) two ways. If it makes sense to him, he may feel relief and think about it. But at the same time, the interpretation interferes with his usual way of reacting and this can either loosen the defences or bring out further defensive behaviour. This continuous shift in the contact of the patient with the analyst – shifts that are provoked by our interpretations – reveals in the analysis, bit by bit, the patient's defensive structure, and we, analyst and patient, can learn how these defences were built up and affected his reactions to his objects. The analyst understands the patient's present relationship to him as a function of the past. Therefore his understanding of the present is the understanding of the patient's past as alive and actual now, in the present.

The changes brought about through interpretation of the transference result in changes in the patient's relationship to his internal objects, and his view of his early family often emerges with greater clarity and realism. By so interpreting, we try to reach towards an emotional awareness in the patient, to resonate in such a way that he can feel and understand our account of what is going on. Only when this has taken place does the linking to the past become meaningful and important. I am speaking of interpreting the past in the present and of integrating this alive past of the transference with the inferred historical past.

In the discussion of the clinical material which follows, I hope to show how by interpreting the transference we are interpreting at one and the same time past and present, and that we do so mainly in the 'here-and-now' of the analytic situation. I will discuss the effect of the interpretations and the movements in the patient that occur in the session, and the reasons why the linking with the inferred past is necessary. I will also speak about modes of verbalisation and refer briefly to the problem of reconstruction.

I will now offer a vignette from an analysis, primarily to show the patient's method of communication and how alive those communications are in the transference. I will also try to show how the interpretation helped the patient to move from repetition towards understanding.

The patient is a very ill young man. Early in his analysis I became aware that very often after I spoke he said 'yes'. Slowly I came to realise that these 'yes's' had a mechanical quality. I also noticed that I myself had spoken, after his yes's, as if nothing had been said. This puzzled me and I became more attentive when he said 'yes'. I had already been somewhat aware that he punctuated his own discourse with 'yes'. For instance, he would say, 'I was reading in the paper – yes – while I was travelling here in the underground'. He would expand on the worrying quality of the news he was reading about, say 'yes', and proceed to his own views on the news.

When he said 'yes' after something I had said to him, it bore no relation whatsoever to what he thought, made of, or felt in relation to what I had said. This would appear in further associations or in occasional direct references. This way of saying yes, which might have been considered a verbal mannerism, impressed itself on my mind. Curiously, at first it made me feel a sense of isolation. Slowly the picture emerged in my mind of a baby crying or trying to communicate something, and being met with a mild, 'Yes, yes, dear', which was an automatic response. From his behaviour and my own reaction, the thought came of a very early relationship with his mother, who, though physically present and, from his account, very devoted to him, seemed mentally to be either absent or incapable of resonating to her baby.

After gradually building a picture of this process in my mind, in a particular session I called his attention to his saying 'yes', to the way he did so after either of us had said something; and I pointed out the unrelatedness of those yes's to what had been spoken. He looked alert, said 'yes' in his usual way, stopped himself, and smiled. Consequently I was able to show him that by those yes's he might without knowing it be trying to reassure me, but that his saying 'yes' to me had no relation to what he felt or thought about what I had said. He was thoughtful, looked responsive, and said 'Strange.' I added that he probably felt me to be vulnerable. He said 'Mmm' – neither doubting nor agreeing. I went on to say that this behaviour towards me seemed also to be taking place inside himself, as if a bit of him were trying to talk about something and another apparently unconnected bit of him, not listening, was soothing him. Later on I told him that there seemed to be in him simultaneously two parallel relationships. In one he had split a part of himself into me and was perceiving me as being in need of reassurance, and himself as having to provide this assurance. At the same time, together with what was going on between us, a part of himself was behaving towards another part of him in the way I have just described. I ended by saying that his lodging a bit of himself in me was done both to get rid of the part of him that felt so unhappy and lonely (a frequent and intense complaint of his) and also to make me know how it feels to be not listened to or understood properly. He looked relaxed and a very broad smile came to his face: a mixture of pleasure and some surprise.

I shall now consider the implications of what I said to the patient. The projective identification process I was describing in him was, in my view, used by him at that moment both as a defence and a communication. He had partially projected into me an infantile aspect of himself while at the same time he was identified with an unresponsive internal object. I suspected that this was an early relationship to his mother, the quality of which had remained frozen in him and separated from other parts of his personality.

I will continue with the session. After my interpretations, he spoke with more warmth in his voice about his hope of being accepted by the university where he had applied for postgraduate work. He expanded a little on what he expected from the course of study, and said that maybe this time he would be able to carry it through, because he was in analysis. This was stated directly and firmly. He returned to talking about the anxiety he had felt when he had attempted to do similar studies in the past. He went into detail, talking both about the coming year and his past problems in the university. (Twice he had had to drop out of a similar course.) While speaking he became progressively more anxious. His way of speaking grew vaguer, the yes's reappeared. He looked dejected and what he said was less coherent than when he had begun to speak.

I said it seemed to me that at first he had felt understood and hopeful about gaining more insight into the strange things in himself, and thus felt more able to cope with the university, but that this hope could not be sustained. He seemed to feel as if he was with someone unresponsive to him, and that hope itself had become tantalising. Following this material and my thinking about it, I was able to show him what was going on, the way the infant in him perceived mother as unresponsive and how sometimes he felt this infant to be in me and sometimes in him.

I have presented this material because I think it gives a picture of how alive the past is in the present and how it affects the analyst. It shows how I was able to use the way it affected me to enhance my understanding of the whole communication, and how I focused the interpretation on the situation immediately present between the patient and myself. In this way I could see the patient's anxieties, the defences that were mobilised, and how the interaction between him and me produced shifts which permitted a view of how his defences operated, and probably how they had originally been built up.

I think that maintaining the focus on the patient's relationship to the analyst permits one to explore in detail the patient's unconscious phantasies. This also forces the analyst to examine closely every issue in relation to himself, which in turn forces the analyst to be emotionally more active, while at the same time remaining, in his behaviour, constant and neutral for the patient. This emotional closeness to the patient, as we all know, can often be very uncomfortable, and the analyst has to be careful not to avoid the discomfort by too quickly explaining the present situation in relation to its probable origin in the past, or by reducing the description to language based on infantile experience.

From what I have been saying, and the brief example, one can see that analysis is an active dialogue. In this dialogue the analyst should, ideally, only communicate verbally to his patient; we also know that this ideal is never completely achieved, since the analyst's tone of voice changes, he moves his body, or he speaks in ways that might communicate more to the patient than he would wish to do. This is inevitable. The analyst should try as far as possible to be alert to such events, and should try to understand the meaning of his own behaviour, as well as the effect it might have had on the patient, and the patient's reaction to it. The analyst needs to distinguish in his reactions what comes from himself and what is provoked by the patient. This should also affect the interpretation. To avoid misunderstanding, I should like to stress that I do not mean that the analyst's involuntary actions are therapeutic in the analysis. On the contrary, they add difficulties to the analytic work, and one should be aware of these so as further to understand and contain the patient.

To summarise: in order for interpretations to be alive and to bring emotional conviction to the patient, they have to be expressed in terms of the immediacy of the relationship to the analyst. On the other hand, the analyst should keep in mind the notion that it is the patient's past that is expressed in his unconscious phantasies. For instance, in the case I have presented, when I started interpreting the yes's, I was examining in my mind the patient's feeling and thinking as an indication of his early relation to his mother. At some point this part should be made explicit for the patient and linked to his actual present experience. I shall return to this later.

I should like to mention here a problem that has occupied analysts for decades, that is, the so-called 'too deep' interpretation.[1] If we agree that interpretations should be made in the emotional heat of the transference situation, as understood by the analyst with the help of the counter-transference, his theoretical background, and his knowledge of the patient, then each correct interpretation is a deep interpretation, since it aims at touching the depths of the patient's feelings. I do not think that the mind of a person is formed of structured layers which we should try to reach one after another.

What are repeated in the transference are conflicts in relation to internal objects. Those conflicts come to light through the patient's shifts in his relationship to the analyst during the session. In these shifts he portrays his anxieties and the defences he puts into action against them. It is this conflict which we interpret when it appears. It is my belief that what has often been described, and feared, as interpretations which are 'too deep', are probably wrong interpretations, in the sense that they derive from theories, often used defensively, rather than being derived from immediate experience.

Now I shall present clinical material and use it to discuss different aspects and problems of interpretation. I will present a complete session from the analysis of the patient I have just been discussing.

Mr A is a young man in his early twenties, exceptionally intelligent and very ill. He is of average height, rather slim, with blond hair and blue eyes. He could be quite handsome, but his appearance and expression change from day to day. He can have an open look and a bright, warm smile. He can also look and dress as a menacing 'punk'. Sometimes he comes to the sessions looking remote and expressionless, but more often he shows anxiety. These striking changes appear from day to day, but are usually not so marked within a session. His immediate reason for seeking analysis was that during the past two years intense anxieties (which he had suffered all his life) had finally prevented him continuing his university studies. He had graduated with one of the best degrees from a prestigious university. Twice he had been accepted for postgraduate work and both times he broke down, suffering from intense anxiety attacks and ideas of reference. If it were not for the devotion of his family in looking after him, he would have been hospitalised.

Among his complaints, a feeling of numbness and of being cut off is very central. He thinks that people can read his mind and that they are talking about him. He oscillates between a grandiose view of himself and a sense of uselessness. Sometimes he fears that he stinks, that he is ugly, and that people are looking at him and thinking 'What is he doing here?' He has never had a relationship with a woman, this being another explicit reason for coming to analysis. His ideal in life is to find the perfect girl. She should be like the heroine of a soap opera, beautiful, intelligent, somehow independent; she should think like he does and be with him always, in the country, where he could work on research with no need to mix socially with other people. He has some friends who appear to like him and seek him out, but he very rarely contacts anybody himself, and often when phoned he feels intruded and imposed upon. From the beginning, in spite of the severity of his problems, I found him amenable to analysis.

Mr A is the elder of two boys. His mother is described as a very fragile, immature person. His maternal grandmother suffers from a severe psychopathology. In the father's family there are several cases of psychosis. Father himself seems to be the strongest and most stable person in the family, and he is a great support to the patient.

The session I wish to present took place in the fourth month of Mr A's analysis. Before starting the analysis he had to wait a term for a vacancy. In the meantime, strongly pushed by his father, he had started a course in education, which he hates. The practical aspect fills him with unbearable anxiety and the training itself bores him, although he likes meeting other students there. At the time of this session he was seriously considering interrupting the training, especially as he would shortly have to start the practical work which would probably prevent him from attending analysis.

Mr A is a person of unusual culture, considering his background. He is well read and has for some time been interested in philosophy. Before his analysis he mainly read existential philosophy but since coming into analysis he has been compulsively buying and reading books on the philosophy of mind. This has been a central theme in the analysis, and has occasionally been spoken of as continuing and substituting for the analysis in my absence. The books and ideas he mentions often make me wonder whether he knows my personal connection with that type of philosophy. Before starting the analysis he knew that I had known a relative of his and that I was South American. In his first session, and often subsequently, he spoke of having 'a Nazi' in himself and daily he speaks of his fear and hatred of President Reagan and Mrs Thatcher. He also hates his maternal grandparents, who are mentioned almost every day, and who seem to have no redeeming qualities.

On the Wednesday of the week preceding the session to be presented, there was a strike of workers on the underground and he phoned me early in the day to tell me he was not coming. That was the first time he had missed a session. When he came the following day, the reason he gave for not having tried to arrange some other means of transport was that this would have proved that analysis was an addiction. He reported on the Thursday that he had been very withdrawn the day before, and, indeed, he was very withdrawn in both the Thursday and Friday sessions. In the latter part of Friday's session he spoke mainly of his desire to go and buy more philosophy books, and said that he planned to spend the whole weekend reading philosophy.

Monday's session[2]

Mr A came in, looking livelier than he had looked the previous week, and he showed some eagerness in his expression when he greeted me at the door. No sooner was he on the couch than he said he had had three dreams, and immediately proceeded to tell me them, one after the other.

First dream. *He dreamed that I, the analyst, was in his house, in his parent's bedroom. I was wearing a nightie and was being very cruel to him. I was teasing him by saying to him that his mother had cancer of the mouth and I was laughing at this. Apparently, it seemed all the time that this was just a tease, that what I said wasn't true. He said that after a short while I left the room and went to the bathroom where I started chatting with his father.* The way he said this last bit had a peculiarly insinuating ring to it that made me think more of 'chatting up' than chatting with.

Second dream. *He was in the United States. There was a horrible woman with two girls. He added that the girls had very long hair and ice-cold eyes. Those girls were wicked and cruel and they had psychic powers. For instance, power to cut a cake with their minds. Later on he added that for some reason the cake seemed to be suspended in the air.* 'Quite peculiar', he said. *The dream went on. Those girls were also rounding up the children in the playground. This was awfully grim;* and he went on repeating and emphasising that they were awful, evil and wicked.

Third dream. *Dave, a friend of his (who is doing the education course with him), phoned to ask the patient if they were still friends. The dream grew vague. Other people were present. The whole scene was happening in an underground train. But instead of going to Chelsea, where he lives, the train turned towards somewhere else. This was very frightening.*

When Mr A had finished narrating the dreams, he said that the previous night he had woken up at 4 a.m. and had written the dreams down. He feared that he would forget them. Then, without a pause, he began talking in a thoughtful way. On Friday he had received a letter from the university informing him that he had been accepted for the postgraduate studies that he had applied for, starting in the next academic year. As soon as he read the letter he began to question whether he wanted it or not. It might have been easier had they rejected him but at the same time this would have made him extremely unhappy.

On Friday he went out to dinner with his parents. His father was worried and did not want him to stop his present studies. His friend Dave had asked him to come on a trip to Europe during the summer vacation. Somewhere at this point he said that the nightgown I was wearing in the dream was like one that his mother had but not the one she was actually wearing during the weekend. He then said that on Saturday night he had gone out with some people from his old university. It was boring. They were, as usual, just drinking beer. He didn't drink too much: only five pints!

He went back to the subject of his education course, his father's attitude to him and to the fact that he does not want to do the next term's practice. He continued along this familiar line. He does not see himself as a teacher. He referred again to the problem of the timetable conflicting with his analysis. Then, sounding very upset, he said that teaching bothered him and then added that if he did not teach he did not know what he would do all day long.

He said that to teach felt to him like supporting the social system of which he disapproves. He then remembered that his friends had said on Saturday that he was an 'armchair socialist'. He added that in a way they were right, since he lives off his father. He felt guilty because of this. And then he remembered that he was feeling guilty, on and off, over the whole weekend. Finally he mumbled something about his not seeing himself doing a nine-to-five job. Then after a brief pause he said that the train in the dream reminded him of a film called *Train to Hell*.

Here I intervened. I said that he felt I was being very cruel in stopping for the weekend. In his mind, I felt like a cake that was out of reach, and it felt as though I were teasing him, as in my 'chatting up' his father in the first dream. I said that he hated wanting something, especially if it was not immediately available. I linked this with his wish for the place at the university to do a doctoral degree and his reaction to the letter. I spoke about the way he dealt with those painful feelings and with his menacing anger; that is, by cutting them off and pushing them out of his mind and lodging them in me. As a consequence of this lodging, he perceived me to be someone like the woman with the girls in the dream: powerful and menacing; and therefore, he did not know today if there was any friendliness left between us or if this would just be a hellish place. At these last remarks, he smiled slightly.

After a short silence he responded warmly to my interpretation. He said that the letter from the tutor at the university was very friendly. He had written that he had enjoyed meeting Mr A at the selection interview and that he was looking forward to their working together. Mr A spoke a bit more about the content of the letter in the same direct way in which he had spoken after my interpretation. But then his tone changed. It became slightly haughty, rather provocative and mocking – almost as if he were teasing me. He continued to speak about the letter, saying, 'Oh, you know the typical things people say in this kind of letter.' In a still more provocative way he said that his father had suggested that he should miss two months of analysis, saying that this could not possibly matter since the analyst also took holidays. These provocative remarks went on a bit longer and then I said I thought that what I had previously said had made sense to him. He responded by saying, 'That is true.' I continued by saying that my having made sense to him was perceived as a friendly contact between us. But that as soon as he felt better, a bit of him became very hostile and started undermining and mocking me, and probably himself. This act of undermining feels like the cancer that cuts into the analysis and into his own feelings; and when he lodges his feelings in me, he also experiences me as having this cancer. That is, he fears that I will not be able to assess properly his need for analysis, as indicated by his remark about his father's comment on the possibility of his skipping two months' analysis.

I will pause here to consider in a rather schematic way the meaning of this material: what I chose to interpret, why I chose it; and the effect of the interpretation on the patient.

I think the three dreams are interconnected and were triggered by the immediate stimuli of the weekend separation, reinforced by the interruption in the previous week. In the first dream he feels his object to be split between a damaged feeding object and a sexual object. He is taunted by my weekend and responds with a destructive biting which is projected into his object, that is now felt to have a cancer of the mouth. The object's separate existence is felt as tantalising to him. And because of his own reaction to this, he feels threatened by a total loss of the good object. A cancer is a fatal illness.

The second dream portrays neatly the tormenting quality of an unavailable object, with increasing conflict between loving and sadistic feelings. As I suggested before, he deals with his problem by cutting. He either cuts off by his withdrawal or he cuts into me with his mockery and then he projects his actions into the object. In the dream the suspended cake is the target of his cutting but the psychic power to cut is felt as belonging to the girls. This is similar to what happened in the first dream, where it was the mother who was said to have cancer of the mouth while in the session he mocked me bitingly.

I think that the third dream points towards the possibility of a more benign response. Thoughts about friendliness re-emerge. He becomes aware of having turned the wrong way, that is, against the object. And he is aware of the frightening consequences of this action, which I think connects with guilt as well as the hellish situation that he has to face.

My interpretation brought a shift in the material. He felt relieved and better. His relief brought an upsurge of envy expressed by sadism. His teasing held a rather veiled sarcasm (he finds it difficult to be directly sarcastic or openly hostile to me but he can be extensively so in a slightly muted way). In this session the sarcasm had a biting, excited quality, and a greedy feeling associated with it.

In interpreting this last shift I reminded him that my previous interpretation had made sense to him and that because it made sense to him it had stimulated his hostility. I also mentioned that he had been pleased by his tutor's letter.

Mr A then spoke of his friend Dave's suggestion that they have a holiday together in the summer. He said that Dave was poor and that travelling with him in Europe would mean having to rough it. He described how exposed he feels in such circumstances, and that having to be social with all kinds of people frightened him very much, adding, 'like what happened to me that time I told you about in Holland'. He then reminded me of how on that occasion his brother had protected him. He talked about these holidays on the Continent which he had taken some years ago with his brother and some friends (all students at the same university). At some point he had parted from them and had returned home while they had gone on to Greece. He finished by saying that Italy, and more especially France, felt 'almost civilised' to him, but the rest he could not face.

I asked him if he spoke French. He looked surprised and said 'Yes.' I said to him that in the analysis we have a common language, when he felt that I understood him and that he could take in what I said. Then we were 'almost civilised'. Whenever, as occurred early in the session, some cruel, hostile bit of him steps in, or something else happens, then he is exposed to incomprehensible feelings which he perceives as dangerous, and he panics.

He said, 'It's like the panic attacks in Holland I have been telling you about. It happened when I was in the red light district and it was not the sex that frightened me. It was the violence.' I linked this with the first dream in which I was in the nightgown and teasing him. I said that when he is faced by sex (me as part of the couple in the first dream) he feels hatred and he perceives me as menacing. He replied, with an expression of puzzlement, 'What you said feels right, but I don't understand why.' I said, 'Because you feel excluded.' He said, 'Yah', and relaxed with a big sigh. After a pause, I did say that perhaps this was how he had felt as a baby, and later on as a child, left in his cot or a playroom: miserable, angry, feeling violent towards his mother, whom he might have felt to be doing something cruelly evil to him by being with his father. I told him that probably when he was an infant this had been felt as the loss of an exclusive relationship with mother, an exclusiveness in which he felt protected. I stressed his need to be protected by these good feelings with mother. I said that he needed to have those old good feelings from when he was very little to protect him when he felt assaulted by 'uncivilised feelings'; that is, hatred, which made him attack when he was not in an exclusive relation, at one with the object. He was thoughtful and silent for a little while, then said that he wondered why the dream had taken place in America.

After a brief pause he returned to the theme of having to rough it, and then in a slightly self-mocking tone said that he is such a socialist but he likes good, comfortable hotels and nice places. Here he made a funny noise that he had made on a few previous occasions in the analysis. In a rather guttural voice, not at all his usual one, he uttered 'Ach', and then went on for a short while on the subject of roughing it and hotels.

His saying 'Ach' had a strong impact on my mind. I sensed that it was central to his communication. I also fleetingly experienced him as someone unknown to me. I asked him if someone in his family said 'Ach'. He reddened a bit and said, 'Yes, my horrible rich grandmother. Why?' (By then I had also remembered an experience he had had when he was in the United States. He had felt utterly helpless, even physically paralysed, so that he had been unable to walk for a while. He had been in a great panic.) I said to him that when he felt limited in the analysis, whether by time (it was nearing the end of the session) or by other people arriving, he finds it rough and feels very powerless, so he quickly turns himself into his grandmother whom he has often described as being anorexic and a kleptomaniac. In this way he does not have to receive from me, but can steal his way into me and have all he wants, a good place, and no socialism; that is, total possession without sharing. However, he then feels himself to be horrible, that is, guilty. He laughed and said, 'Strange', and started talking about Dave. I interrupted and stopped the session.

I hope that I have been able to show with this clinical material the way the analytic session is an active dialogue about a relationship of which the dialogue itself is a part. As I said earlier in this paper, it is the immediacy of the relationship with the analyst which is the focal point of the interpretation. The careful scrutiny of the details of the patient's responses to the interpretation is of central importance. We see from the session how, once he felt understood, my patient reacted both with hope and with envy towards myself as object. The analysis of that reaction unravelled further anxieties connected to incomprehensible states of confusion that were probably the result of his attacks. This in turn permitted us a clearer view of his possessiveness and of the mechanisms he uses to avoid both the awareness of his possessiveness and the conflict he experiences by wanting an object, feeling separate from it, and having to share it. His solution to this conflict is to become the object, which at that moment is a rich, anorexic kleptomaniac, and thus, someone who has everything and needs nothing.

This solution made him feel guilty, and then the analysis began to focus on those guilt feelings.

As I have shown, most of my interpretations focused on his relationship with me. The person of the analyst comes to stand for the internal object through which the conflicts are experienced. Throughout this session, I thought he experienced me in a maternal role. When my interpretation about this was heard and felt by the patient, I could branch out into explorations of other aspects of the material. Some of these can be seen in the material, but for the sake of brevity I have had to condense much of what went on. It can still be seen, however, that not everything was interpretation. I made comments and asked direct questions. In this last, of course, I depended on my judgement of the nature of the contact with him.

The way I spoke was direct and ordinary. Some of the patient's material, especially his dreams, had a powerful evocative quality, bringing to my mind imagery of earlier infantile relationships, but, as can be seen, I did not express my interpretations in terms of the archaic experience. I think that using a language derived from the archaic experience (which has sometimes been called 'symbolic language'), creates a number of problems. First, it employs repetitive words, on the meaning of which both patient and analyst believe there is mutual understanding but which in fact lose the quality of specificity which should belong to each element of the session. Therefore, these terms stand in the way of further exploration of the material in the transference. Second, it is an artificial language that hinders ordinary communication and renders itself open to idealisation. My third (and most important) objection relates to my earlier remarks on so-called 'too deep' interpretations. Using symbolic language bypasses the depths of the transference experience. It destroys the live contact between analyst and patient and turns the analysis into *talking about* unconscious phantasies, rather than experiencing them in their crude impact.

My last point concerns the linking of the interpretation of the present to the historical past. I think that the main reason for doing this is that, by connecting the historical past with the past as it appears in the transference, we enable our patients to gain a sense of the continuity of their lives. By analysing the past in the present, the ego of the patient becomes more integrated and therefore stronger.

By linking the interpretations to the historical past we also allow the patient to distance himself both from the immediacy of his experience and from the closeness to the analyst. The distancing from his own immediate experience helps the patient to gain perspective on his problems and stimulates his thinking about his own ways of viewing the past. The distancing from the immediacy of the relationship to the analyst allows the patient at moments to view his analyst as separate and different from his internal object, as someone with whom he is working out his problems. But in order for the links to the inferred historical past to be useful, they can be made only when the patient has experienced and understood the past situation in the present. It will be noticed that I have mainly used the expression 'linking to the past' rather than 'reconstruction'.[3] I think that the real work of reconstruction goes on in the transference. The patient, by repeating with us again and again his problems with his internal objects, portrays in the analysis the way that his relationship with those objects evolved. The interpretations mobilise defences which correspond to the old defences used in infancy and childhood. The understanding of those defences is formulated in new interpretations. Those interpretations form the actual reconstruction. It is only here that the patient understands his own past and his relation to his real external objects.

When the analyst interprets the present the patient will often remember scenes from the past, incidents that occurred with different people, or he will narrate episodes of the past. The interpretations of the present are more definite and precise than those which link to the patient's history, which I think should be done in a way that is loose enough to allow the patient himself to provide more precise connections with his own past. As we interpret the present, the patient's relationships to his internal objects change, revealing bit by bit under our very eyes how those relationships were built up. And as I have been emphasising, those changes are achieved by interpreting past and present at one and the same time.

Summary

In this paper I maintain, and illustrate clinically, the point that the analyst, by analysing the transference, is analysing past and present at the same time.

Following the Kleinian understanding of the internal object relationships, and using case material to illustrate my point, I support the view that the past is alive in the present, and that transference is an alloy of past and present. By understanding and interpreting the transference the analyst deals with the patient's early conflicts, which can only be understood and resolved when lived through in the present with the analyst.

I argue that the work of reconstruction is done in the analysis of the transference, and that references to the past have an important linking value for the patient, in that they help him to get a sense of continuity in his life which helps him toward integration.

I also discuss the level of interpretations and the language in which I think they should be expressed.

3

The constitution and operation of the superego

I will try to explain the history of the development of the superego, which I take to be the history of the evolution of internal objects from birth through infancy and childhood. I will first emphasise those aspects of the objects that do not ever become totally altered by further development, but remain forever as part of the personality. I will present two examples. In the first one I shall present a fragment of the beginning of an analysis to show how in that patient her objects had not changed and then I will describe three sessions of another patient to show how the objects changed in the sessions.

Freud considered superego formation to be mainly the result of the resolution and demolition of the Oedipus Complex. He thought the ego was formed earlier than the superego. Freud was aware of the role which early identifications as well as Oedipal phenomena play in the formation of the superego. In *The Ego and the Id* he says:

> the effect of the identifications made in earliest childhood will be general and lasting. This leads us back to the origin of the ego ideal; for behind there lies hidden an individual's first and most important identification, his identification with the father in his own prehistory [in a footnote he adds that perhaps it would be safer to add with the 'parents'].
>
> (31)

He describes this early identification as 'apparently...not a consequence of an object cathexes...and it takes place earlier than object cathexes'. He adds

---

This paper was a contribution to a symposium on 'The superego' held on 21 March 1984 at the Institute of Psycho-Analysis, London. A different version of this paper was first published in the *International Journal of Psychoanalytic Psychotherapy*, volume 3 (1988): 149–55.

'But the object-choices belonging to the first sexual period and relating to the father and mother seem normally to find their outcome in an identification of this kind, and would reinforce the primary one' (1923–7: 31). Though Freud clearly expresses the importance of these early identifications, he does not explicitly link them to the character of the superego.

In his paper, 'The nature of the therapeutic action of psycho-analysis' (1934), Strachey calls attention to the central role of the superego in the therapeutic process as well as in therapeutic achievements and suggests that when Freud said that 'a favourable change in the patient is made possible by alterations in the ego' he was referring to that part of the ego he subsequently separated into the superego.

Strachey was familiar with and influenced by Klein's work when he wrote this paper. He noted the importance of projection and introjection in the development of individuals, and he accepted the idea that 'internal objects' are the bases of the 'superego'; in his paper he uses these terms interchangeably. Though he refers to the different views of Klein and Freud about the origins of the superego, he agrees with them both that superego formation ends with the onset of latency and becomes fixed by then. In his paper his main interest is not in the evolution of the superego in the child, but in how it can alter in psychoanalytic treatment.

Strachey maintains that it is the internal objects or superego that have to change if any lasting progress in the patient is to be achieved. He stresses the fact that each new relation in the neurotic is based on an archaic object-relation pattern, which perpetuates the neurotic vicious circle. He postulates that when introjected in analysis, because of the peculiarities of the analytic circumstances and his special behaviour, the analyst will remain in part separated from the rest of the superego, and will form what Strachey calls an auxiliary superego. Its 'advice to the ego' will be realistically based, and will help to change the original superego, making it less sadistic and allowing for further development.

One of Klein's great contributions to the psychoanalytic theory of mind was her idea that the infant relates to an object, originally the mother, from birth onwards. With this idea she brings a whole different view of mental development. For Freud an object comes into (mental) existence only after 'repeated situations of satisfaction have created an object out of the mother' (1926). Klein differed from Freud in thinking that the object (the mother) exists for the baby from the beginning of life and that the baby relates to it. For this capacity to relate the baby is born with an elementary ego. Though this appears to be fundamentally different from Freud's ideas, there are indications in some of his writings that he conceived of an early ego or ego nuclei (1915, 1920). Following Freud, Klein assumed that the infant is born with two instinctual drives, for life and for death, which are active and instrumental in the infant's development as well as in the way he relates to his mother, therefore laying the foundations for the internal world. The conflict between the two instincts is felt as anxiety. The predominance at any moment of one or the other force will determine the quality of the baby's experience, and the mother's ministrations to her baby will of course influence this quality. A feeling derived from a loving impulse will be experienced as good and satisfying and the object will be felt as good, while a feeling derived from a hostile impulse (derived from the death instinct) will be felt as painfully persecuting, persecution felt to come from a bad object.

Klein's conception that psychically as well as physically a relationship between baby and mother exists from birth has centred our understanding of mental phenomena on what is always an interaction between people: at first, mother and child, increased later by father and other members of the immediate family. Impulses, anxieties, feelings, defences, and their results always exist in a relationship, externally or internally. They have no meaning in isolation.

In Klein's view a baby at first feels a pain, a gratification, hunger, and so on, as being caused by the mother. As soon as he has his first contact with his mother, it is with her or through her that the infant feels everything. It is the relation to the object which centres the experience and it is the instinctual drive which gives it its character.

To understand how ego and superego are thought to develop, I will first describe briefly the state of affairs at a very early period and will describe as well the main mental mechanisms that are active from the beginning. First it is important to mention that in Klein's view introjection and projection operate from the start. Babies tend to spit things out or take them in mentally as well as physically. Objects are constantly mentally projected into and introjected, which makes the baby perceive the object as coloured by the feelings that he has projected into it (projective identification). This means in turn that the object is internalised not as it really is but as it is felt to be. Since feelings do not operate in a vacuum, what is projected is a part of the self which feels those feelings. This operates as well for introjections, since what is taken in is mother, or the part of mother that has been perceived, and it gets installed in the child's mind, creating the basis of his inner world. Together with introjection and projection a third mechanism is assumed to operate: splitting. To protect himself from anxiety produced by the conflict created by the coexistence of both instincts, the baby has to split himself and his object, to keep apart good from bad, love from hate. This splitting is fundamental to development because it organises the baby's (chaotic) functioning, it divides in his mind the quality of his object. The one perceived and taken in when felt to be gratifying is perceived as good, or, at first, since feelings are absolute, it is 'superb', that is, ideal, while in frustration, pain or hatred, the object is felt as bad or totally persecuting. So the internal world begins from early on to become populated by all kinds of objects. When objects are felt to be good they protect the self and permit the accretion of good experiences, which in turn promote growth.

Together with this primary splitting used both as defence and, as I said, as an organising factor, the baby splits in many other ways and for many different reasons, that is, he splits himself to be able to project unwanted feelings (parts) of himself. He can use splitting as a hostile attack on the object, resulting in the phantasy of the object being split in bits. What I wish to emphasise here is that whatever the infant's reasons for splitting parts of the self and for projecting some of these split-off parts into the mother, these split-off parts contain the possibility of being understood by the mother. This will depend on the mother's capacity to make sense of her baby's communications and on the baby's constitutional endowment. This constitutional endowment will affect his mother's understanding of her baby. It may help, it may make it more difficult, or it may even prevent this understanding taking place.

Because of what is projected into the objects when they are introjected in the first months of life, they form a conglomerate of extremely fantastic entities: horrific, dangerous blissful, marvellous, etc., depending on the predominant feeling with which they are perceived and taken in by the infant. Though the external object is the mother, the combination of multiple introjections, as well as splitting processes, makes for the existence of many internal objects, apparently at first unconnected from one another. Since these objects are not yet connected, the experiences with them are felt to be 'ever present', that is, timeless. What is 'ideal' is there for as long as it lasts, to be replaced by what is persecuting, with no continuity or reference to the previous state. It is assumed that at first there is no notion of space and, therefore, of time: there is no memory, no awareness of anticipation.

The introjection of objects that starts from the first introjection and forms this conglomerate of internal objects which I have described leads to the formation of a multiplicity of separate introjections of experiences of the baby with its mother, and they eventually (if all goes well) tend to fuse into one another to form the superego. At this time child and object become more integrated, and the inner world becomes more coherent. The assimilation into the self of these more integrated introjects adds to the construction of the ego, that is the 'organ' through which the individual functions. The introjection of bad objects has a different effect in the formation of the ego. Since bad experiences produce anxiety, the ego has to split itself to get rid of the bad feelings; such splitting makes it weaker. If such anxieties and splitting are too intense, impossible to bear, symptoms often result.

As I said before, for Freud the ego does not appear to exist at the beginning of life, and I would agree with Laplanche and Pontalis when they say that 'the idea of the genesis of the ego [in Freud's work] is laden with ambiguity' (1973: 140). In *The Ego and the Id* Freud says: 'It is easy to see that the ego is that part of the id which has been modified by the direct influence of the external world' (25); but, as I have already mentioned, in the same work Freud speaks of the ego as deriving from early identifications, and he also is explicit that its energy derives from drives (that is, the id). Returning to Laplanche and Pontalis' summary of Freud's concepts in their chapter on the ego, they say 'it becomes an internal formation originating from certain privileged perceptions which derived not from the external world in general, but specifically from the interhuman world' (1973: 142).

Following Laplanche and Pontalis' statement, I will turn now to what I said earlier, that is, to the view that it is the introjection of experiences with the original object that goes into the formation of the ego. In my view the formation of the ego depends on the assimilation of the object's qualities into the self. Mother's feeding, her understanding, her thinking, etc., are not only introjected into the inner world as separate objects, but the qualities of the maternal function are also assimilated as such into the ego. But, as I have stated, they are also internalised and remain as objects, and this internalisation of objects begins the building up of the internal world. These early introjected objects, persecuting and ideal, form the basis of the superego, and will go on relating to the ego. One could say that the internalisation of objects yields three interrelated outcomes:

(a) the assimilation of the qualities of the object, a process that adds to the construction of the ego;
(b) a normative, protective or punitive relationship of the introjected objects towards the ego;
(c) a benign or ego syntonic relationship that allows an independent existence of these internal objects in a friendly attitude towards the self.

Klein differed from Freud, both in the date of the origin of the formation of the superego, and in the nature of the objects that form it. For Klein, the superego begins to form from birth. Freud says that the superego derives from the introjection and identification with the real parents, while Klein says that the objects introjected are highly coloured by the child's projections, and contain his feelings. Hostile feelings projected into the mother turn her into a terrifying and persecuting object which, when internalised to form the core of the superego, are responsible for its harshness and cruelty. Good feelings experienced at the beginning of life as ideal are also projected into the mother; this accounts first for the idealisation of the mother and can lead to an idealised ego.

I think it of great interest to observe that Freud sensed this fact, but did not seem to understand how it took place. He says in *Civilization and its Discontents*:

> His aggressiveness is introjected, internalized; it is, in point of fact, sent back to where it came from – that is, it is directed towards his own ego. There it is taken over by a portion of the ego, which sets itself over against the rest of the ego as super-ego, and which now in the form 'conscience' is ready to put into action against the ego the same harsh aggressiveness that the ego would have liked to satisfy upon other, extraneous individuals.
>
> (Freud 1930: 123)

In my view, the understanding of projective and introjective identification, that is, the projection of the attacking aspects of the infant and their subsequent re-introjection in the very early months of life, permits us to enrich Freud's formulation by enabling us to understand how the ego actually has already experienced and expressed this aggressiveness towards an object, and how this object, containing the aggression, has become internal rather than external.

Melanie Klein called these very early, disconnected and highly distorted objects the 'foundations of the superego'. In most of her writings Klein expressed the view that all internal objects, however terrifying, form part of the superego. In her early papers especially, she expresses the view that the hallmark of the superego is the terrifying, persecuting objects. According to Klein, in early life the superego has an extreme harshness and cruelty, usually very different from the actual parents, due to the extreme nature of the feelings that the infant has projected into his objects; Klein's view was that with repetitive good experiences over time, the projections are withdrawn and the nature of the objects changes. But in 1958 in her paper 'On the development of mental functioning', she seems to contradict herself. While discussing the states of instinctual fusion by which the superego is formed, she says:

> but under the stress of acute anxiety they [I think she refers to the most destructive objects, possibly ones that cannot be assimilated] and other terrifying figures, are split off in a manner different from that by which the superego is formed, and are relegated to the deeper layers of the unconscious.

This is a puzzling contradiction which she never clarified. The way I understand this remark is that very primitive emotions, especially, but not exclusively, negative ones, can never be totally modified; their severity being possibly due to constitutional factors or a mixture of constitutive and extremely unfortunate negative experiences. I think that through many mergers such archaic phantasies can be considerably transformed, but they leave a mark or trace which remains forever a potentiality or disposition that may be partially reactivated. The 'deep unconscious' that Klein speaks about is for me the core of the internal objects, that is, of that specific kind of superego. My own view corresponds to Bion's ideas as expressed in 'Differentiation of the psychotic from the non-psychotic personalities' (1957). There are cases in which the basis of psychotic illness derives primarily from the baby's constitutional endowment, which makes it impossible for the mother to process and modify it (however he also takes account of the double aspect of nature and nurture). I am referring to something so destructive and eviscerating in the infant's reaction to his object that when his projections are re-introjected they leave a trace that really can never be completely modified. I believe that Bion's (1962) description of the kind of superego that results from the operation of minus K describes this very primitive (possibly only partially or very partially changeable) superego that results from the constitutional strength of the death instinct, and the reactions to it, taking the form of hatred and destructiveness which denudes the baby/mother relationship of any positive feature, leaving it just as a negative 'anti' experience.

Though in her paper Klein only speaks of the most terrifying objects, and we know that the idealised ones tend to integrate more easily with each other, and to be modified into less ideal, more ordinary, that is good objects, nevertheless I think that when the early objects are so terrifying, their idealised counterpart is so extreme and so precariously maintained that they too leave a certain permanent trace in the core of the objects, that is, the ego-ideal.

Freud talked about the ego-ideal and the conscience in many papers before he finally linked both concepts into one, 'the superego'. This superego included prohibitions and punishments as well as aspirations, such as 'you should or should not be like this or that'. Though I think the difference between the concepts of conscience and ego-ideal can be quite tenuous, I believe there is a difference. It seems to me that the punitive and cruel aspects of the superego derive from the very early *terrifying* introjects, while the ego-ideal or ideal ego, if one could call it that, derives from a vestige left by the very early idealised objects.

So far I have been speaking about the formation and constitution of the superego as derived from the internal objects and their evolution. I have referred to these as being one and the same thing; in other words I consider the internal world to consist of the ego and the internal objects or superego. In his 1934 paper, Strachey also uses the concepts of superego and internal objects interchangeably.

An important question remains to be addressed, however, when we consider that internal objects, differentiated from the ego, are often not subjectively associated with superego functioning. Does this suggest that there may, in fact, be internal objects which do not form part of the superego?

Attempts to answer this question must, of course, remain as metapsychological speculation. My own clinical experience, observation and theoretical position lead me to the view that it is most useful to regard all internal objects as constituent parts of the superego. There can be little problem in seeing very early internal objects, or pathological expressions of conflicts between internal objects, as contributing to the early superego; they attack, persecute or are excessively laudatory. There may be more difficulty assessing the role and location of internal objects once mental growth and greater cohesion have begun to be established. I would suggest that as maturational processes take place, internal objects remain as the remnants of early introjected relationships and that they continue to exist in the mind, relating amongst themselves and to the ego. When these internal relationships are not in serious conflict either amongst themselves or with the ego, they remain unconscious, parts of our mental being, reflected in moods, ways of thinking and states of mind throughout our lives.

Internal objects described in this way appear to be ego syntonic. Another way of describing this situation is to say that ego and superego are functioning harmoniously. It is at moments when an internal conflict is felt to take on a moralising quality, that the internal objects are experienced in more familiarly superego way: they moralise, admonish, condemn, attack, persecute, or, under other circumstances, become over-praising or laudatory, they idealise the ego.

Freud and Klein (and with them most analysts) see the superego as a definite aspect of the personality; I have no quarrel with this description. Freud links superego formation mainly but not totally to the resolution of the Oedipus complex. Klein also sees the influence of Oedipal conflicts in superego formation, but sees such conflicts as occurring much earlier in infantile development than did Freud, and she eventually linked the origins of superego formation to the introjections of the earliest experiences with the primary object. Most Kleinians think of the superego as a particular function of those internal objects. I personally believe that *all* internal objects operate as the superego. When all goes well in life these objects and the ego seem to be functioning in harmony and a reasonably benign state of mind predominates. But when there are problems of any kind these are experienced as conflicts between the ego and the internal objects. And following Strachey once again, lasting change in our patients can only be achieved by change in their internal objects.

Before proceeding with the description of the evolution of internal objects into their more integrated state, I will present a case that illustrates a situation in which the object did *not* change through a patient's life previous to her analysis, it seemed to have remained undigested and active in the patient's mind, keeping her trapped in a nightmare state, in spite of the fact that many other areas of her personality did evolve. This is a vignette from an analysis that finished a long time ago. I hope to show through this material the fixed unchangeability of certain early experiences and the relentless way in which it expressed itself, together with the total lack of integration of it with any other sorts of experience in which change had occurred.

Clinical material

Dr X, a young endocrinologist, an unmarried mother of two, came to analysis because she felt herself to be on the verge of collapse. She suffered from extreme anxiety. In the initial assessment interview she complained at length about her life, but her complaints were vague, conveying very little substance. And though she thought herself attractive and very intelligent, she lacked friends and felt that people in the hospital where she worked were hostile to her and disliked her. She oscillated between grandiose aspirations and intense feelings of being worthless. She perceived relatives and acquaintances as both intrusive and mean.

Shortly after starting analysis, when I knew almost nothing about her, she began complaining that I criticised, scolded and shouted at her. She began to scream at me in an almost incomprehensible way. At times, what she shouted sounded like gibberish, and even when the words had meaning the sentences seemed to have none. She screamed at the top of her voice for almost fifty minutes, day after day. As far as I could make sense of what she said, she complained that I was shouting at her and 'pushing' her. At first I felt frightened and bewildered. This was followed by a mixture of irritation, puzzlement and sorrow for her. Guided by her behaviour and my own feelings, I tried after a time to convey to her that we seemed to be in a situation in which on the one hand she seemed to be bombarded by me whilst, at the same time, she wanted to convey something to me but felt me to be walled off from any communication from her. Sometimes these interpretations seemed to bring some relief to her. She seemed to feel better, spoke in a different manner, and there was a certain sparkle in her. But she behaved the following day as if this experience had never taken place, and returned to her usual screaming. After a very long time and very slowly we could unravel an early relationship to her mother. I learned that when Dr X was born, her mother had a severe psychotic breakdown, and that she was separated from her when she was about three weeks old, for several months. She was looked after by a relative.

The analysis of this patient continued for several years, and she achieved many changes, but there remained in her a sharp core of harshness that did not ever allow her to establish the close relationships she longed for.

Her mother's breakdown suggested that not only could she not offer her baby proper containment (in Bion's sense) but that she also very likely projected massively into her baby. This could be seen when early in the analysis the patient shouted incomprehensibly at me, identified, I believe, with this projecting object, while reacting to my speaking as if I were pushing something into her. As can be imagined the situation was fraught and it was extremely difficult to talk to her. When eventually we managed to overcome it (and surprisingly it cleared up to a considerable degree) what emerged was a cruel and envious streak, which I felt was coming from herself and not just originating in an identification with an inadequate object; with this cruelty and envy she used to punish me relentlessly. Over time she got considerable insight into it, but there seemed to be something so relentless that we both could see something very destructive inherent to herself that could only partially be modified in the analysis. Of course one will never know for certain whether if Dr X had had a better beginning she might not have developed differently and tamed her hostility better.

The material I have presented shows not only the consequences of having been projected into as a baby, which as I said were eventually worked through, but her own projections into her objects which we were not able to transform, and which locked her into a repetitive process of disconnected episodes with neither memory nor much hope.

The important meaning of this material is the relentless unchangeability of the patient's internal objects. This constellation operated in a seemingly endless way, keeping her experiences both in her life and at the beginning of her analysis fixed and completely disconnected from one another. In the analysis, by projective identification, she communicated to me the experience of being a baby with an object that is not only unreceptive of the baby's feelings but also is projecting massively into it; once this could be overcome and understood we could both learn about her intense envious attacks, but we were somehow unable to modify them sufficiently.

Development and fluctuations of the superego

I return now to a description of the evolution of the internal objects, and I will present clinical material to show the developmental movements of internal object relations as expressed in the transference. As I said before, one of the functions of splitting is to keep separate two kinds of experience, the good ones, and the persecuting ones. This broad division groups the objects into *clusters* of ideal and persecuting objects.

As the infant grows in the relationship to its mother, its perception of her evolves from that of a conglomerate of part objects, present in different emotional contexts, to the notion of one mother who can be wholly present or absent. Due to continuous introjections, there is an evolution of the internal objects. These previously unconnected objects begin slowly to link with one another and to merge into one another. These mergers are helped by new introjections, which also merge with the previous ones, thus transforming the split internal objects into more whole objects. I think that in each transformation of the internal objects by merging old and new experiences, something of each is retained in the new outcome.

Of course this development is not straightforward but is subject to many progressive and regressive movements. Integration is assumed to bring into the baby new feelings, some of them extremely painful, which make him regress to paranoid-schizoid defences that can temporarily halt the integration, or disturb it more permanently (as we saw in my previous example). But, on the other hand, further integration strengthens the internal objects, which can then protect the infant better against new outbursts of anxiety.

As the baby becomes more integrated, this integration ushers the infant into the depressive position. His objects, by becoming more integrated, strengthen his ego. He begins to become more aware of himself and therefore of his actions as being his own. He also becomes more aware of his mother. This greater awareness of separateness allows for the beginning of a rudimentary notion of space, which brings the notion of time and therefore of memory. The absoluteness and timelessness of the previous experience lessens and changes into awareness of continuity and expectation.

With the increasing awareness of the infant as separate from his mother, the awareness of psychic reality becomes possible. The baby now evolves from the absolute polarity between ideal and persecuting relationships into feeling that he loves his mother and feels loved by her. He can also now begin to perceive his own hate, that is, he does not automatically feel persecuted, but begins in a rudimentary way to be aware of what he does to his mother. The perception that he loves and hates the same person brings a whole new series of emotions. He feels ambivalence. The fact that he hates his mother means that his hatred is directed to the same mother he loves, which makes him feel concerned for her, so that he feels guilty and frightened of losing her.

At this point of integration of good and bad objects of self and of both external and internal objects, the child recognises the father, and the triangularity of the Oedipus complex begins its development.

To repeat: the early internal objects are highly distorted, since they are shaped and coloured by the baby's projections of good or bad feelings. In order for progressive integration to occur, there has to be a predominance of love over destructiveness. The life instinct, by furthering good experiences with the mother, more and more binds the death forces by increasing the strength of the good internal objects.

The characteristics of the real mother, including her relationship to the father, as well as other external circumstances, are of course of great importance in development. The clinical material of Dr X, the first case I discussed in this paper, exemplifies this fact. The relative contribution of constitutional factors and environmental ones leaves questions that are more often than not impossible to answer. In *Learning from Experience*, Bion brought forcefully to our attention one of the ways in which the external environment acts upon the infant. We know that not only do babies project, but that some mothers also massively project into their babies (as shown in my example). Where Bion expresses more certainty in the predominance of constitutional factors is in the development of schizophrenic illness (1957).

Symbol-formation, together with the recognition of and relation to the father, and later to other members of the family, facilitates the protection of the good objects, by dispersing or displacing destructive feelings. The continuing, more realistic, loving relation with the actual parents allows the withdrawal of projections from the internal objects, which then become more benign and realistically based. The superego becomes less harsh.

As we all know, this development is never straightforward and permanent. In the depressive position the continuous impact of ambivalent feelings, love and hate towards the same object, results in what Freud called 'the fatal inevitability of the sense of guilt' (1930). The way the infant will deal with guilt will depend on how strong the guilt is as well as on the degree of integration of his ego and the quality of his internal objects.

The intensity of the pain produced by guilt may throw the child back to his old, disintegrative defences, which make him feel his objects to be persecuting and force him to go on defending himself.

Guilt may also bring a movement towards repairing the damage he feels he has inflicted on his objects by his destructiveness. This reparation will help the objects to become more integrated, and they will be felt as more loving and forgiving. This in turn will relieve the feelings of guilt and push the child towards growth and better relations, with both internal and external objects.

This constant to-ing and fro-ing is characteristic of the depressive position. As Freud said, the struggle between Eros and the death instinct is eternal. The type of *internal objects* that will emerge from childhood (that is, the type of superego), will depend on which kind of experiences prevail.

But one has to keep in mind yet another point. In addition to the progressive and regressive movement that takes place, there is the fact that, as Strachey puts it, 'his superego is in any case neither homogeneous nor well organised'. One can understand and explain this by the fact that different internal objects and different constellations of internal object relationships do coexist and have different superego functions, which can not only be different from each other but even opposed to one another. In such cases the ego seems to be divided or to function in a divided way. This can be illustrated with examples from those patients, often encountered, who can be highly responsible and strict in some areas of their life, in work for instance, while in other areas they are habitual liars. Stability of the superego is the result of the integration achieved by the working through in the depressive position. But as is well known, this is not an easy task and the intense pain and anxieties that it involves often militate against stability and result in a divided superego.

I will now present some clinical material to illustrate the operation of and changes in the superego in the transference.

Clinical material

Mr Smith is a man in his twenties of short and stocky build. He has been in analysis for three years. He consulted me originally because of sexual problems, shyness, difficulties in making stable relationships, and difficulty in concentration at work. He is an engineer specialising in oil production. During adolescence he went through a short period of intense disturbance, in which he occasionally hallucinated, was impotent, and was generally in a state of anxiety. Though he had some friends, he was isolated and withdrawn.

During his first two years of analysis he felt intensely persecuted. He was very cold in the sessions. After my interventions he reacted with silence, speaking only after he rehearsed in his mind several times what to say. He had frequent cruel fantasies about me, which occurred apparently in isolation. They had a static though very pictorial quality.

The third year of his analysis was marked by substantial progress in his external life as well as in the analysis. He spoke more directly and freely; there was more warmth. He himself felt much better. He acknowledged this improvement in the analysis, and also became more aware of dependency. He found that he trusted me more and felt that I was more friendly. At first he wondered if I had changed.

I turn now to three consecutive sessions which occurred at the start of the fourth year, which I shall first summarise as follows: At the end of the first session, Mr Smith felt me to be helpful and supportive. Something that happened between sessions one and two made him feel intensely guilty.

This guilt increased his hatred towards me because, as his internal object, I was felt to be accusing. Besides expressing this in the transference situation, he also projected it into his external world. Further analytic work in sessions two and three both clarified this situation and allowed the patient to feel that I could tolerate what was going on. He felt better and felt me to be more benign, and this allowed us to continue to work on severe underlying anxieties.

Session one

Mr Smith spent a considerable time complaining in a monotonous, repetitive way, which sounded like an incantation. The subject of his complaint was his car. After considerable analytic work, he could see that what he was doing was aimed at paralysing me in order to keep his most troubling immediate problems at bay. Then he could talk about what was upsetting him, which referred to problems at work. He could understand some things that were blocking him. He felt helped and said that he felt very relieved.

Session two

Mr Smith came looking glum. After some silence, he said that he was feeling shut in himself ever since he woke up. He reported an incident with his girlfriend in which she had been cruelly teasing him. The whole incident ended in intercourse. All this was said in a fairly direct, rather sad way. He then spoke about his day. He had gone for a walk, spent a long time in the garage discussing his car, then went home. Whilst speaking about all this, his tone had changed considerably. His voice became low; he spoke in a very mannered and slow way. He became more repetitive and provided further minute details of these events. This all took a lot of time and, while he spoke, I could detect something provocative in his manner. While this was going on I felt pressurised to intervene, but was quite unclear as to what it was all about. I knew he had felt better last session and remembered that he was supposed to have spent the day in a course of study. (This is partly a compulsory course paid for by the firm, which also provides him with the day free to attend it.) I also remembered that he had missed the course the previous week.

I started saying something that I then felt unclear about, trying to call his attention to what he had told me at the beginning of the session, and to his subsequent manner of speaking, which seemed to be aimed at provoking me into saying something which he could feel was critical of him, and thereby he could have a row with me. I reminded him that this type of quarrelling is often exciting to him, and I said that he was trying to whip up some excitement in order to avoid feelings that seemed very painful. (In analysis he used to call this quarrelling 'having a party'.) Thinking about what was going on, it would appear that his guilt related to a hostile attack against me when he felt relieved by the session and became aware that he had to wait for the next one. His impatience drove him to attack his good experience in the analysis. To cover up the unhappiness brought to him by guilt he tried to whip up excitement, but the central issue is that he had felt better and I knew it.

Returning to the session, he responded rather quickly, in a strikingly cold way: 'Mr O'Hara would probably not be very happy.' (Mr O'Hara is his immediate boss.) I began saying that it appeared to me that he was not feeling very happy; he interrupted furiously, responding as if I had mentioned the course (which I had not). He said in his very cold way, why did I not complain when he missed the previous week? He continued for quite a long time to complain about my 'accusations', he said that all I did was to scold him; and that I well knew that he could not attend the course and come to analysis. (This last, again, was not quite true.)

Looking at this piece of material, I think that he had sensed that he had felt bad about what he had done and was still doing, and felt that I not only knew it, but could also understand his feelings and help him. These sentiments were apparently very precarious, since internally he felt both that I was accusing him and that he had done something wrong to me and the analysis, and he tried to cut all this out with his withdrawal.

Between sessions one and two something had happened that changed me (his object) in his mind from the helpful analyst who provided understanding into someone very accusatory. I think that the help obtained the previous day increased his desire for more, and his intolerance of waiting. (A characteristic of this patient is intense impatience.) I believe that the waiting between sessions was perceived by him as my teasing him, and this triggered off his usual negative reaction and hostility. When he feels helped by me he often feels split between wanting help and envying me the ability to provide it. But this particular attack on me in his mind did not eliminate completely from his mind that what he was doing was to a me whom he also valued, that is, he was attacking his good internal object. The intensity of his guilt made him regress to paranoid-schizoid defences; he split off his awareness of what had happened and projected it internally and also externally into me. The projecting it internally into me made him experience me as blaming and criticising so he did not have to know that he was feeling guilty, fearing that this knowledge might prove too painful for him. He then tried to enact this internal situation by provoking me so as to misunderstand what I did or distort it into what he could tell himself was my accusing him. He acted out this destructive behaviour so as to provoke criticism and punishment. When he felt this provocation was being carried out in the session, he felt criticised and persecuted, and then fully justified in protecting himself by fighting me off.

After some considerable time I tried to convey to him that I thought he was feeling guilty about something that apparently happened during the evening, since he had awakened with the sense of being shut in. I told him that when he left the previous session he was feeling well, but that he experienced his going away as my teasing him, and that this teasing me was projected into the girlfriend. I also mentioned that I thought he was attacking not only me but also the two of us working together.

While talking I was watching him. He seemed to be listening very carefully. After a pause, I said that by missing his course, as well as by trying to provoke me into a row about it, he could then experience me as criticising and hurting him. But I added that he was feeling very unhappy and that he knew something about this (certainly more than he was letting on).

His posture relaxed, a vague smile seemed to come and go on his face, but he tensed up again and looked very withdrawn. After a provocative remark about changing the time of the session, he was silent for some ten minutes. Though he appeared to be very tense, I thought it better to tolerate with him his silence and tension. Near the end of the session he asked in a rather cruel way: 'When is this torture going to end?' I pointed out to him that he seemed to me to be prolonging something beyond his own need, and he believed that if he could turn the session into so-called 'torture' he could produce some excitement that would avoid his real feeling of misery. Here the session ended. He sneered and left.

In a summary of the following session I will try to show that in the one just described he seemed to have taken in more than he was acknowledging to me. Already his object seemed to have improved, as will be seen from a remark of his, but was still felt to be fragile inside him. Once this improvement was reinforced, Mr Smith felt the object stronger and proceeded to reveal more of his most central anxieties, but those brought further problems.

Session three

He started in a mildly provocative way, without much conviction, by asking: 'When are you going to start criticising, or are you going to wait for me to say something?' In spite of his provocativeness, by his remark I realised he was not feeling criticised by me. I said he wanted us to clarify something left unclear the previous day – that is, what it was that he felt was keeping us shut in a torturing situation. He interrupted in an unusual way for him – unusual in the sense of openness and directness, saying:

'What do you mean, unclear? It was *you* of course.' I pointed out to him that the torture seemed to have started when I said that he seemed to me to be unhappy, and that my saying so felt to him like an accusation, because internally he felt me to be quarrelling with his view of what had happened after the previous session. This interpretation (rather condensed here) was not different from the one of the previous day, but I think it allowed him to focus more clearly.

After a pause he said that he met Mr O'Hara in the pub: O'Hara was very friendly, and even suggested to him how to use his practical experience in the rigs in Scotland for his present studies. Then he said: 'You know, your voice is different today: yesterday it was harsh and scolding.' (Of course, it is possible that my voice was more relaxed.) I responded by saying that this could be true, but that there could also be something different in his perception; that, for instance, he feels different, he feels people to be friendlier, and I sound different to him. He then said that while I was just speaking, the feeling of a dream of two or three days before came into his mind, and that he could not catch the dream. It was a nice dream and he thought it was about a girl.

From here on his attitude to me was more trusting and warm. He spoke about work; he remembered an event that happened that day. Someone had described a hospital for mental defectives. He said that the people described sounded horrible and amorphous, really as if they were not human. He said he could not face going there or looking at such horrors. This was said in the context that actually he felt it to be his duty to accompany a close friend of the family to visit a brother in such an institution.

The session continued and opened up areas of severe anxieties. He left with tears in his eyes and, very uncharacteristically, said 'Thank you.'

This example illustrates the change in the internal objects as viewed in the transference relationship. The object kept changing because of internal pressures and the effects of the interpretative work. I felt good to him; parting felt tantalising. This stimulated hatred and he turned internally against me. As a result of his hostility he felt guilty, and this guilt felt too painful to him, so he resorted to further splitting and projection into me. The internal object (me in the analysis) was now felt as cruel and accusing, and he acted out the conflict in his external world. Further interpretations provided him with understanding that helped to change the object into a benign, stronger and helpful object. One could say that the superego (the object) underwent several regressive and progressive changes during these sessions.

Discussion

I think it interesting to note the differences between the two examples. In the case of Dr X (the screaming woman) the analytic situation had for a long time a considerable immobility. The insistent characteristic of her object relations seemed to be fixed and kept repeating itself almost unchanged. It was as if her inner world remained untouchable. The patient and I experienced it as interminable. In the case of Mr Smith, much progress had been achieved and the patient's relationship to his objects had evolved considerably. The objects had developed, and with their characteristic oscillations continued developing in the sessions.

Returning now to Strachey's idea that it is the internal objects, that is, the superego, that need to be modified in the analysis, I not only agree with him but hope to have shown how, in the frame of Klein's ideas, these modifications take place.

It has been my aim to show that the superego is the internal objects. It evolves from the first introjections of part objects which form the foundations of the superego. In the many vicissitudes of this evolution some of the characteristics of the very early objects remain unchangeable. In the clinical material, I have illustrated how the modifications of the objects take place, and the way they are experienced in the sessions and are modified by the analysis of the transference, which is the place in which the archaic object relationships are experienced, but where the analyst, by not entering blindly into this repetitiveness, helps them then to be modified.

Summary

In this paper I have tried to describe the different outcomes of introjection, that is, the ego, the superego and the internal world. I have also emphasised the interaction between environment and constitutional instinctive factors.

4

Construction as reliving history

A former patient of mine once wrote to me: 'Analysis is a relationship and an autobiography that is re-written'. The truth in this remark is that in the relationship to his analyst the patient relives his emotional biography, that is, he relives the history of his relationship to his internal and external objects, including the anxieties and defences he used against them.

I am using 'construction' in this context to signify the analyst's understanding of the patient's emotional phenomena as expressed in the transference, an understanding which is presented to the patient in the form of interpretations. I think it may be useful to reserve the word 'construction' for the work the analyst does in his own mind, and 'interpreting' for that which he communicates to the patient.

The continuous construction of the meaning of what goes on between patient and analyst reconstructs, in the transference, something of the history of the patient's relationship to his objects, the anxieties involved and the way defences were built up.

This construction which takes place in the analyst's mind and is conveyed to the patient in interpretations of the transference is, wherever possible, linked to the patient's history as remembered by him or inferred by the analyst. ('Reconstruction' as distinct from 'construction' will be used for an actual reconstruction of historical events, whether remembered or not.)

The work of reconstruction in analysis is a continuous interweaving of the threads of history as experienced in the analysis, and the threads of remembered history. This combination helps the patient to distance himself

---

This paper was read at a European Federation symposium on 'Construction and reconstruction', Stockholm, March 1998. It is published here for the first time.

from the transference and enriches his understanding of himself, thus providing him with a new autobiography.

In his paper 'Constructions in analysis', Freud says: 'It is a "construction" when one lays before the subject of the analysis a piece of his early history that he has forgotten' (1937: 261). Throughout his paper he stresses the importance of recollections as a means of lifting repression. For Freud the forgetting that results from repression, and the act of remembering, are fundamental to the analytic work, which he compares with archaeology, with the distinction that in analysis construction is only the preliminary work, whose aim is to elicit further material which is then used for further constructions that can recover further fragments of lost experiences. Analysis also differs from archaeology in that the elements from which we construct are alive, and Freud emphasises the importance of the transference. He also makes it clear that it is the analyst's work to construct from the material and offer these constructions to the patient.

Melanie Klein's theories of early infantile development allow us to forgo the requirement of verbal remembering. Her understanding of splitting, projective identification and introjection throws light on very early mental phenomena, many of which come before language. These experiences remain in the individual as emotional memories; Melanie Klein called them 'memories in feeling'. In the analysis they are not verbally recollected by the patient, but re-experienced and communicated by projective identification. It is the analyst who puts those memories into words.

But Freud was also puzzled in his paper by those constructions which do not result in recollections. He says: 'if the analysis is carried out correctly we produce in him [the patient] an assured conviction of the truth of the construction which achieves the same therapeutic result as a recaptured memory', and he states the need for further enquiry. In my view, this assured conviction to which Freud refers is achieved by the work we do in the transference. In the transference the patient relives with the analyst his archaic object relationships – those relationships to internal objects that for some reason or other have not developed. He experiences his analyst as if the analyst were the externalisation of an internal object, that is, the embodiment of his view of his historical objects past and present. The patient communicates these feelings to the analyst by action and words and by evoking feelings in the analyst through the mechanism that Klein called 'projective identification', to which I shall return. The analyst understands the patient's communications and his own feelings in relation to the patient's history in the live expression of the transference. He gradually constructs explanations for what is happening, for why it is happening and, where possible, how it originated.

The continuous construction of aspects of the conjoint experience of patient and analyst which are communicated to the patient as interpretations, mainly of the transference, allows the patient to come to feel and gradually know different aspects of his mental experience, thus providing him with the conviction of truth and the therapeutic result described by Freud.

Bion (1962), in his theory of container and contained, described the mother's unconscious perception and the working through in her own mind of the baby's anxieties, making those raw experiences bearable for her child, and thus allowing the infant to introject the modified experience and, more gradually, to introject the maternal function itself. Bion called this function 'reverie'.

The analyst's 'sensing' of the patient's projective identification is similar to maternal reverie, but differs from it insofar as the analyst always requires a conscious perception and further elaboration of what he has sensed; only then can he understand it as a communication. What I am describing is the use of counter-transference as a tool to help the analyst perceive and understand the patient's material and to construct it meaningfully for him.

I will be using the term projective identification to describe an important mechanism by which the patient communicates in analysis. In early development the baby relates to parts of mother as if they were the whole mother. They are parts due to limited perceptual development. They are parts due to the feelings experienced by the baby, who needs at first to keep apart different emotional experiences – good from bad. These feelings are experienced as absolute at the moment of the experience; they are totally bad and persecuting or totally good, ideal. These feelings are always experienced in relation to the object, the mother at first (or that part of her that is being sensed: feeding breast, holding lap, understanding, etc.), and are projected into her in such a way that they greatly colour the baby's perceptions of her; that is, for the baby, she *is* as he feels towards her. At first the infant who has good feelings is felt to be different from the one who feels something bad, just as we assume that the good mother has little to do in the baby's mind with the mother perceived as bad. This splitting helps to organise the baby's emotional experiences and to build up a more integrated self. Splitting can also be of a different nature. It can be an attack, or can be used defensively. These different splitting processes bring about a whole series of different experiences and consequences. Projective identification, splitting and introjection together constitute the main mental phenomena at this stage. Melanie Klein called this the paranoid-schizoid position – paranoid in its anxiety, schizoid in its defences.

When all goes well and integrative processes prevail over disintegrative ones, the infant begins gradually to experience his mother as a whole person; he perceives her as 'one mother' and also gradually begins to be able to sense his own feelings as being his. At this point feelings of guilt and ambivalence set in. This Klein called the depressive position. Throughout life there exists an oscillation between the paranoid-schizoid and depressive positions, between these two modes of feeling and reacting. Understanding this mobility, together with understanding splitting mechanisms, helps to explain the coexistence of different strands of development in our patients' personalities which can manifest themselves in the analysis sometimes simultaneously, sometimes sequentially and often with many contradictions.

I will apply these concepts to the clinical material of three patients. The first patient is a psychotic boy for whom the past as past seemed to have little or no significance. In my second example I will try to illustrate the use of the counter-transference in the understanding of my patient's projective identification and how the interpretation of this brought back early memories and permitted us to get through a block in the session. My third example is of a different kind of patient altogether, a woman with a lively awareness of her past. I will attempt to illustrate with her material the interweaving of the construction of the transference with the patient's recollections, which were brought spontaneously to her by the insight which she had gained through the interpretations.

I hope to show, through these three examples, different types of transference constructions and the ways constructions take place.

Jim, a pre-adolescent boy

I saw Jim in a child guidance clinic. He was thirteen when the school referred him to the clinic. The main complaint was encopresis, which the school felt they could no longer tolerate. The teacher reported that Jim was a very strange child, that he spoke to no-one, that he did not relate to either teacher or children, but that apart from soiling, he did not cause trouble at school.

His mother, a reserved, closed-in woman with a discontented air, reported that he had been a quiet, withdrawn child, and that at home he soiled at night. She gave no details of his history nor of his encopresis.

Jim was very thin and small for his age. He came easily to the treatment room, but neither looked at nor spoke to me. He had an 'angelic' smile directed nowhere. At first he sat rigidly in front of me and for a time did not seem to respond to what I said, as if in spite of his rigidity, he was totally enveloped in his smile, with apparently no contact with me or the world around him.

Later, after some encouragement, he took some paper and a black crayon. With the pencil he covered about half the sheet with messy, scrawling black strokes. This continued for quite a number of sessions. I spoke of his feeling something black and incomprehensible inside himself. I also spoke of his not expecting me to understand or make sense of this. For several weeks I could detect no response. I spoke little while he went on blackening the paper. I attempted to verbalise my communications in different ways. Sometimes I linked them to his symptom. In spite of the apparent lack of response, I did not feel disconnected from Jim; I felt puzzled, not anxious.

After some time I received some oblique glances from him, and I noticed that the smile was not there.

Finally, in one session, after occupying himself for a while with his usual scribbling, and when about two-thirds of the sheet was a solid black mess, he drew two circles in the blank space on the paper. Those circles were clearly delineated, separated from each other, and attached by the rim to the black mass. He did not fill them in. This made me think of the lights of a car, and I said so to him. He nodded. Then I told him that my words threw some light either on the mess that he felt himself to be or that he felt he had inside him, and that now he was experiencing some slight hope that we could understand this. More or less at this point he stopped using pencil and crayon and began to talk.

He spoke mainly about two animals. One was a highly idealised cat, 'Fluffy', so good that he even spent the night on Jim's tummy to comfort and warm him; the other was a horribly vicious dog, 'Puffy', that messed everywhere, always trying to attack Jim or Fluffy and even soiling his mother's kitchen table. There was a highly delusional quality in the way he portrayed both animals (there were no animals at home). He spoke of them in session after session in a manner that made me think that in his mind I held the position of the idealised cat.

Jim generally inspected me rapidly on arrival. During the session he smiled very warmly. Sometimes he took in what I said, which mainly concerned his relationship to me as this highly idealised cat (breast), split off from the horrible dog, which he feared I might (or had) become when I spoke about a division between good and bad feelings as expressed through cat and dog. He did not much like my talking since sometimes it disturbed his idealisation of me. Also, when what I said gave him relief or was experienced as good, this seemed to arouse his envy, which he expressed by quickly speaking of how the dog had just made a mess in the kitchen or bedroom, or how it had gnawed at a piece of furniture. He then looked at me in disgust and fear: I was the dog. He had dislodged his hostile feelings and put them into me. He tried to cut me off and ignore what I had to say as much as possible.

During this time, on a day I was to see Jim, I was wearing a different watch from my usual one. On entering the room he gave me his usual quick encompassing glance. He then looked at me in a strange way and tensed up, as if expecting something, after which he grew increasingly rigid. I did not understand what was going on, and felt confused and anxious. He then started moving rather slowly, whirling rhythmically round and round and moving mainly from the waist up. I realised that he was revolving in a clockwise direction, and at that point I remembered that I had on a different watch. I said he was being a watch. With evident relief he said 'Yes', and his movement slowed and eventually stopped as I continued talking. I told him that he had been frightened by a change in me, by my different watch; that when I did not recognise his fear he felt I had changed. He felt I had become a different analyst, a bad one who did not understand him, and he felt terrified. To protect himself he had to control this bad watch (me) by becoming it, by getting inside it and taking possession of it.

Looking at this vignette, we can see coexisting in Jim different strands of development. He could understand what I said, and, what is more, he responded to me. He symbolised this understanding, as can be seen, in his drawing of the circles and in his movement in communicating with me verbally. Verbal language often broke down under pressure of anxiety, as shown, for instance, in the episode of the watch. Jim's mental functioning was pathologically archaic, that is, psychotic. His objects were part objects, as expressed through cat and dog. As such, they possessed absolute qualities and were kept split apart form each other. His experiences kept changing from one to another, however, and these two part objects easily became entangled. The dog, containing his hostility, attacked the good cat, resulting in total confusion, which he dreaded. I often felt very confused and had difficulty following the rapid changes and what resulted from them. It is interesting to note that the animals had similar names: Fluffy and Puffy. Although this material lacks detail, I hope that my reasoning can be followed.

My constructions in Jim's case were of very primitive unconscious phantasies. Though some of them were partially expressed in language, they referred primarily to pre-verbal experiences, such as a confusional state resulting from the unsuccessful attempt to maintain a clean split between good and bad feelings. This resulted in further splitting and projective identification, as when, for instance, the 'cat' sometimes landed up inside me.

My trying to convey to Jim something of what I thought to be his early history had no meaning for him. His history was being worked out in the Fluffy/Puffy material. He did not seem to have a sense of past or present, only of past/present timelessness.

I will now present my second example to illustrate the use of my feelings in the counter-transference to understand a patient. Interpreting this brought memories of early events to the patient which helped us to understand the reasons for a block in the analysis.

Dr L, a woman doctor in her early thirties

Dr L is an only child born into an Irish Catholic family in Boston. When she was small, because of her mother's work (she was a professional pianist) the family moved to England for a few years. When Dr L started secondary school they went back for another period to the USA. They finally settled in Dublin after she had graduated from an American university. Dr L was taught by her mother to play the piano from the time she was very young.

The material I will present comes from the third year of a difficult analysis. She often brought many childhood memories, but these had an anecdotal quality, lacked feeling, and often were a barrier to analytic work.

I will present a short fragment from a Monday session, prior to which she had missed a few sessions in order to attend a conference in her speciality.

She spoke at first in a rather plaintive tone, but then more normally. She talked of not having enough time, and referred to the neglected state of her house and the fact that she was not spending enough time with her children. She said that the only thing she felt like doing was sitting in her garden, and that she never had time to enjoy it properly. She went on to speak of her worry about a difficult situation between her daughter Laura and Laura's godmother, who had been very sharp with the girl, accusing her of being too demanding, something that the patient thought was more characteristic of the godmother than of Laura, who had felt hurt and unfairly treated.

From early on in the session I felt under great pressure, accompanied by a sense of urgency. I made several attempts to interpret the material. I addressed myself to her possibly feeling neglected, which I linked to the long gap caused by the summation of her missing sessions and the weekend. She seemed to agree, but this did not take us any further. I tried to explore other areas with her, referring to her fears of my finding her too demanding. During this time, I felt my interpretations to be limp and flat. The patient responded to all of them with some agreement and further associations that had a perfunctory quality. She seemed to be trying very hard, while I felt a considerable increase in my sense of discomfort and urgency to communicate with her, but we seemed to be going nowhere.

I felt as if we were in the presence of an unconcerned critical object whom she had to please no matter what. Guided by these feelings, and influenced by the disparate elements scattered in her speech, such as 'the neglected house', 'the missed sessions', etc., I told her that we seemed to be speaking past one another. She nodded. I said that she felt that I was unreceptive to something she experienced and she needed to get this across to me; and the only way she could do so was by making me feel how it was to be with someone who was emotionally unavailable, but apparently demanding that she behave nicely. She answered directly, saying 'This is very true,' and then told me she had suddenly developed an acute stomach ache. Though she often reported stomach aches, at that moment I felt quite puzzled. The fact that I had been puzzled by this particular occurrence of what was a frequent symptom of hers, was puzzling in itself. She then proceeded to say that she had an image of herself when she was three or maybe it was five years old. She would be sitting practising the piano, and her mother was in another part of the room listening to the radio while at the same time correcting one or another aspect of her playing. They had just come to London from the States, and she remembered the radio programme, a soap opera which she named. Her mother listened daily to it while supervising her daughter's piano practice. Dr L by now was looking puzzled, very pale and upset. She said:

'Odd what comes to my mind. The first year at school, in England, we had to eat lunch every day at school. It was awful, I felt sick every day and couldn't cope with it…of course, that's funny…I must have been five then, this is the time that grade school starts in this country. I told my mother about how I felt when made to eat; she said glibly: "No problem dear: just don't eat it."'

Dr L remained silent, then said after a short while: 'This explains the confusion about whether I was three or five. Five is when I started school, in this country. The lunch issue made me feel terribly ashamed, tongue-tied and paralysed, not knowing how to speak at all, let alone to dare to say I won't have it!' Then she added, somehow dutifully: 'But it worked, and my mother was right!' She continued speaking, with difficulty, about how helpful this remark of her mother had been.

This further material helped me to understand my having been puzzled by what was a frequent reaction of hers, that is, her tendency to somatise. Her physical pain came after what I believed was a helpful interpretation, but she seemed to react to it in a way that made me think that she might have experienced the interpretation as a re-projection of something which was difficult to tolerate. The fact that I was surprised by her stomach ache made me reconsider this. It was only after her further associations about the school lunch problems, that I realised that her somatic reaction was an expression in the transference of an early experience between Dr L and her mother. Although my interpretation had been felt to be true, as her mother's solution had appeared to be good, the patient remained at some level unconvinced. Her rapid acceptance of her mother's remark seems to have been to reassure her mother, to 'cure mother of her [mother's] own anxieties'. After we understood this we could go on working on it as it appeared in the transference.

The session continued and we were actually able to address ourselves to the problems of the first part of the hour in a more meaningful way, and with some understanding.

I hope I have shown through this material how, by understanding Dr L's projective identification, we were able to locate and reconstruct her experience of an object felt to be out of touch, unresponsive and confusing to the patient. It was frequent in this analysis that the patient expected little from me, but on the contrary experienced me as someone who expected her to give a very good performance, apparently interested in her but really with my mind closed to her. Of course I did not know what her mother really was like, and my picture of her at that time of the analysis was very dim. When I verbalised the experience of the session, Dr L was able to connect my interpretation of it with a personal experience of a kind that felt real and helped to clarify the issues that had so far been muddled and obscure and thereby to overcome the impasse in the session. This eventually provided an opening towards understanding better her perfunctory way of addressing my interpretations, which in turn brought, later on in the analysis, a picture of one aspect of her relationship to her mother which portrayed the patient's loyalty to a mother who appeared to be rather unreal and self-centred.

Ms Y, a lecturer in economics

My third example will serve as a contrast to the constructions described in these first two cases. Ms Y is in her late thirties, a lecturer in economics. She had recently been awarded her Ph.D. and obtained a better university post, and she had been invited to take part in a discussion group chaired by a leading authority in her field. She was in her sixth year of analysis at the time of the session I wish to describe.

The previous session had been concerned with Ms Y's 'active passivity' in relation to asking for or accepting help, and how this resulted in her feeling excluded by a good object. She had recognised this session as being very helpful; she had been moved and had left feeling hopeful and pleased.

At the beginning of the following session Ms Y came in looking pale and dejected. She spoke about the coming meeting of her study group in a week's time, at which she had to present a draft of her paper. She said she was terrified; she feared that the group would criticise her and that the professor would be very disapproving of her work. She then referred to Joanna, a colleague of her own generation who had been severely criticised at the previous meeting. She expanded by saying that she herself was feeling very critical of Joanna, who had not prepared her paper properly and had got her statistics wrong. She said that now the same thing would happen to her, and that as a result her whole career would be damaged: she would not obtain tenure. The more she spoke of this, the more it sounded as if she had already failed.

While listening to her, my first reaction was surprise at the change from the previous session. I was puzzled by what she was saying. She had spoken before about her work in writing her paper, and as far as I could judge her preparations had been very thorough. I also had a sinking feeling of 'here we go again'. I remarked that she had felt better in the previous session and had also reported on an earlier occasion that she was pleased with her paper. She now seemed to have turned against those feelings and plunged into a masochistic self-beating which kept us both in a state of useless immobility. She looked more alert. I then said that she attacked my work because she resented feeling hopeful, since this opened up new avenues for her and made her feel uncertain. She responded directly, saying, 'It must be the dream.' She had been feeling very bad since she woke up because she had thought she had gone back on her own understanding. She sounded quite hopeless.

She then explained that *the dream had been about John, a boyfriend she had had in her teens who had been involved with drugs. In the dream she and John were going about together. She did not know if she was there as his girlfriend or as a companion. John had just come out of prison. They went around meeting people. John seemed to want to settle old scores. They met a couple who ignored her completely. They were very tight-lipped and wary of John. She tried to introduce herself, saying 'I am Yolande' to the woman, who did not respond. At first John spoke in a threatening manner but finally he seemed somehow forgiving. At this the couple loosened up, and the woman spoke to Yolande, recognising her as a person. She thought she must have been about twenty years old in the dream.*

After the dream she felt very downcast. In a strongly self-accusatory tone she spoke about how much work had been done in the analysis on the reasons for her participation in the drug scene in the 1960s and on her idealisation of it (a familiar topic in our sessions). She also spoke of what we called in the analysis her 'mental drugging'. (This referred to moods in which she was passive, withdrawn, vague and disconnected. These states were often expressed through complaints similar to those at the beginning of the session, in which there was a hidden excitement.) She said, 'Only last week it all was so clear to me and now this dream...slipping back.'

I said that actually she seemed to have gone back *after* the dream and *in* the session, so as not to have to stand by her understanding in the last session – not to have to explore the meaning of the dream which I thought she perhaps sensed. She reacted somewhat belligerently and argumentatively.

I pointed out that she had forced herself into Joanna's position, and Joanna had already failed, so no good could come of our work today. But still, John in the dream had come out of prison, and in the last session she had felt recognised, that is, understood by me, and been helped to integrate the diverse aspects of her life. This had made her freer 'to come out of prison'. This increased freedom made her aware that she could be accepted by me and that it was she who excluded herself. She was thoughtful; she made some associations, and I proceeded to link these with events in the 1960s. I said it was true that at Oxford she had been very much part of the marijuana crowd, but this had also been for her a period of friendship, exploration and intense intellectual activity and growth. By now Ms Y's mood had changed and she was very surprised. She tried to argue the harmfulness of the marijuana scene, but what kept coming to her mind were thoughts of her student days, the music of those years, the people she knew. Finally she made a weak attempt to emphasise the negative aspect of those times.

I said that at this moment, when things had come together for her, she felt, as in the dream, that she was facing a couple, and she felt excluded. The couple represented myself and my own thinking as well as myself and my husband in the coming holidays. It was because of her hostility to the couple that they became a critical pair in the dream. I also pointed out that by joining in the criticism, she avoids having to deal with feelings of both resentment and forgiveness, keeping in that way a whole area of her mind and of her feelings cut off from the rest.

Ms Y was thoughtful and a bit tearful. She said she was reminded of her period of agoraphobia. (This fact was known in the analysis, but so far had not been well understood. It had occurred shortly after she left university, and had had to go to live with her parents for a while.) She spoke about that period, and how during it, and especially after, she stopped seeing most of her friends. I made the interpretation that this phobic situation had been partly present in the session; that by trying to join and inflate whatever she felt as negative she believed that she could keep other experiences out, thus avoiding having to face conflict and painful issues, in the same way as in her phobic period she had cut off her vitality and enjoyment. In the session she tried to join with a very punitive internal object-analyst and exclude myself as I really was, especially to exclude awareness of the hostility generated by her perception of me as helpful and also part of a couple, accentuated by the coming holidays. To do this she had lodged in me as the woman of the dream the her that did not wish to recognise something. But there seemed also to be — active and in evidence — another aspect of her that knew better and was striving towards acknowledging something, as did the woman who finally recognised her.

In this material we can follow the movement of the transference: from negative reaction to increased paranoid-schizoid defences to further integration; and from there to her spontaneously remembering her past. All this made it possible to bring together the enactment of her phobic mechanisms in the session with her recollection of her agoraphobia and further elucidation of the past.

Discussion

In the analysis of these three patients, all the constructions took place in the transference and were of the transference. In the material I have presented from both Jim and Ms Y, I used my counter-transference as an element in understanding the material. In the session presented from Dr L's analysis, my counter-transference was my main resource for understanding that aspect of her material. For Jim, present and past were one and the same thing; at least with me he did not seem to know any difference; in the analysis we were just Fluffy and Puffy.[1] When he felt a bit understood by me I was immediately idealised. The Fluffy-me replaced in the sessions his 'angelic' smile, and this replacement would suggest that the angelic smile was itself a sign of his having been living as an ideal object or in an ideal state, precariously protected from further disintegration. His encopresis, as far as I understood it, seemed to express, in part, an uncontrollable oozing-out of bits of himself. The black mess and angelic smile were replaced by the dog and cat.

Dr L had always made frequent references to her history, which so far had been no more than superficial anecdotes which she tried to believe were psychoanalytic insights. I think they were the expressions of identifications with a confused and partly unavailable object. It was only when I could understand and sense what kind of object and situation was being enacted in the session that her history became alive in the analysis and reconstruction begun to take place. This later brought very important information about how she had remained fixed in such a relationship to her object.

In the material of Ms Y one can see in an interweaving of transference and counter-transference phenomena, verbal communication and enactment, which marked her return to masochistic defences in order to protect herself from facing a painful awareness of her reactions to Oedipal feelings. Understanding this permitted us to explore issues to do with early defences against similar problems which had expressed themselves in a severe agoraphobia. Once this was understood we could continue to work on it in the transference.

Summary

In this paper I have presented three clinical examples to show how the work of construction takes place in the transference, and also to show how the early conflicts, both those susceptible to recall and those not recallable in words, are experienced live in the transference.

PART II
Defences against anxieties of the depressive position

Introduction
Priscilla Roth

In this section are grouped five papers which concern organised defences against experiencing various aspects of the depressive position; Riesenberg-Malcolm shows how these defences emerge in analysis. These defences protect the patient from unbearable feelings of sorrow, regret, remorse and loss, but when organised and structured to such an extent that they become inseparable from what we call personality or character, may also severely limit his capacity to grow, to learn, or to feel real contact with his objects.

The first paper in this section, 'Self-punishment as defence', (originally published as 'Expiation as a defence'), was written in 1980 and is one of a number of papers published by Kleinian writers around that time on the subject of pathological organisations (see Steiner 1993: 47–53). The particular defensive structure which Riesenberg-Malcolm addresses is one in which the patient uses continuous self-punishment to avoid knowing about the damaged state of his internal objects, and thereby to avoid guilt. He constantly blames himself, but does nothing to put right the damage he feels he has caused.

This patient had in his mind a picture of an idealised mother; he had to cling to this picture to protect himself from an unconscious guilty belief that his hatred had destroyed his love for his mother, and, indeed, had destroyed his mother herself. In his first meeting with his analyst he told her that he had never told his mother that he loved her; that she had died when he was seventeen, and that therefore it was now 'too late'. This despairing conviction that it was too late to repair the damage he felt he had done, was to be repeated many times in the analysis. Despairing of being able to protect and repair his good object *internally*, and terrified of the guilt that thereby threatened him, he turned to an organising structure which would protect him from guilt by continuously submitting him to punishment. Such a structure, of course, continues and compounds the guilt-inducing relationship with his objects, and thus feeds on itself. This, then, is a defensive organisation dominated by masochism, and the strong presence of erotic elements – the fact that the patient achieves not only protection against psychic pain, but also sexual gratification from the maintaining of the organisation, complicated the analytic work. In the first phase of the analysis Mr K used the analyst to contain and digest the fragmented and then projected bits of his mind – he spilled himself out in meaningless words and inarticulate sounds. When she understood the meaning of what he was doing, and could tell him about it (after having tolerated the chaotic nature of it until she could understand) he became more able to think and to make meaningful links: his ego became somewhat stronger and he could speak more coherently.

But as soon as his mind was less fragmented he was faced with the problem of knowing about it, and this seemed to be almost intolerable. At this point, phase two, the patient made every effort to exert absolute control over the analyst. Riesenberg-Malcolm describes a split within him in which one part of him wanted to look at what was going on between them and inside himself, to learn and to know about himself; and another part, identified with a cruel, torturing gang of criminals, attacked both the aspect of himself which wanted to learn, and the analyst upon whom he was dependent. Through careful monitoring of interpretations to help him to struggle with his cruelty without being overwhelmed by it (or by guilt and envy) Riesenberg-Malcolm managed to establish a more benign relationship with her patient and to help him to strengthen his ego further. Knowing about himself, however, exposed him again to knowing about his guilty feelings – now about the way he had treated his analyst as well as how he treated his original objects in his mind.

Mr K could not bear this guilt, and he escaped from it into a static state of sado-masochistic triumph. This static, unchanging state was a new and more powerful means of controlling his inner and outer world: he could prevent his analyst from being useful, could thereby obviate his envy of her, and, by his incessant self-punishment, could keep at bay feelings of guilt at what he was doing to her. It is this pathological organisation which is explored in this paper.

Working painstakingly with her counter-transference feelings during this prolonged and difficult period, Riesenberg-Malcolm enabled the patient increasingly to tolerate looking at and knowing about himself and his treatment of his objects, past and present. Eventually, however, his guilt became too strong for him to bear and, after a period of separation and a temporary resumption of the treatment, the analysis broke down.

The case study gives us insight into the way such pathological organisations work, and helps us address the problems we have dealing with these patients.

It is interesting to compare this patient's use of a perverse defensive organisation with the way the patient in The Mirror paper used her perverse sexual phantasy. For The Mirror patient, the perversion could be more encapsulated, allowing her to develop in other areas outside the perverse organisation. For Mr K, the patient described in 'Self-punishment as a defence', the sexual gratification in the organisation was more pervasive and more destructive, in such a way as to preclude change and development.

The second paper in this section, 'Technical problems in the analysis of a pseudo-compliant patient', continues the exploration of pathological structures against the anxieties of the depressive position. For Mr K, the self-punishment patient, integration threatened to bring intolerable guilt. For Mrs H, the patient discussed in this paper, integration and development were threatened by a terrible fear of dependency on an object felt to be too weak to depend on. Like Mr K, Mrs H attempted to immobilise the relationship with her analyst so that it could continue, but could not seriously threaten an internal status quo. She did this by means of a pseudo-compliant relationship, in which she appeared to be fully cooperating and participating, when she was in fact setting up a mental wall through which interpretations were never allowed to penetrate. In this way she could seem to enjoy a friendly relationship within a friendly 'analysis', while not allowing her actual analyst to get through to her, thereby avoiding any genuine dependence.

Mrs H was not as ill as Mr K – her internal object was not in such a disintegrated state. Although it felt to her to be weak, her internal object contained loveable qualities and therefore did not have to be idealised in such a schizoid way. Thus, although she idealised her analyst, and herself as analyst/mother, she also seemed to be able to appreciate, use and identify with some genuinely good qualities in her object. She was not idealising her object in order to protect it from the kind of powerful hatred with which Mr K was dealing. For Mrs H, the object was weak and therefore would not protect her – she had to create a falsely idealised object with whom she could identify. Later, when she began more fully to recognise her analyst's strengths, she became prey to Oedipal anxieties, but so long as the falsely cooperative stage remained operative, she was internally in control of her object, and therefore had no need to worry about jealousy or rivalry.

Especially important in this paper is the sensitive handling, once again, of the particular counter-transference problems presented by such a patient. Riesenberg-Malcolm became aware that what presented itself as cooperation and appreciation – following a long period of intense denigration – was in fact only pseudo-cooperation, pseudo-compliance, and she demonstrates how she tackled this often intransigent situation.

The patients described in 'As-if: the phenomenon of not learning' suffer from different degrees of pathology, but all manifest what Helene Deutsch originally called the 'as-if' personality. Ruth Riesenberg-Malcolm links this to Bion's 'reversible perspective' and describes the way that in the analyses of these patients the analyst's interventions are heard, repeated and applied, but without any depth or meaning or specificity. Each of the patients has a different way of rendering interpretations meaningless: patient A immediately applies every interpretation, 'as if' correctly understood, to someone else in his life; patient B instantly connects the interpretation with some other event in her life again, 'as if' it had meaning, but actually in order to divest it of analytic meaning. Riesenberg-Malcolm calls this reaction to interpretations 'slicing', by which she means to convey the thinness of what is left after the patient's response to the interpretation has robbed it of depth and meaning.

She describes the peculiar nature of the analyst's counter-transference response to such patients, the shifting back and forth between feeling the patient's behaviour is conscious and deliberate and therefore highly provocative, and believing it to be unconscious. This uncertainty and even suspicion, characteristic of the analysis of 'as-if' patients, leads to questions about the nature of their early objects, and to the coexistence in their histories of severe maternal pathology and the patients' own endowment of envy.

Riesenberg-Malcolm begins the next paper, 'Hyperbole in hysteria', with a description of Bion's (1965) understanding of hysterical behaviour: that the hysteric resorts to hyperbole (exaggerated behaviour) in order to communicate or get rid of emotions which he feels are not received by his object, and which he therefore finds impossible to manage in any other way. To this formulation she adds another: that the nature of the hysterical behaviour itself gives a picture of the hysteric's internal objects and his relations with them.

This understanding of why an hysterical patient is behaving the way he is, and of the importance of paying attention to what the behaviour is communicating, allows Riesenberg-Malcolm to adopt a position in relation to her extremely difficult patient in which it is possible for her to be tolerant, patient and perceptive. As is often clear in her work, she trusts the meaningfulness of the patient's communication, and she trusts the process of analysis. This leads to interpretations which have none of the quality of static, repetitive, theory-driven responses; she is enabled by her theory (and by her own internal objects, which include her psychoanalytic forbears) to allow movement, change and transformation in the work.

She sees histrionic hysteria, as manifested by the patient whose material she discusses, as a pathological organisation: as such it serves some of the same defensive functions as Mr K's self-punishing (Chapter 5) and Mrs H's pseudo-compliance (Chapter 6). The patient moves back and forth, within the session and in response to interpretations, between avoiding fragmentation and avoiding depressive pain, as, for example, in the form of guilt.

'Dramatising patients', she writes (p. 145),

> show great difficulty tolerating frustration...when they are confronted with experiences that produce pain, they react to them in a way that results in some sort of swelling of the total experience, which then gets inflated and exaggerated but in some way remains integrated.

This is an important observation about this patient's material – it is not disintegrated. Although reading it on the page, such material looks very disturbed, and indeed can feel very disturbing to listen to, in fact Riesenberg-Malcolm believes that the behaviour may be less disturbed than it appears. The patient manifests a rapid oscillation between different levels of functioning – between believing in the action he stages and seeing it as metaphorical. This is understood as an enactment in the presence of the analyst of an internal situation of hopeless despair. The audience (the analyst) is obliged to witness helplessly the cruelty and mockery with which he is being treated, and to experience the despair. The patient himself is at least partially identified with a sadistic object: rejecting, cruel and contemptuous.

Riesenberg-Malcolm stresses that in order to understand and treat histrionic patients the analyst has to be aware of and follow the various splittings and the multiple projective identifications the splittings result in. This paper, written in 1995, demonstrates a further development and increased sophistication in her own capacity to follow the shifts between different internal objects as they express themselves in the transference.

'Pain, sorrow and resolution', written in 1997, is the last paper in this section and extends Riesenberg-Malcolm's study of depressive position phenomena into new areas. As I have noted, each of the previous papers in Part II describes a particular pathological organisation defensive against the anxieties of the depressive position. In 'Pain, sorrow and resolution', Riesenberg-Malcolm looks at the working through of the depressive position as a process in which the individual has to relinquish his control of his object. She is exploring two areas in this paper. First, she is drawing attention to the centrality of problems of separation from the object in the working through of the depressive position; second, she is describing progressive stages in this working through, each stage being characterised by a particular kind of psychic pain. The three patients she describes are each at a different stage in working through the depressive position; each is at a different point in the process of establishing separateness from his object; each experiences a different sort of psychic pain. Riesenberg-

Malcolm's work in this area continues and adds to the recent work of other British Kleinian analysts, notably Joseph (1989), Segal (1958, 1983) and Steiner (1993).

Finally, Riesenberg-Malcolm makes explicit in this paper something which is implicit in all her work: her conviction that our patients introject not only the *content* of our interpretations, but our *attitude* to our interpretations, our patients and the analytic endeavour itself. Bit by bit, over time, both analytic understanding (the content of interpretations) and the analytic function are introjected by the patient. It is the introjection of these two aspects of the analyst which allows the patient eventually to take back his projections, to have and use his own mind and to properly separate from his analyst.

5

Self-punishment as defence

In this paper I wish to deal with a specific type of defence which organises itself in analysis into tight, closed, and rigid behaviour that creates an impasse which may make continuation of analysis, as well as termination, impossible. I am referring to those patients who use self-punishment and suffering to avoid what for them is feared as even greater suffering and danger, namely their perception of the damaged state of their internal objects – a perception indispensable for any real reparative work.

The patients I shall discuss feel their internal world to be populated by damaged or destroyed objects. They are afraid of being responsible for this destruction and feel helpless and hopeless to do anything about it. They have often reached a point in analysis in which some of the persecutory anxiety and schizoid defences have diminished, they appear more integrated, and they have experienced relief. They are on the verge of realising how they perceive the state of their loved internal objects. But here they experience a pain of such intensity that it quickly becomes persecutory. They fear this pain to be unendurable and this makes them turn away with hatred from analytical work, into a pathological organisation.[1]

One such an organisation is achieved by those patients who seem to operate on the principle that 'no change provides safety from pain and disaster'. Bion (1963) refers to a phenomenon similar to the one I am referring to here. In what he calls 'reversible perspective', he describes a situation in which the patient tries to achieve a static condition, and he says the patient does it secretly.

This paper was first published under the title of 'Expiation as a defense' in the *International Journal of Psychoanalytic Psychotherapy*, volume 8 (1980–1). It was also published in Spanish, under the same title, in Asociacion Psicoanalitica de Buenos Aires, *Revista de la Asociacion Psicoanalitica de Buenos Aires*, volume III (1981).

The patients I will be discussing here turn from the analytic work by leaning towards masochistic behavior, which serves the purpose of preventing the emergence of any awareness of their feelings of guilt. They feel they are making expiation by being incessantly punished for what they believe is the damage they have done. This self-punitive behaviour takes the place of what should be reparation.

In most analyses we get momentary or temporary self-punishing reactions, but in the patients I am talking about the whole analysis is turned into a continual failure of the analysis, with the aim of making the analyst and the analysis be punitive. Self-punitive patients organise their behaviour in the analysis so as to create a static situation which consists of their own suffering and misery plus the analyst's immobilisation. They feel that this static condition encapsulates or puts their dread within limits; it contains it in such a way that the patient does not actually have to face it.

Contrary to the static state described by Bion in reversible perspective, the immobilisation caused by an unending punitiveness is not a secret. The patient clings to a situation of non-analysis in a setting that is nominally analysis, and feels that this state of affairs should last for life. The patient's awareness of being able to produce the halt in the analysis also brings feelings of triumph, often linked with sexual excitation. This erotic satisfaction contributes, in part, to the perpetuation of this type of behaviour. The patient believes that he avoids or denies his helplessness through keeping things as they are. He projects his helpless self into the analyst, and also his own potential for feeling guilty. Through the use of these mechanisms of projective identification, he not only feels that he has rid himself of undesirable feelings and problems, but also he avoids responsibility, for now the analyst is the guilty one.

These dynamics, the belief in having succeeded in ridding himself of the dread of madness or death, together with the sexual gratification, both masochistic and sadistic, place this problem close to the area of perversion. Here I think it worth remembering Glover's paper, 'The relation of perversion formation to the reality sense' (1933), in which he describes sexual perversions as defences used by the patient against psychosis.[2]

Along with the patient's fear of harbouring damaging and accusing objects, the patient also has a relation to an idealised omnipotent primary object. The emergence in the analysis of contact with this ideal object (experienced in the transference as the analyst), and the patient's own good feeling towards the ideal object, sometimes permits a breach in the otherwise steel-like enclosure, and proper analytic work can take place. But the patient will generally react to this achievement in two ways. On the one hand he will feel pleased, sometimes relieved, and will be more generous. This encouragement makes the patient feel that the analyst has been sufficiently reassured, so that the patient feels he has removed any danger of the analysis coming to an end. On the other hand, progress fosters the patient's hatred because he quickly feels exposed to those very conflicts that he is trying to avoid, and thus he will reinforce his attacks on the analyst's competence. From the analyst's point of view, this type of encapsulation, and the occasional breakthrough that permits a more hopeful view of the patient's loving and constructive capacities, undoubtedly complicates the whole range of counter-transference responses.

The combination of these factors makes the analysis go in circles. The patient's interest is to prevent it from progressing, since the so-called 'analysis' is perceived by him as confining his problems to the analytic sessions without further consequence. The analyst feels that he can neither help the patient nor terminate the analysis, because the patient's expiatory behaviour presents a continuous danger of suicide or disintegration. Both analyst and patient are locked in a difficult, even impossible, situation. Should termination be contemplated, both patient and analyst are faced with a sense of absolute irreparability.

Clinical presentation

Mr K came to analysis primarily with the desire to become an analyst, but also to get some help with his problems, the most important of which he felt to be indecisiveness. He described himself as a 'compulsive doubter' and 'the most successful failure'. In his first interview he reported a profuse symptomatology. His aspirations were bizarre and he was intensely arrogant and incoherent. He was also obviously in considerable pain. He showed some warmth as well as a fine sense of humour. It was very difficult for him to leave the interview.

Previous diagnostic consultations with different psychiatrists had resulted in apparently different diagnoses, all along lines of psychosis or borderline conditions. A previous analysis had lasted three years, and turned into a three-times-a-week psychotherapy. The analyst ended it abruptly in a way that seemed to me to be very traumatic, but Mr K spoke of this with both glee and triumph.

Mr K was the only son of what appeared to be a very disturbed family. He described his mother as an 'extremely good person': 'She always wanted the best for me.' From the beginning he repeated that she had used influence to get him into exclusive schools and other circles. But she worked full-time, and actually took no personal care of him because of what appeared to be excessive anxiety. Mr K nonetheless always spoke of her with reverence. The little time she spent with him was spoken of as not merely good, but nearly perfect. He used to say this in a flat voice with no feeling. He also said that she worried very much about him, fearing that he did not grow, put on sufficient weight as a baby, or was not pretty enough. In the preliminary interview he communicated something that would recur frequently in the analysis, namely that he had never told her that he loved her and that she died before he thought of doing so, when he was seventeen.

The father emerged from the patient's description as hard and indifferent, not sharing much of his life with the family. The parents were separated for approximately two years when the patient was two years old. Mr K's father had died before the analysis began.

During Mr K's first year of life he was looked after by a quick succession of nurses. Then a permanent nanny arrived, who stayed until he grew up. Despite many problems in infancy and childhood, Mr K finished school, studied at a university, and obtained a degree and a professional qualification. He emigrated to Australia partly because he could not get along with his father and also because his mother used to tell him that this would be 'the best place in the world to live!' In Sydney lived his mother's sister, of whom he said he was very fond. He went to Melbourne and there suffered his first major breakdown and had to return to England. He spoke of his coming back in many ways. He stressed how besieged he was by doubts about returning but also said that he needed 'to make it up with father before it was too late'. But when he returned trouble with his father started again, and during a very violent row his father told him to go to his room. He stayed there, literally, doing nothing for a year. Finally he made himself leave the room, studied his father's craft, making jewellery, and in spite of disliking it, worked at it part-time.

Phase one: the psychotic transference

I want to divide the account of his analysis into three phases. In the first, the patient was highly disturbed. He often had flights of ideas, made many puns, constantly mocked everything, and sometimes hallucinated. In the first week of his analysis he spoke of a dream and an incident with his father, both of which would have considerable importance in his treatment. The dream occurred during the night before his first analytic session with me.

He was in a village inside a ditch, and had to climb up to get to freedom. He had in his hand a kind of miner's pick, but when he proceeded to make his way up, an enormous amount of rocks, earth and all kinds of heavy things fell on his head. To his surprise, the first association that came into his mind was a very thin girl whom he knew. At that time she was about to leave London to go south.

My interpretations of this material were very tentative. They were related to his fear of what the analysis might do to him or what he might do in it.

I also mentioned that he might be worried about my strength: would I have to run away? (My accent as well as my appearance suggest that I might be native to a southern Latin country.)

The incident he told me about had occurred when he was ten years old, and he related it with a mixture of worry, satisfaction and hatred. His father asked him to go and buy cigars for him. The patient provocatively asked 'Where?' His father, irritated, said 'Stanmore', the location of the jewellery workshop, in a London suburb some forty-five minutes from home. Mr K did exactly that, going to Stanmore and coming back some two hours later. He spontaneously volunteered an explanation. He said that he had always been very passive and wanted to be told what to do. He said this in a strange, very flat voice, sneering at the same time. He also said that the actual place where his father wanted him to go was in fact opposite their home, but the patient did not like the place. He thought it was frequented by prostitutes and he felt ill at ease there. He said that he had always hoped that his parents or grown-ups would guess how he felt.

At the time, I noted how immensely heavy Mr K felt and how despairingly he experienced the approach of the analytic task. I also noted that I felt uncomfortable about the way he spoke of the incident with his father. I wondered how much he would use sadistic sexual acting out.

From the beginning of the analysis Mr K reacted very intensely to weekend separations. After the first analytic holiday he came back in a severe state of depression.

In this phase, as in the following one, he often communicated concretely through action rather than verbally. He used to wear ragged clothes, especially a pair of old trousers, full of holes, as a way of showing me how impoverished, miserable and broken he felt. He usually came in a long coat, several sizes too large for him, that had belonged to his father, and he kept emphasising that it was 'my dead father's coat!' (When we started the treatment, his father had been dead for several years.) In the sessions, he moved around the room, sat on the floor, or stood immobile near the door. He often felt that I suffered from delusions.

In this first phase there emerged material that threw light on his early infancy. For one thing, we learned about his severe feeding problems. He often reacted to my interpretations by turning them into a meaningless mash which he would let ooze out in the form of fragmented sentences, words and mere sounds. I learned in this way that disintegrative processes were operating and also that he had to get rid of their products very quickly. In response to my interpretation of this material, he told me that he had been informed that he had suffered a severe diarrhoea during most of his first year of life or a bit longer, and that this had made his mother frantic. We then were able to link his behaviour in the transference to experiences in his early infancy.

In the transference, I stood for all kinds of part or whole objects. There emerged with great clarity a division of me as a very powerful mother (or breast), that could give him anything if I so wished. For example, I could make him normal, I could be his analyst or make him into an analyst, that is, somehow let him become me. Or else I was felt to be rigid, just giving him interpretations, keeping set times, a harsh nurse determined only to feed and clean him. Occasionally I was a more intermediate figure: not too bright, quite insensitive, just wanting him 'to adjust', the nanny who wanted him to be a well behaved child.

In a paternal transference, he perceived me as stronger and more aggressive, ready to criticise. He had to win me to his side, conquer me or fight me. All this was done in a highly eroticised and teasing way and it felt very homosexual.

In spite of the severity of pathology, genuine progress took place. Mr K's relation to me changed and his material became more coherent. He started again to report dreams (which had stopped for quite some time); he developed a passion for them because their analysis brought him great relief, as well as convincing understanding.

Phase two: extreme control

Together with these positive changes, new aspects began to appear in the sessions; it is these which I refer to as the second phase. Mr K began to control me more and more. He produced two or three repetitive themes with the aim of proving that I could do nothing; at the same time, he really expected me to provide an answer that would solve his problems at a stroke. For example, he would ask me a question, generally practical and referring to an actual situation in his everyday life – for instance, whether he should post a letter. I was ordered to answer in one of four ways: 'yes' or 'no', 'I don't know', or 'I cannot answer because it is against the psychoanalytic technique'. What I interpreted was irrelevant if I actually answered as he demanded, because when I did so he proceeded to find a flaw in the answer. Whatever I said, or if I said nothing, it always drove him to recite the alphabet again and again, sometimes for the duration of several sessions.

Initially I tried to deal with this development as ordinary material to be interpreted in the whole of the transference context. Since I could not reach him this way, I would begin my intervention with 'I don't know', and try to explain the reason why I was in no position to know, and how the problem seemed to go further than the realm of the question and answer. I added that he might be very determined to get an 'answer' from me, but that I thought he also might perceive my interpretation differently. He would answer that all that was irrelevant since I had spoiled 'his orders' by going beyond the sentence, 'I don't know'. He would ask why I could not just say, 'I don't know', or why I could not just say 'that it was against the technique!' My attempts to remind him that he knew (from his own statements in previous sessions) that the technique was no more than a part of a process would be interrupted.

At some point I managed to get across to him (and I wish to remind the reader that most of the time he was monotonously reciting the alphabet) that his questioning me, together with his need to make me obey orders, seemed to suggest other questions that might feel upsetting to him, which probably felt too painful and were related to the way he was treating me. Therefore, by turning me into a mechanical answering machine he believed he could avoid those potential upsets. Sometimes his whole manner would show that he was touched by my words. But the hatred of having been touched and therefore losing successful control would increase his anxiety, driving him to intensify the monotonous recitations.

On the occasions in which I would just say 'I don't know', he might speak about something else, but then promptly repeat the original question. He would say he was not sure if my response was 'the answer' or just a 'catch'. I tried as far as I could to point out both his controlling behaviour and also the fears I thought underlay this control. I remarked that the dread he might be experiencing made him fear that everything was a trick. I also attempted to link this fear of guilt with the sadistic satisfaction he was getting from his behaviour, and how this in turn made it more difficult for him to get out of his psychological state.

Another theme, his complaints about his life and work, also applied to the analysis. Mr K would say in a very tormented way: 'I drill holes and fill them up with silver; that is all I do.' He drilled into all my attempts to interpret and filled the sessions with repetitions of the alphabet. In turn, I often felt as if my mind were a sieve. I could remember very little from the sessions, but was preoccupied with what was going on in them. My mind was not functioning during sessions, but it did not wander. The reason for this, I believe, is that he had a powerful hold on me, probably through a minute type of projective identification. I remember an occasion in which I was very preoccupied by a problem of my own, and it came fleetingly into my mind during a session. Mr K stopped saying whatever he was saying, and sat up in a panic.

This behaviour lasted for many months. I think that because of all the effort, very slowly one could see a mixed response. He tried to harden himself even more against my interpretations. He even brought a tape recorder into the sessions with the explanation that he had no memory.

I felt very uncomfortable with this new development, but I accepted the machine at first, knowing that should I refuse it, the likelihood was that I would not be able to enforce my refusal. I also thought that should I succeed, it was very probable that Mr K would perceive it as an increased success: I would be doing what he had been demanding all the time: 'giving direct orders'. With him, I kept my instructions to an absolute minimum; the analysis took place in the consulting room at set times and the door would be closed. I tried to deal with the rest of his actions through analytic interpretations.

I felt that the tape recorder, moreover, showed two main things: his behaviour was leaving him without a memory, that is, without a mind, and that he also had a desire to remember. I oriented my interpretations from this second aspect. I emphasised the pains and difficulties arising from his continually trying to put out of his mind almost everything by questioning and, even more, by his monotonous chanting of the alphabet. There was some positive explicit acknowledgement from him in the midst of his acting in.

Together with the appearance of the tape recorder there was, at first, increased bizarre behaviour, I think probably as a response to how he perceived my feelings. But in spite of some mockery, his desire to remember was taking first priority, to the point of his genuinely stating, 'I did not want to lose what you were saying.' His recitations diminished and an increase of violence in his associations came to the fore.

Once, upon entering the room, he looked with horror at the couch, stood very still, and asked me if there was a four-poster bed where the couch used to be. He said that he saw it. I will try to summarise the content of many weeks of work on this issue. The main associative theme was prostitution and a pub called the Blind Beggar. During this time, news reports were following a trial that was taking place. A criminal gang that used to terrorise the East End of London was being tried. It had just come to light that the gang's means of achieving their objectives was torture. The gang operated from the Blind Beggar pub.

As I have mentioned before, Mr K's main mode of communication was through actions or tone of voice. From the way he was speaking, I felt that something very dangerous was going on at this point, and for the first time in this analysis I actually became frightened for my safety. I used my fears as an orientation of where to put the emphasis in the interpretations. (I also took some practical measures of protection, such as having a nurse in the flat who would come should I ring an electric bell near my chair.)

The interpretations pointed mainly towards the operation of a torturing gang inside himself, directed against both me and the self who wanted 'to remember', to learn, and to know so that he could feel better. This cruelty in him was so terrifying that he felt we had to submit to it to prevent further and worse consequences. I linked it to blindness – so as not to get insight, not to know, since the guilt of seeing what was going on was threatening the most intense pain. In that way, he felt it was better to be a beggar, to get nothing, rather than experience the awareness of this awful sight. I also, very slowly, emphasised that now, in spite of the torturing terror, he was more able to look at what was going on in his mind. He could bring it more into the open, speak about it and, though half-heartedly, try to remember the meaning it had for him. The half-heartedness came from the question: Who was remembering? Himself, or a machine without responsibility?

While working in this area, my fears progressively diminished and I dispensed with the nurse. Mr K made repetitive attempts to increase and harden his control, while at the same time his cruelty towards me became more vicious. Nevertheless, I felt that he could keep an increasingly continuous contact, mainly through interpretations that he could take and which allowed for an alternation between cruelty and genuine understanding. This allowed him to attempt to control the cruel behaviour, and he tried to work with me. Those attempts, however slight and shortlived, had a real constructive quality, and marked changes occurred in the sessions. The recitation disappeared almost totally. He began to bring dreams again and to work at them. Glimpses of changes in his external life emerged. He seemed less isolated, spoke about people, and resumed his original profession part-time (which he liked better than jewellery and which he had stopped practising because of excessive anxiety). His relation to a girlfriend seemed to become less bizarre.

It seems to me that many factors had played a part in producing those modifications (I am speaking of work done over a period of years). The decrease in the need for such sadistic control was partly due to his perceiving me as a strong analyst who could contain his 'horrors' without being completely overwhelmed by his anxieties, and therefore he felt that I was able to present them back to him (re-introjection) in a modified way (Bion 1962). He experienced gratitude and a desire to make good, which in turn brought new incentives towards further understanding which, in small quantities, could be used by him.

In other words, through the increase of introjective processes a more benign relationship was setting in which allowed for the possibility of structural modifications. His superego became less cruel and punitive. His ego also became stronger and therefore much less in need of resorting to extreme modes of defence. The following vignette might bring a clearer feeling of what I am trying to say. In one session, he said rather angrily that I was like one of the nurses he had as a baby: 'She must have been a brutal beast.' He had been told that she even sat him on top of a wardrobe to get him to eat. I said that this could be taken as beastly, but that I also wondered if he might not be saying, however angry it made him, that he recognised my efforts as like that of the nurses in childhood: not letting him starve or go hungry. I added that we might have been trying to get the baby in him to take something in, since food, mental food, is important for life and growth. He was moved by this and felt thankful. He said, 'I have to give it to you, you do try and if something does not work you try something else, in spite of me being so beastly to you. Either you are not too frightened or you still go on in spite whatever!'

This improvement in the analysis lasted for some time, after which I began again to feel myself progressively more limited in my thinking (this time it felt differently, more oppressive) and in my capacity to reach him with my interpretations. A new repetitive theme started to establish itself in the material. He began to produce endless variations of one sentence: 'I made a mistake'; 'A mistake happened'; 'It is all because of a mistake!' The mistake to which he referred was that he came back to England instead of staying in the ideal place, Australia. As one may imagine, I tried to deal with this material from many angles, all to no avail; and then I realised that I was totally stuck. We were in what I call the third phase.

Phase three: stagnation

With phase three, Mr K had reached the most difficult point in his analysis, for along with the improvement, feelings of guilt became paramount. However difficult the previous two phases were, for the patient this last one appeared to be insurmountable.

The themes were very repetitive, circling mainly around the same contents. For example, Mr K would walk into the room, not looking at me. Once on the couch, instead of speaking directly, he would say something like, 'Shall I talk to you or not?' Or he would recite a long rigmarole, always the same, which amounted to asking me whether he should write an application to the Institute of Psycho-Analysis.

In spite of the immense repetitiveness of these sentences, the feeling they conveyed to me was far from being always the same. Sometimes it seemed to be a plea to give him a helping hand that would allow him to start. Sometimes he did accept the help and began to speak directly about the issues that were in his mind. But of course this did not always happen. There were very subtle nuances in how he said things that did allow me to sense different things.

On other occasions he sounded more excited, and whatever I said then was discarded. If I said nothing, this was taken as a hostile provocation or as proof that I had been put out of action. When I did speak, be it an interpretation or a description, Mr K would meet it with great contempt. He would tear it to pieces and the 'mistake' was brought to the fore, generally in a very plaintive, monotonous, nasal tone, immediately followed by a superior attitude to prove that, since the mistake took place twenty years ago, it was of no use for either of us to try to understand anything at all.

During this period Mr K suffered intensely, but according to him, I also had to suffer, so he had to 'drill it into me'. One of his fears was that otherwise I would not know how he felt. He again resorted to the use of massive projective methods and concrete behaviour. Also he believed that this was sexually stimulating for me, that it must be exciting, 'kept me on my toes', particularly if he could believe that he was hurting me. (My main feelings were very painful, and a couple of times I did actually get a very short-lasting, sharp stomach pain. He perceived the whole situation as turning into a flirtation, a sexual game.)

He also had the conviction that I had the power to put things right, but, of course, not through analysis. For him this meant putting the clock back twenty years, and turning him into an analyst. He believed firmly that a word of mine would make him accepted into the Institute of Psycho-Analysis. He felt that I was very cruel not to do this, and it stimulated him to further cruelty to prove how useless I was.

Through very careful listening to his way of talking, rather than its content, since what he said was usually very much the same, I could sense a possibility of making contact with his anxiety. It is possible that I felt him to be more receptive and felt myself to be less tied up. I tried to do something that I had done before, to produce just descriptive summaries. As in most of my interpretations, I would usually start from his state of pain, his desire to draw me into attacking him, so that I would become actively 'the punisher'. On other occasions I could sense from the way he was speaking that he was actually aware of thinking something else, or was preoccupied by something, and I would try to point this out to him. He would show surprise at my noticing it, and would allow associations to flow and would listen to interpretations. For example, one day he was reciting his litany: 'Oh! that terrible mistake, why, why did I do it?' I felt that in spite of his usual monotonous voice, which he called 'tuned-down-flat', he was agitated. I also felt myself becoming more alert. I ventured a comment in which I said that I thought that he was agitated, and that this monotonous litany might also refer to something else. He was startled, and started speaking about having been very worried because of something he said to a colleague that he thought might have been very unkind.

This instance, as well as others, allowed for some analytic work to take place. He could then take in some understanding about his unkindness to me – originally the nurse – and the fear it gave him to look at it. We also worked on the fact that the 'not looking' made him feel that he lived eternally in 'a mistake'. He became more depressed, his whole demeanour changed, and he would appear very worried. During these times he shrank from any interpretation of his positive qualities as a person, since this seemed to increase his feelings of guilt as well as his fears about his ability to sustain his good qualities. For example, when I would refer to his concern about someone at work, he would react with a mixture of pleasure and fear, fear that would often lead him to mock me and himself or try to prove the contrary. 'Me, doing something good? You must suffer from excessive imagination!'

I believe that 'the mistake' was also an attempt at encapsulation, though of course not exclusively that. But a mistake, just one, however badly it made him feel, also allowed him not to have to look at many things, many so-called mistakes, in his behaviour towards his objects. Furthermore, *the* mistake consisted in leaving the land felt to be ideal by his mother. He had behaved very nastily to many people in Australia; he did break down; he 'was expelled from Paradise'.

At other times, Mr K was in a more receptive and sad frame of mind. He would puzzle about why he behaved towards me as he did. He would question whether he was a pervert. These questions were sometimes mocking, but more often they were serious and concerned. Sometimes my interpretations were oriented towards how much he worried about this. In spite of trying to laugh it off or reassure himself that I was a masochist and that was the reason I put up with him, he had doubts. He felt that his behaviour was not only hard on me but incomprehensible to him, that just to say that he was 'a pervert' did not mean much, and that he needed to look into this cruel, gruelling behaviour that he called 'perversion'. I sometimes also pointed out to him how much he wanted me to call him a pervert; the word would then acquire a moralistic meaning and he could feel me as accusing and punishing. In other words, through projective identification, I would be the punisher, and he thought that then he could avoid his own anxieties. When I managed to get this across to him and he did not feel me to be punitive, he experienced intense pain that drove him into panic, which in turn prompted him to intensify the cruelty of his behaviour by a total grinding of my interpretations, rendering everything, both what I had said and his own understanding, meaningless.

If he did not succeed in this, and my words had some impact on him, he would force himself to sleep in the session in order to cut off all contact. He would also force himself into sleep when he came with the desire to tell me something he felt important. This felt too dangerous to him.

One of my greatest difficulties with this patient was to avoid being too repetitive, and to try to be alert to any minimal change in his way of speaking or inflections that could be used for either a new approach or for a new way of addressing him.

I also felt more and more under internal pressure. The idea of the scarcity of time kept creeping into my mind. I often found myself thinking that 'I have to do something' or it would become 'too late'. 'I have to think of something'. I think that I may have contributed to his own fears by 'trying too hard', until I realised and became clearer about the projections into me of feelings of irreparability. I could then orient my interpretations, starting from my feelings of pressure and his feelings about time passing. (He spoke often about this, but I do not think that my reactions were due to actual, external reality.) I became more watchful so as not to overinterpret, and tried to increase my containment of the situation for longer stretches of time. During the whole analysis I had let him talk or act at length, but I felt at this point, maybe not sufficiently, that he needed even a longer time. In spite of his intense suffering he needed me to wait and wait, and only then to interpret. This projective identification was aimed at testing whether I could endure him without going out of my mind. But it required a careful balance, since if waiting was perceived just 'a fraction too long', it was felt to be a proof that my mind was out of action.

In spite of all these difficulties, he managed to convey something that made me feel slightly hopeful and also very sorry for him. After a period in which the balance between a total paralysis of the analysis and some more sensitive understanding was tipped slightly towards the latter, Mr K became very depressed. His external life deteriorated. He complained often that he could not cope any longer and he interrupted analysis for some time. Guilt became very prominent.

He warned about the possibility of his stopping several weeks before he actually did so. I think that the idea might have been in his mind for a longer time, considering the intense pressure I kept experiencing of 'having to do something'.

He approached the subject of stopping the analysis in two ways. First, he said he had no money, that he was spending more than he was earning, and he could not afford it. Of course, I think what he could not afford were his depressive feelings. Second, he just had to stop. His explanations were so muddled that I cannot reproduce them here. His language was almost incomprehensible. He moved as someone attacked by intense pains that could not be described in words. He acted as if under a tormenting force that dragged him away from me. He could not 'stand coming to analysis'. I think I was then experienced as internally pulling him to the struggles between love and hate, life or death (externally he could be more warm and friendly to me). He maintained that he could not stand this, that he had more to lose than to gain, much like a baby who, as soon as it allows itself to be fed, gets bouts of colic and diarrhoea. Mostly those feelings were projected into me, so that he was convinced that stopping would bring relief and possibly freedom.

He broke away from analysis, kept telephone contact with me, and eventually asked to come back. During the interruption he had pulled himself together. He had started working full-time. He felt triumphant and hypomanic. He felt that he had cured himself in the same way, whatever that was, that he had got himself out of the room in his father's house. He also reacted triumphantly to my taking him back.

Why did he come back? And why did I take him back? It soon appeared that the flight into so-called 'health' couldn't be maintained and that he was in panicky fear of collapsing, of becoming very depressed and of falling to pieces. He acknowledged only some of this when he asked to be taken back, but he did agree that now he was not coming for analytical training but as a patient in need of treatment.

My reasons for taking him back into analysis were mixed. I was aware of the dangers of not doing so. But I think it was predominantly his capacity to stimulate hope in me about making some fundamental change, as well as the projection into me of the need to do something. Looking back, I think I felt trapped in the situation which I described at the beginning of this paper, which is what makes it impossible to terminate such an analysis. I think that I, as well as he, found it impossible to face the idea that he might be beyond repair. Though I was doubtful about the wisdom of taking him back, I discussed it with a colleague; I think I was more inclined to cling to hope.

I would like for a moment to consider some aspects of what I have been saying about this patient.

I think Mr K had achieved a relationship to an object, a whole object, but this relationship was never firmly established and developed. It is my opinion that his tendency to idealisation when he was an infant was expressed in multiple associations and reactions to interpretations. 'Mother was extraordinarily good', 'kind to a superhuman degree, she rushed from her death bed to take a gift to a charitable society'. In the analysis, when something really did satisfy him he used to have a very strange, blissful smile or he would praise an interpretation or my capacity to make it, in a way that had no basis at all, either in what I did or said. For instance, when I once made an ordinary, pedestrian interpretation, not new, but to which he had not listened before, he said, with a kind of radiance, 'You are Shakespeare!'

The idealisation, a normal factor in any infant development, was probably accentuated in Mr K by constitutional weakness. The split was between the very bad mother (breast) and the extremely good mother as expressed in his analytic material. This split was much stronger than in ordinary patients and, I think, probably was also reinforced by his mother.

Not only could she not contain his anxieties but she projected her own anxieties into the child and needed continuous reassurance from him. She was always worried that he might not be well, and dragged him from doctor to doctor. This was to the intense annoyance of the patient's father, who found no sign of things going badly, and it was contrary to the view of the paediatricians. He had also been told that, when little, as soon as he and mother were together, he laughed and made all kinds of 'cute things for her'. Whatever he told me about things that went on at home with his mother, some of which sounded either harsh or bizarre, there was never a note of criticism for her. Also, there was never any praise for a nurse or nanny.

In the analysis, when he felt me to be the ideal mother, he invested me with omnipotent powers. I could turn him into someone else: a very successful analyst. I think that as an ideal mother I was to get him right inside me, through his being fused with me, becoming me. I was the mother who got him into 'exclusive places' (the only child). He also felt compelled to tell me ever so often how intelligent I was or how my interpretations sounded poetic – often when these remarks were completely alien to the general feelings he was having at the moment.

The deep split between the ideal mother and the bad persecuting nurses, and the difficulty of bringing those aspects closer together, was also influenced by another factor. It is my impression that as soon as he would get close to his mother physically he became very excited. This excitement seems to have spoilt the contact, confusing him about the quality of the object he was in contact with.

This confusion was seen in ample transference manifestations; deeply hostile as well as friendly actions were so intermingled with excitement, that it was often impossible to discern what was going on. It required a very lengthy, patient and minute observation while holding the situation.

This extreme idealisation of his mother made it much more difficult for him to work through guilt. Since his perception of his mother was of a perfect object, any damage to it made the guilt enormous. And he felt helpless to repair the damage unless he himself was omnipotently perfect.

The conjunction of these factors made his capacity to bear pain, which was probably constitutionally limited, almost non-existent. Therefore guilt was perceived as a horrible experience and had to be avoided at all costs.

Finally, the paralysing of the analyst, together with the avoidance of guilt, seemed to express a passive early experience of an inadequate mother, and perhaps had the aim of communicating the experience of a passive helpless mother; but at the same time this communication was turned into something pleasurable in itself. This eroticisation, which in the analysis appears so perverse, may have stemmed from an early experience, probably perceived as very confusing by the child, in which he felt that if he could act sexually, he would enliven the object and make it less anxious. I think this explains, at least partially, his conviction that somewhere there was some pleasure for me in all this.

Once Mr K was back in analysis, after the short period at the beginning in which he was hypomanic, he made a genuine effort to work in the analytic sessions. But he soon relapsed in the ways I have previously described, this time in a worse form. He sometimes reported dreams literally in only the last one or two minutes of the session. They were often of concern to me and contained elements indicating potential suicidal danger. When I tried to refer to them the following day, Mr K would not let me talk, or would go to sleep.

Two dreams were the last ones he reported before a complete paralysis took over. Unusually early in the session, looking very depressed, he reported the following.

I was walking through a very dangerous path, probably mined, full of barbed wire. It was surrounded by police, just standing there. It was in Connaught Square [in central London] and I felt that if I managed to walk through, I would be free. This last remark was painfully sincere. Then his tone changed. He seemed to force himself to mock me. He said, 'Well, we lived right next to that place. Nanny used to take me there for walks. All right, come on. What can you make out of this?'

I pointed out that perhaps Connaught Square might also refer to something else. To my surprise, this silenced him and after some thought he reported that when watching television the previous night, he had seen a programme about the siege in Connaught Square. The Provisional IRA were holding a couple as hostages in a flat. He added that in the dream, he did reach the other side and was safe. He looked very subdued.

My interpretation was that he seemed to be suffering a severe conflict that had been with him since childhood. He knew he had to go through something very difficult to reach safety and real freedom. These difficulties felt horrible to him, both internally and externally. If he attempted to walk, he feared that he would be torn into pieces (the wire), this probably having to do with separation from his objects, both me and the original one. His insides would explode like the mines. It is striking that no helping hand existed and so he surrendered to an aspect of himself that ordered him to freeze everything, including the transactions between the analytical couple. There is a connection here to the imprisoned couple in the flat.

The patient was extremely quiet. After a moment he went on to say that he had 'a bit of a dream' following the previous one and with the same theme. He described it as follows: *I want to reach freedom and safety. To do so I have to dig a tunnel and go through it. While I am digging it, I see the gravel and rubbish piling up into a terrible mess that makes me feel that I will never be able to clear it up.* He had awakened abruptly at 3 a.m., feeling extremely depressed. After this description he complained about becoming increasingly slow in whatever he did. He could not function.

This session was drawing to an end. I tried in my interpretation to link the two dreams. I said that if he functioned in the analysis and he used me properly, he would see such a mess that he feels hopeless to put it right. But that he also felt me to be helpless, as somebody held in a siege, paralysed like the policemen, paralysed by his behaviour in the previous sessions. It is his perception of me as being helpless that added to his hopelessness. If I was allowed to help him, and also, if he was aware of the mess, then both of us would have to clean it up. He felt very badly about it, so badly that he became panic-stricken with the fear that he would not be able to bear it. So he had to stop everything, even the dream by waking himself. He left the session looking extremely depressed. The next session he slept the entire time. I tried to reach him by reminding him of the similarity between the dream he told last session and the one he dreamed at the very beginning of his analysis. He jerked, opened his eyes, and went back to sleep. I don't know how much he had listened, but I think that he heard something.

I waited. I tried now to link both dreams to the anecdote he also had told me in his first session (both of those memories from that first session came suddenly and spontaneously into my mind).

I pointed out that his fears of the consequences of his provocative and stubborn behaviour made him not only feel awful but also made him perceive me as an internal father, impotent to help him with the gravel. So he had to shut himself in by going to sleep. Again he jerked opened his eyes, closed them, and started a rhythmical breathing so as to induce sleep.

He slept the entire time as well as in many subsequent sessions. It was impossible to re-establish any contact with him until he finally resumed the old pattern of repetitiveness which made the analysis static.

I want to end this clinical presentation with these dreams, which I consider to be very revealing, because they express his hopelessness as well as his determination to paralyse and maintain the siege. As a result of his own determined effort, he returned to his usual mode of stultifying behaviour. I was totally paralysed, while he suffered, complained, and demanded, as an immediate omnipotent cure, that I should make him into an analyst.

The analysis went on in this manner for many months. It became progressively impossible to reach him. By now I was faced with a decision. Was it advisable to go on in a situation in which I was no more than a guardian-nursemaid or a perverse sexual partner? This, of course, in addition to its uselessness, increases the patient's guilt. Or does the analyst have to take steps to end the treatment, facing the consequences this may have?

I finally decided in favour of ending the analysis. I waited for some time before actually telling him, in order to see how this decision might influence my work with the patient. I felt freer, but things did not change at all.

I gave the patient slightly less than a term of notice (approximately two months, a considerably shorter time than is my usual practice). I decided on this shorter time to give him a chance to do some work toward termination but also in order not to make the termination time so distant that my announcement might appear to him as more threat than fact. Also, in my wording of the announcement I did not leave open the possibility of continuing with me.

Discussion

I want to limit my discussion to four main points extracted from the vast range of problems that a patient such as the one I have spoken about presents:

(a) specific difficulties in the contemplation of terminating an analysis with this type of patient;
(b) some comments on the problem of self-punishment;
(c) the impingement of this type of psychopathology on the analyst's emotional responses; and
(d) some considerations about technique.

Early in the paper I mentioned that from the patient's point of view, stopping the analysis carries serious dangers of suicide or disintegration. As many authors have already pointed out, this danger underlies many of the problems that bring about a negative therapeutic reaction. I think that the specificity of suicidal danger in a defensive constellation of self-punishment consists in the patient's carrying his expiation to the last consequences, for himself as well as for his internal objects. These patients will reach the climax of suffering by dying, which is what they fear most. The other specific causation in this syndrome is that they disintegrate when they do not have an external container in which to encapsulate the problems. Those problems, when having to be kept in themselves, drive them to defensive fragmentation, which may end in a permanent state of disintegration.

Riviere (1936) wrote that what the patient fears most, should he make contact with his inner world, is suicide and disintegration. It is my belief that for the type of patient presented, it is the analyst who actually fears those two possible outcomes much more than the patient himself. This fear in the analyst, conscious or unconscious, creates a state of anxiety closely linked with guilt, which I think in turn is stimulated and increased by the patient's projective identifications.

My experience, both directly in treating patients as well as in supervising colleagues, has shown me that the sense of failure, the incapacity to effect reparation with these patients, makes the analyst react in an anxious way. I do not mean acute anxiety, which is easier to detect and therefore to attempt to understand, but a kind of diffuse anxious state that expresses itself in a 'pressure to help to alleviate pain'. This may explain the sometimes overextended length of the treatment, when the same analyst, with other patients, could have decided either to interrupt or to suggest a change of therapist, with more clarity of judgement. He will experience the usual pain and difficulty, but without the agonising feeling that 'one has to go on' or that the patient cannot be abandoned. I have seen the same type of response in different analysts with very different personalities, as well as some with different analytic theoretical backgrounds.

In dealing with this kind of problem, and especially in treating Mr K, I often asked myself if the difficulty was something specific to the patient's mental make-up or whether it was due to something shared by the analysts who treat these patients. I do not think I can answer the question with any accuracy. My observations incline me to think that the reactions of the analyst are mainly caused by the specific problems of the patients, especially their use of projective identification. But I am also led to suspect, with not enough evidence at present to substantiate my suspicion, that there may be a common factor in the therapists' reactions, probably related to their personal modes of dealing with depressive anxieties.

In relation to the psychopathology of self-punishment, one aspect deserves emphasis. I have spoken of this defence as a perverse organisation, or even a perversion. I have mentioned the frequent use of eroticised and excited manifestations in the analytic relationship. What I have not spoken about is my belief that what is sexualised is 'the pain' itself. I do not mean the suffering, which I think can be more easily deduced from the self-punishment behaviour and is a common character in masochistic pathology. What I mean is that the perception of any contact – physical at first in early infancy and mental later on – is perceived as painful. This pain is immediately sexualised. This sexualisation of very elemental units of pain serves to facilitate a pervasive expanding of generalised eroticisation. How does this take place? I do not think I can give an answer at this point. I can only state that in my observation it does take place and it could be of interest to find out why.[3]

To finish, I want to make a brief reference to my technique. The patient's behaviour in the consulting room at most times was very bizarre, to say the least. Still, I consider that what was going on was a classical analysis, inasmuch as my method did not deviate from ordinary analytic technique. The patient behaved as did some psychotics and children that I have had in analysis. I took his behaviour as analytic communication which I tried to understand and interpret in the framework of the transference relationship. My interpretations, whenever possible, were guided by what I felt to be the predominant anxiety. I did not interpret symbolic contents, but I worded my interpretations in such a way as to deal with what I believed to be preconscious expressions of his defences, as well as of contents which I hoped would lead to my understanding of genetic explanations.

The idea of introducing what Eissler (1953) has called 'parameters' crossed my mind several times. I concluded that such an action would only be a way of bypassing what I felt most difficult to bear. In reflecting on the patient's possible reaction to the introduction of parameters, I became convinced that they would not only be unhelpful but actually damaging, since they might make him perceive my behaviour as an expression of my having been destroyed analytically. I also thought that it could increase his anxiety as well as his feelings of triumph. In fact, I hold the view that extra-analytic interventions are in no case of any use. In an analysis, if there is any chance of helping a patient it is only by analysing (Riesenberg-Malcolm 1971).

As to whether patients with self-punishing behaviour can be helped, I do not have an answer. From my limited experience, I suggest that better results are possible in patients whose self-punishing organisation is not so impenetrable that it both prevents the analysis from continuing and also makes the analyst feel that it cannot be terminated.

6

Technical problems in the analysis of a pseudo-compliant patient

I would like to discuss in this paper a technical difficulty in which a patient used apparent agreement with the analyst and an intense idealised transference to stop the analysis working by totally disregarding the interpretive work. In this way she maintained a narcissistic structure as a defence against dependency, which, for this patient, was felt to be a catastrophe.

Mrs H, a good-looking, professional woman, mother of two children, came to analysis when she was twenty-nine years old. She said her main reason for doing so was a vague state of dissatisfaction, connected with what she felt to be her incapacity to love. She wanted to get analytical understanding to facilitate her work, which was related to people. She also reported marital problems, which she quickly tried to play down by saying that her husband loved her very much. From the beginning of her treatment it emerged that she had very severe problems. She was totally frigid and had always been so. She had serious difficulties in learning; she had managed to pass her examinations thanks to her high intelligence, but her performance was below her capacity. Her relationships with people were based either on her being idealised by them or on her suffering intense fears and suspicions to a degree that often paralysed her. She also had persistent insomnia. Mrs H was a potentially gifted person, intelligent, sensitive, capable of passion and warmth.

The patient was born in a Scandinavian country, months before the German invasion. Her family, being well known, had to flee into the countryside of a neighbouring country, also occupied by the Nazis. The parents never got on with each other. The father, a highly successful politician, was authoritarian, violent and cruel.

She describes her mother as scatty, nagging, always suspicious and very

This paper was first published in the *International Journal of Psycho-Analysis*, 62 (1981): 477–84.

unhappy. Her mother loved and cared for her, but she has never been able to remember or know anything about the patient. As a child, Mrs H felt isolated and unhappy. She is the younger of two sisters. When she was five years old she suffered a trauma. While crossing a road with a cousin some years older than herself, the cousin was hit by a car. There was profuse bleeding and the cousin remained partially crippled for life.

A big change occurred in her adolescence. She became very popular. She obtained great pleasure from this and felt superior. At home this popularity also brought her relief. She had a long and unsatisfactory affair with a very cruel man, followed by a succession of love affairs, after which she decided to marry her husband.

The analysis can be divided into four phases related to the predominant defences she used against dependency:

1 fragmentative-evacuative;
2 perverse;
3 idealisation of self and projection into her own daughter;
4 compliant.

The first eighteen months were characterised by intense fragmentative and evacuative processes. In the sessions she quarrelled and attacked systematically whatever I did or did not do. Her attitude was extremely grandiose but she suffered from crippling anxieties and was very unhappy. The interpretive work was directed towards providing a situation in which the patient could feel safe. Once this was partially achieved, some shift towards increased introjection occurred, which brought about more integrated behaviour.

The second phase, lasting about one year, brought the emergence of a perverse constellation in the transference, in which, by identification with her father, she sadistically kept me in the role of an ill-treated mother or a despised child. But her behaviour became more meaningful and her life outside improved. It seemed that the sado-masochistic syndrome served to stop the disintegrative process, prevalent in the previous phase, and to keep at bay dreaded feelings of dependency, which had been defended against in the previous phase by fragmentation.

In the third phase, the perverse transference diminished and her fears of dependency increased. Her main defences were based on maintaining, in the transference, an egalitarian relationship with me as a sister. During this period she got pregnant and had a baby, Karen, who became a depository for her infantile self. In the analysis there appeared a split between a part of herself in identification with an idealised mother, which made her 'be' a very good mother, and a baby self projected into her daughter, who also was perceived as very good and special.

This idealised relation with Karen presented serious difficulties in the analysis for a while, as I was kept in the position of a subservient listener whose principal function was to admire both of them and occasionally give some practical advice.

In the fourth year of her analysis, while considerable working through of maternal transference occurred, acute problems of dependency came to the fore. This development was very strongly feared and defended against by the patient. The experience of being penetrated by interpretations was felt by her to be a threat to her omnipotence and to her grandiosity, which had made her feel safe and protected because she was 'the source of everything'.

In a dream at this time, *she was in a bathroom and a woman handed her something to put into her mouth. She thought it was something with which to brush her teeth. Then she felt terrified because she noticed that what she had put into her mouth was a razor blade. She began to bleed profusely.* Among her associations were the following: the woman reminded her of myself, the bleeding and cutting reminded her of the accident of her cousin. There were some associations to sexuality and also to something that should somehow be perceived as dangerous and horrible and which felt to her exciting, in a sense that made her feel special.

I interpreted the dream mainly along the lines that as soon as I handed her new interpretations, they felt like razors cutting into the armour of her grandiosity and she felt in danger, like the terrible situation of bleeding to death. I related it to a nipple feeding her, which was felt to be like something that was going to cut into her and cripple her for life. By working on this dream we could also see that because of fears and persecution, understanding was bypassed by becoming sexualised, perceived as exciting, and turned into food for self-aggrandisement, as in some sense her cousin's accident had been treated, as well as other illnesses or misfortunes of the family. In subsequent sessions, we could go on working in the context of her fears of accepting needs and having someone to fulfil them.

This dream brought a change in her approach to analysis. She became more receptive and interested in what was said. She became slightly more responsive sexually with her husband, and for the first time glimpses of interest in myself and dreams with more Oedipal content began to appear. Mrs H's attitudes towards analysis and herself changed considerably. Up till then she seemed to organise her life as a path from one disconnected episode to another. At this time in her analysis, she became more aware of mental activities, of meanings and causations. For a considerable time while this was going on, the patient cooperated in the treatment and ordinary analytical work could be achieved.

But slowly a new situation began to emerge and I gradually realised that compliance was the underlying problem. Mrs H began to behave in a more friendly way. She seemed to accept easily most of what I said. At first I could not pinpoint what was really happening, but I began to feel a sense of stagnation and oppression. She spoke in a very lively way, but the issues became more repetitive and dreams disappeared. I then began to scrutinise very carefully her associations and general behaviour in the sessions. She would come on time, and start speaking almost immediately, telling me about her daily events, work, Karen, problems with her husband, thoughts she had. Sometimes she spoke at some length, sometimes she would pause for interpretations. When I interpreted, she listened with what appeared to be thoughtful interest. She would pause as if to think about what I had said and would then proceed to bring new associations. As I listened, at first I got a feeling of uneasiness and impotence, and I soon came to realise that although she had seemed to agree with what I said, my interpretations actually did not appear to make any impact. She would go on talking, untouched by what I had said. Of course, I thought I might have made the wrong interpretation. But upon careful examination, this attitude of hers was repeated, no matter what I said. She would nod, say yes, or nothing, look as if thoughtful, and then continue talking from where she had left off.

Here, for instance, is an example taken at random from a session. She started telling me about the previous night, saying that she could not sleep. She had had intense worries about the head of the place where she worked, particularly about the head's opinion of the work the patient had to discuss the following day with her. Also, Karen worried her. She quarrelled so much that she could not leave her alone with other children. 'She has to have every toy, she is so possessive.' The patient did not prepare her report at all. She said she had met someone who knew me – this, in a tone of some satisfaction – and went on talking about Karen. I tried to make a tentative interpretation, saying that perhaps she was expressing something about her work with me, probably stimulated by her having heard about me. I also tried to link it with her worry during the night about Karen, saying that she probably feared feelings like the ones she was expressing through Karen. While I spoke, Mrs H seemed to be listening attentively. She nodded, said 'Mmm, I see,' and went on exactly from where she had left her repetitive account of Karen's behaviour. I thought, from this, that I might have disregarded her anxieties about her actual work. I tried to include them in my next interpretation. She then spoke amicably about her work and again lightly about Karen and events of the previous day. I tried again to take up her worries about Karen, although now they were expressed in a rather casual way. I reminded her about previous situations in which she knew she had been expressing her own feelings through her child. I also pointed out to her that her way of speaking did not bring about or express a feeling of openness that would allow examination of what she felt, as it all came as a pleasant report of events. Again, the interpretation was met with some approval, but Mrs H went on speaking, untouched by it.

The situation I have just illustrated repeated itself for some time in most sessions. I tried to reach the patient with different interpretations about her not listening or taking notice of what I said, at first by pointing out to her the evidence of this and then trying to link it with her underlying anxieties. These interpretations, also given in different ways, sessions and materials, got the same reception as all the others. She politely stopped talking while I spoke and proceeded to ignore what I said. Sometimes when I managed to come close to a more responsive part of her, it was very quickly disposed of by behaviour meant to make me feel better and reassure me of our good relationship. For instance: on one of the many occasions when I told her that she seemed to have completely bypassed what I had said, she was silent, then she referred to some friends of hers, also in analysis, and made a favourable comment on my style of work as compared with the style of her friends' analysts. This seemed to have been aimed mainly at reassuring me of her appreciation of myself, and perhaps especially of her own satisfaction in her own analysis, and that everything remained all right and unchanged.

My attempts to link this with her perception of myself as her unhappy mother, for whom she felt she had to provide and to whom she had to be the sparkling adolescent, were later proved to be correct, but were, at this time, again totally ignored, while she went on being complacent and charming. In spite of my continuous and systematic attempts to try to acquaint the patient with what was happening, not only did I not have any success, but her 'good feelings' towards me remained unaltered. I realised that under my very eyes she had built a wall against me, solid and impenetrable.

She was living out a very strong phantasy in the analysis, with which she not only felt happy and excited, but which kept her out of touch with her real needs and awareness of dependency, and would not allow for any real analytic progress. This situation seemed to be mainly achieved by projective identification. She was, in phantasy, inhabiting an ideal me as mother and was identified with this ideal object. In this sense, there was no awareness of separateness. Therefore, things did not exist either in motion or time, which explains her total lack of concern about progress, getting older or the analysis eventually ending. In her mind, things would go on, unchanged, forever. Externally, some problems seemed to persist, especially continuous difficulties with her husband, and insomnia. She dealt with the marital problems by pushing them aside, for which she used the well-being she obtained from things in her everyday life and eventual reconciliations with her husband. She tried to forget the insomnia when she was awake, or took sleeping pills. Although I think by now I had a fairly correct picture of the complacent situation, the possibilities of making contact with the patient seemed remote.

As most of the interpretation had been unsuccessful, I decided to modify my approach slightly. In a session when the patient brought an association that made me feel fairly confident of my understanding of it, I made an interpretation which was taken in her easy manner. After she spoke again, I asked her what had happened to what I had said. Mrs H was very surprised, tried to gain control and said pleasantly, 'I heard it,' and tried to proceed with her own thoughts. I asked her again what she had done with what she heard. Mrs H said, 'What do you mean? I just heard.' From then on I proceeded to stop her often, asking what she had heard, what she had done with it, and how did she dispose of it? Mrs H at first felt very persecuted by this behaviour and tried to tell me how disagreeably I was behaving. She tried to seduce and placate me so as to re-establish the previous equilibrium. She became frightened and tried to deal with her fear and anger by splitting and projecting it outside the analytical situation so as to preserve her ideal relationship.

For a long time I had to resort, in the sessions, after she had ignored my interpretations, to questioning as described above. I also had to be careful about two things. First, when possible, I tried to link my questions with explanations of what I thought was the cause for her behaviour in that specific material, that is, why she was not listening. Second, I tried to modulate the questioning so as not to transform it into a *tour de force*, and to allow her to act out in the transference without blocking it excessively.

Following this approach systematically, I saw her attitude loosen, and she started to make an effort to listen to me and to take notice of what I was saying. What came to the fore was that most of the time she had not heard my interpretation at all. At other times she seemed to have picked up some words in what appeared to be a random fashion, and bunched them together with no regard to whether they made sense or not.

It became clear that to prevent awareness and development of a relationship of infantile dependency with its ambivalent feelings, she resorted mainly to splitting and projection. As her analyst, she split me into two. In the sessions she experienced me as perfect. She felt that I liked her very much, that she was my favourite patient and on the whole we were as one.

She perceived another person, often her husband's close friend, as useless, weak and impotent, though nice. She often became frightened that the head of the school she worked in would find her out and sack her from her job. All the things I had been made into by her behaviour in the sessions were split off from her perception of me and projected into those people. Slowly the meaning of this became more available to the patient, the splitting tended to narrow or be resolved more rapidly.

She then brought a dream. *She was in a strange house. It was her house. She heard a noise and went upstairs to see what it was. To her surprise she saw a woman, a servant or washer woman, who was looking very helpless and upset at the washing machine that seemed to have gone berserk. The machine was overflowing because it was burst at the seams. It looked uncanny.* Mrs H felt frightened and woke herself up. She tried at first to talk about something else, but her fears of the night came back into the session. She made some association about overloading and helplessness. I interpreted this dream as a picture of what she felt to be her relationship to me and to the analysis. I said I thought she felt that her way of talking and not listening was overloading me. Her contention had often been that I was just an analyst, so that nothing could affect me. I pointed out that this belief often gave her a feeling of my so-called strength and seemed to free her from guilt. But now she felt frightened that she had overdone it and that she was making me burst at the seams. I tried to link what seemed to me to be her fears of my having broken apart in my capacity to contain or remember, and Mrs H's fears of having caused her mother's disability. I also said that if she did perceive me as human, I would feel helpless and hopeless about how to deal with what she did to me. I reminded her of an early dream in which a woman – part myself, part her mother – was suffering from breast cancer, and I linked it with what I thought she felt she might be doing to the breast in the analysis by not allowing it to function.

In response to these interpretations, the patient felt upset and anxious. She was going to speak and said that her thought was interfered with by a sentence which said 'Karen is very lovely'. Then she told me something that had only now come into the open, namely that often when she felt about to listen or think, or felt she understood something, she was interrupted in her mind by sentences which were admiring of her daughter. She said also that she always seemed to seize upon these sentences and enjoy them. But now she felt upset, as she realised that this stopped her from thinking.

We could see here how Mrs H resorted to self-idealisations as a means to break the perception of the analyst's train of thought. By doing so, she felt even more grandiose. She did not have to listen, as she could submerge herself in an ideal phantasy, but she could not think, and she then felt identified with the analyst's broken mind that did not function properly.

This material was followed by other sessions in which more understanding could be obtained.

The patient, who had never been able to make contact with any feelings about separation, had a dream in which *Johnny, a six-month-old son of her friend, was screaming and crying in his pram because his mother was not there. He got blue with rage and died.* Mrs H woke up in a sweat. She realised that this dream had to do with her own feelings in relation to myself and particularly to separation. She herself connected the fear of rage with her incapacity to perceive any rage in herself. I pointed out that probably it was very difficult for her to feel separation from me because, as with Johnny, she might not only feel furious and angry, but was also terrified about having to cope with these feelings inside, as well as helpless about being able to recover, or having a helpful me she could depend upon to stop her from dying. I linked this with feelings of despair. The patient was touched and moved after this session. She began wondering about her future. By now the stultifying compliance was loosening its grip.

I would like to bring, in some detail, the fragment of a session some days after the Johnny dream, which I think illustrates how the patient resorted to pseudo-compliance when anxiety about separation, fear about collapse because of it, and jealousy came more to the fore.

Mrs H started the session by making a remark about work. She went on to say that she had been extremely upset the previous afternoon. She also had a dream which she thought was related to what she felt in the afternoon. Then she told me in some considerable detail what had happened. She took Karen to play with a little girl, Anna, in Anna's house. While the girls were playing, she stayed with Anna's mother and some other people. She knew Anna's mother very slightly. She thinks of her as very clever and smart and she felt shy and somewhat worried, as she used to feel when with people years ago, particularly when they talked about a party that took place the previous Sunday. They mocked and laughed at the people who gave it and at how it went. During the afternoon Karen got progressively more difficult. She started quite well and seemed to enjoy herself, but then she began to fight over toys. She became very quarrelsome and when it was time to go, she made a tremendous fuss, did not want to leave, and cried and screamed. Mrs H said that she was worried about why Karen behaved like that, and she added that Karen woke up at 6 a.m. and by 4 p.m. she was exhausted. When she was not tired, her behaviour was different. In the evening, Mrs H tried to discuss Karen with her husband. He would not take much notice and Mrs H thinks he is too anxious to listen to his daughter's psychological problems. As she was giving an account of her conversation with her husband, she repeated again at considerable length her description of Karen's behaviour, now as part of that conversation. She also said that she herself felt extremely passive and tired when the girl was misbehaving and could not attend to her. I started interpreting by pointing out to her that it did not seem clear to me where those problems were located and whose problems they were, because when she was explaining what she felt were Karen's psychological problems, she also made it clear that when Karen was not too tired, she behaved well and there were no difficulties between the girl and other children. While I spoke she listened politely, paused, said 'I want to tell you so I can understand Karen's problems,' and proceeded for the third time, more vivaciously, with the same story. I pointed out to her that she seemed not to have listened to me and that in this way she tried to involve me in a conversation of a kind in which two parents would discuss the child's problems. She seemed to be stuck with those problems because she did not seem to be able to make sufficient contact with them in herself, perhaps feeling too anxious, as she believed her husband to be. She seemed to have put these problems into her daughter (facilitated by Karen's behaviour) but could not deal with them in Karen because they did not seem to belong there. Her attitude then changed. She mumbled something and said it had to do with the dream, which she proceeded to tell me.

She was in treatment with Peter. She corrected herself with another slip, saying she was being taught by Peter. She corrected herself again quickly, saying that Peter, a little boy whom she had taught, was back having lessons from her. When she told him that the class was over, he behaved like Karen the previous day. He grabbed things, started throwing them around, became violent and desperate and would not leave the room. Finally she said to him, 'All right, I will give you Karen, you can take her with you if you agree to leave.' He said, 'Yes,' took the girl by the hand, and left. She did not hear any more from them. Her husband said she was mad to entrust a child to another child. She then felt despair, started looking for the children, but could not find them. No one knew where they were. Finally she learned that Peter was in Germany. She went there. She saw many concrete, cold, depressing looking blocks of flats, all alike. She felt dismal. Finally, someone said that the children were in one of those buildings called the 'The Nose'. She found them there, but somehow she felt that this ending of the dream was untrue, as if she would not have been able to bear any other ending.

I will mention here that Peter was a 10-year-old boy whom Mrs H had taught and who had to leave London unexpectedly. She often used to refer to him in her analysis, impressed by the child's capacity to express deep feelings, his intelligence, and also his high excitability. She was particularly moved by the boy's attachment to herself and his suffering when he had to leave her.

Selecting from the associations to the dream: She spoke about the previous day and her state of collapse which she linked to Peter's not wanting to part from her. The two children together reminded her of Proust's description of Marcel and Gilberte as being such an idealised couple of children, but in spite of the beauty of their relationship, Marcel seemed to her to be more interested in Gilberte's parents than in the girl herself. 'The Nose' made her think of curiosity, being nosy. She spoke about Germany, the Nazis; Peter was half-German, and she remembered a film, *Fear Eats The Soul*, in which a woman was proud of her Nazi past, but she immediately said that the woman was very simple and knew no better.

It can be understood from this material how important it was for Mrs H to come close to her feelings and capacities to experience them, but one can also see how frightening this was for her. The double slip at the beginning indicates, I think, how to be aware of those feelings was for her to be completely dominated by them, helpless – as being treated or taught by Peter.

What are the main feelings that seemed to be so frightening to her? I think they pertained mainly to two areas: first, being aware of needs and second, Oedipal preoccupation.

To Mrs H, having needs was being not only very weak and exposed, but also in continual danger of collapse. She felt her object to be weak, so the whole situation seemed to her to be hopeless.

The other aspect was Oedipal. If the object was not so weak and she was separated from it, she became curious about the relationships that occurred in her absence; this parental relationship that excluded her brought out sadism with its frightening consequences. In the dream, Peter, who in reality had many qualities highly valued by Mrs H, seemed mainly to represent her sadistic self as identified with her father, whom she always spoke of as cruel and dominating. She was frightened of this sadism, as she feared her father in childhood, and felt she had to placate his sadism by surrendering to it the idealised self, Karen. With this she hoped for peace. By sending the children away, she split off a whole area of her mind into an independent entity that she believed would not have anything to do with her anymore. That is, infantile feelings, ideas about a couple, interest in parents, were all separated from her.

But of course this splitting did not work, for she feared that she would become mad. She feared the loss of parts of herself and the loss of her objects – losing contact with me – the result of which made her feel empty and lifeless.

Still, she wanted so much to live, she valued passion and strong feelings. To regain all this, she had to resort again to curiosity, to find 'The Nose', that is, to acquire knowledge about herself and her relationship to me as a maternal object.

This knowledge, which on the one hand was indispensable for her growth and sanity, would in turn confront her with her own hatred and its consequences. She was terrified that if she came to know about herself her soul would be eaten up by fears. Nevertheless, she was aware that if she did not, she would remain in a world of gloom and coldness.

The beginning of the session shows how she tried to act out the content of the dream in the relationship with me. She would not listen, and she flatly repeated again and again the same story, while trying to establish with me a relationship of two partners, the parents, discussing someone else's troubles. In this so-called partnership her behaviour, as in all her pseudo-compliant behaviour, was of great cruelty, since my work was ignored and made useless. Only when the pseudo-compliance of her agreeing with me and at the same time not listening to me, was worked through in the session, could we move on to the dream and the problems it was expressing. It is of interest to note that by this time in the analysis, after long and laborious work, her not listening and apparently agreeing attitude could be understood and modified in a part of a session, allowing the rest of the session for work on the anxieties against which such defences were being used.

In considering the role that this pseudo-compliance occupied in this patient's analysis, it can be seen that it had been evolved from previous defences aimed mainly against the same types of anxieties. At first she used fragmentation as a defence, then, when some introjection had been achieved and a more dependent part of the patient began to emerge, she defended herself in a sado-masochistic way in the analysis, based mainly on identification with the father. When contact with the infantile area could again be established, she became pregnant, among other reasons, to try to deposit in the baby all her main problems about dependency and so that she could deal legitimately with them there. But when, in spite of this, in the transference the patient's anxieties about dependency came to the fore again, she next began to resort to a type of self-idealisation based on splitting and projective identification. I, as the maternal object in the analysis, had once been able to help the patient to reach some integration. She began to split me into first, an ideal object based on a previous containing capacity that had brought her relief, and with whom she had become identified; and second, a devalued, subservient one, an inanimate machine, a despised person/servant, also based on the same container, but this time contaminated by containing the bad aspects of herself. The purpose of this split was to preserve a state of non-anxiety which had to be achieved through a situation that did not change. This, of course, was threatened by the analytical process itself, expressed mainly in the interpretations, so that interpretations had to be split from the rest of the analysis and defended against by deafness or mental deafness. So when questions about what had happened to the interpretations were called upon to help, they were felt by this patient as a menace, as this technique may, by bringing together the splitting, bring on the so-much feared dependency.

Historically, dependency seemed to the patient to be linked with what she consistently described as her mother's incapacity to know or remember, that is, to contain. The situation in the analysis of pseudo-compliance can be traced in the patient's life history to the way she overcame most of her childhood depression and misery in adolescence through resorting to a narcissistic structure, which now, as well as earlier on, had become mainly defensive and to which she felt she must cling as to a lifeline.

The analysis of the compliance as defence did allow us to penetrate more into the narcissistic armour, but this quickly built and rebuilt into other forms, and the treatment moved very slowly. When I had to interrupt for a year, the patient could not stand the narcissistic wound. This, I think, was too painful for her and she terminated the analysis and went back to her own country.

Summary

This is a clinical paper which describes the analysis of a defensive narcissistic personality. The emphasis is on studying and illustrating the behaviour in the sessions which I have called that of pseudo-compliance. This behaviour was aimed at maintaining a split between an idealised relationship with the analyst and the projection into external objects of persecuting and painful aspects of this relationship. By appearing to agree with almost everything and listening to almost nothing, the patient felt that she could avoid contact with the feelings of dependency that seemed to terrify her.

7

As-if
The phenomenon of not learning

Analysis is a process which aims to achieve psychic change through understanding, that is, an emotional experience of learning.

It was Helene Deutsch who in 1942 coined the term 'as-if personality' to describe certain types of people about whom she says: 'The whole relation to life has something about it which is lacking in genuineness and yet outwardly it runs as-if it were complete' (1942: 301). In this presentation I want to speak of the patient's 'as-if' response to analysis, a false connection with the analyst and the interpretations in the sessions, which gives an outward impression of understanding and progress, while in fact the whole process lacks something real, does not feel genuine and seems to be going nowhere. In most, if not all analyses, we can find as-if behaviour in our patients, operating like any other defence or resistance against insight. But in some patients, this 'as-ifness', as behaviour in analysis, comes to constitute their basic mode of responding to the analyst's attempts to bring insight and change. This way of functioning aims at keeping an appearance of an analysis in progress, while the patient's main objective will be to keep the situation immobilised. A static situation acts for such people as a kind of reassurance, a kind of proof that they are all right, do not need any change, which they prove by perceiving themselves endowed with keen analytic perceptions and gifts and rich emotions.

Many of these patients come to analysis for reasons that they find difficult to be precise about – a general malaise, some vague anxieties and discomfort, also on occasions the hope for some professional gain. The fact is that they are near breaking point, a fact more often than not unrecognised by them. I think they are patients who have barely managed to

---

This paper was presented at the 36th International Psychoanalytical Congress, Rome, July 1989, and was published in the *International Journal of Psycho-Analysis*, 71 (1990), Part 3.

survive psychically, by maintaining a particular split in their personality. A vast area of fragmentation is encapsulated by a false structure.

Winnicott (1960) described very vividly the formation of a 'false self' as a protection of a 'true self' that could not develop due to maternal failure. He says that in an early stage the infant is most of the time unintegrated and very rarely fully integrated. I would very much agree with Winnicott's description, but I would like to add that the infant, when not met by what he calls mother's 'devotion' and which I, following Bion (1962), would call mother's 'alpha function', not only fails to integrate, but is also exposed to active processes of disintegration derived from destructive as well as from defensive sources, which increase and complicate the unintegrated states, creating an abnormal development. As I said above, this results in fragmentation which becomes precariously enclosed in a false structure.

I think that this false structure is based on a falsely idealised object. It is doubly false, not only because excessive idealisation falsifies, but also because of the object's own pathology. The patient's equilibrium is threatened by life.

The state I am describing can be illustrated by the way patient B presented herself in the preliminary interview. She wore a long knitted pullover, too big for her, and probably belonging to somebody else. It was scruffy and dirty, literally covered with holes, big and small. The patient spoke in a grandiose way of her ambitions and plans for her future work. While listening to her I kept asking myself, 'Are holes the substance of this garment, and will the wool hold them together?'

A common characteristic of these patients is the desperate need they seem to have to agree with most of what the analyst says: sometimes even disagreement gives the impression of being orchestrated to emphasise the points of agreement. They also often balance what the analyst says by interventions that maintain the equilibrium.

In these analyses many areas are apparently addressed by the analyst's interpreting and furthered by the patient's associations – only for it eventually to be realised by the analyst that nothing has been achieved. The patient has learned a lot about 'psychoanalysis' but achieved no insight.

In this situation it appears that both patient and analyst are speaking the same language, meeting for the same reason, namely, to get analytic understanding. More often than not there would appear to be many points of agreement. The analyst believes he is doing analysis with the aim of furthering therapeutic insight. The patient behaves as if this were true. But actually he is coming to analysis, as I said before, for a different reason. His aim is precisely to avoid any emotional learning. I think that in fact such people feel hopeless of ever being understood, and they need to maintain a relationship with an object, the analyst, who is not expected, or allowed, to function. What he is expected to do (omnipotently) is to declare the patient 'well' and if possible make the patient an analyst or an expert in analysis. Simultaneously, something called 'The Analysis' is highly idealised and felt to be full of promise, and somehow expected to last for life. In the 'as-if' analytical situation there are common traits in patients' reactions. They will often refer to what the analyst has interpreted in such general ways that the analyst gets very little information about what the patient did hear or understand. Common expressions are 'that', 'what you said', 'it', or 'that which you think'. Another rather common phenomenon is that these patients will often get hold of that part of the analyst's wording that actually had been unnecessary, or was of very secondary importance, and will elaborate on that peripheral point, ignoring the important points.

On occasion, the patients report intense suffering, pain or difficulties, but the analyst's feelings usually do not correspond to those reports, as they do with other patients. There is often an atmosphere of morality, and the analyst has vague feelings of guilt, sometimes mingled with irritation or despondency.

Bion used the expression 'reversible perspective' to describe this clinical situation. In the various chapters on this subject in *Elements of Psycho-Analysis* (1963), he presents an inspiring clinical picture, which he examines in the light of his ideas on pre-conception, realisation, minus L, H and K, and the Oedipal myth, and he links the phenomenon predominantly to (unbearable) pain. I will not review his ideas here, but I will draw from some of those which I feel to be directly pertinent to my subject.

In his description of 'reversible perspective' he compares it to the agreement two people would appear to have about the disposition of lines, light and shade, but in those lines one sees a vase and the other sees two faces, yet they think they see the same thing. Bion says *'the interpretation is accepted, but the premises have been rejected and others silently substituted'* (1963: 54, my emphasis). In my view this replacement is generally done by the patient very subtly shifting his focus: while stating his acceptance of the analyst's interpretation he has actually neutralised it or emptied it of substance. The result of this action is an accumulation of meaninglessness.

I will present some material from several patients.

Patient A is a headmaster in a secondary school. He is a very ill man in his sixth year of analysis. The example is from a session in which his behaviour was typical.

In the session, A was complaining about one thing and another. He had quarrelled with several people. He complained especially about Nancy, a teacher at his school, who did not support him when the situation at school was breaking down. My attempts to say something were brushed off. He seemed irritated by my speaking, while at the same time he seemed impatient to get something from me. He kept going back to Nancy and her lack of help. Finally I managed to say that I thought that something was going on which we were not managing to confront, and that most of my attempts to say something were interrupted and discarded by him, and that his preventing me from talking must make him feel me to be unsupportive and unhelpful. I added that he was feeling pressured and angry, and feared he might break down with my not helping him.

Patient A relaxed. His posture and manner changed; he became thoughtful; and after some moments he started speaking about one of his pupils who was under such pressure that he feared that he might have a mental breakdown. From this association onwards we seemed to get involved in a dialogue in which whatever I said, whether interpretation, elaboration of it, or just repetition of what I had said, was accepted, somehow agreed with, and immediately applied to one of his pupils and expanded in the context of that child's experience. Several times I tried to describe what was going on, and finally, when he once again said 'It is like Peter...' I interrupted him and pointed out there and then what was happening. At this time he managed to listen and take in what I said. I interpreted that this breaking the connections with me kept us immobilised and did not allow him to apply the understanding to himself. He interrupted me here, sounding very depressed, and said that what I was speaking about was schizophrenic thinking. My patient, up to a point, could get the gist of what I said, but, by transferring it to one of his students, kept some of the meaning of the interpretation but in such a way that what I said did not affect him, and the situation remained unchanged, while he believed himself to be very understanding.

Patient B, who could be called 'Once upon a time', had some similarity with A, but here the focus was moved not to other people, but to situations from her past that my interpretations seemed to remind her of. Her most common phrase was 'It is like when...', going on to expand on relations with aunts, grandparents, school, etc., in a way which was appropriate, but useless analytically. These seemed to be displays of illustrations of my interventions. During this period, when I was trying to make her aware of what she was doing, she had the following dream.

She was going up a slope, which seemed to lead to something that could be an eating house, but when she arrived there was a small plateau that led immediately to a slope leading down and ending in the original place.

I will not go into details and associations to the dream, but there was some understanding between us that the main meaning of the dream was the realisation of the static position created in the analysis; we go up and down, that is, nowhere.

This in turn led us to further manoeuvres of the same kind: now we seemed to agree on the lack of movement, appeared to be analysing it, that is, talking about many kinds of expressions of static situations. In other words, the so-called agreement on a static situation simply replaced the 'It is like when…'

This material shows that both patients heard and retained the gist of the interpretation. The meaning of the words was correctly grasped and remembered, the formal content apparently intact. But something happened to make the interpretation useless and devitalised.

Bion thinks that in situations of 'reversible perspective' 'splitting had been arrested in a static pose'. I have already spoken of how those patients invest in a static situation. I differ from Bion in that I do not think that the splitting is arrested, but rather that what happens is that a different type of splitting takes place. It would appear as if the interpretations are being cut or sliced longitudinally. Everything said by the analyst seems to be there, as if each segment had been photocopied and repeats itself, scattered among different situations and people. Each new situation reproduces the interpretation as a faint, thin echo of itself.

What has been taken away by this slicing is the actual specificity, the substance of the interpretation, which is meant to bring meaning for the patient.

The slicing of the analyst's interpretations differs from a fragmentative type of splitting, and does arrest the latter, at least for the time being.

I have called this type of splitting 'slicing'. I have taken the word from a dream of a patient, C, which took place when I was trying to get some cooperation from her in facing the kind of situation I have been describing. *In the dream a woman was insisting that the patient should go to a patisserie. The patient, though liking sweets, did not particularly want to go, because she knew that the woman would force her to buy a cream bun, which she does like, but did not want to get because, for some reason, she knew that it was the woman who would enjoy the cream. Suddenly she saw in the shop that there was on display a beautifully, symmetrically cut cake, each slice so thin that no cream was noticeable.*

In this patient's analysis, my interpretations, or parts of them, were repeated and displayed in her associations, but out of focus. This was done through slight, rather clever shifts. The impression in the session was of a great activity, giving the illusion of something continually happening, when actually from an analytic point of view the main thing that was happening was the neutralisation and destruction of my work. As in my patient's dream, slicing was the solution. The woman would not get the cream, neither would the patient be affected. Nothing would change.

This common phenomenon I am describing often gives the analyst a curious feeling of hovering between thinking that the patient's action is voluntary or conscious, or an unconscious bizarre behaviour, and thinking that the patient is re-enacting something or that he is plainly lying.

The thin barrier between the levels in which the patient is functioning expresses the peculiar division of his personality which I described previously, the division that the as-if analysis helps to maintain. What happens is that it provides an artificial sense of wholeness, which is continually threatened by real and basic conflicts: by a terror of feelings of hopelessness in facing an internal world of disintegration, and of objects felt as dead and beyond repair. The pull of the existing destructive impulses attacks any feeling of real relief and help from the analyst.

I will illustrate this with material from patient D. He is French and has been coming for several years to analysis. He works in an international corporation and speaks several languages perfectly, including Spanish and English. The analysis was conducted in English. The patient often had to take short trips for his business.

During a period in the analysis in which there was the problem of having to make us equal, as well as the emergence of some real depression, he had the following dream (this version of the dream, as well as the associations to it, is abridged):

He was in a party in a big house that belonged to some people called Corbeaux. [He stopped to tell me that 'corbeau' meant raven.] There were quite a number of people around and lots of things were going on. Mme Corbeaux started to show him around. The house was very luxurious. They stopped in a room that he found impressive. It had belonged to the au-pair girl who had left. The room was full of empty shells, on tables and shelves, and they were very pretty. But what was most impressive was that the floor was completely covered by them. He found it all quite disturbing and woke up.

He associated, rather fluently, to many things, but he kept coming back to the shell-covered room, and the strange effect it had on him. The subject of 'au-pair' was a familiar one in the analysis, meaning literally that we were equals. I asked if he had any association to the shells. A little shame-facedly he said that it reminded him of his last trip to the Middle East. He went to the Dead Sea. There were many notices asking people not to remove shells, stones or any other objects from the shore. He took several shells with him. After some more remarks about this, he told me that he was reminded of a saying in Spanish: 'Cria cuervos y te sacaran los ojos', which roughly translated means 'Nurse ravens and they will pick your eyes out'.

I wish to show with this material how, when the patient feels his defences not functioning any more, he feels exposed to a situation he believes to be unfaceable.

Let us look first at his expression in the dream, 'the au-pair who had left'. As I said before, during the time of the dream the subject of he and I being equals was very much in the foreground of the analytic work, and it was one of the ways he used to try to keep a balance to which the pair of us contributed, but to no avail. At this time in the analysis my interpretations had managed to touch him, and his sense of 'our equality' had left him.

Once this defence lost its effectiveness he felt exposed to the sight of the state of his internal objects. Those, though idealised (the beautiful shells), were stolen, empty and dead. In the analysis, by his continuous use of as-if behaviour, the interpretations were appropriated and deadened by being emptied of meaning. They were robbed of their potential usefulness. His own association to the shells had to do with stealing them from the Dead Sea.

In the dream there was also an awareness of the shells being disturbing, and he was embarrassed and uncomfortable in telling me about his thieving. In this sense one can see that he was becoming aware not only of his state, but also of his own contribution to this. This incipient awareness was very disturbing for the patient.

Melanie Klein spoke about the difficulties that the baby experiences when it begins to integrate parts of the object and parts of the self with the ensuing awareness of psychic reality. John Steiner (1993) describes the specific difficulties of the transition from the paranoid-schizoid position to the depressive position. He refers to the intense anxieties and pain inherent in this transition, which on some occasions results in a compromise: a pathological organisation, which perpetuates the vicious circle.

Coming back to D's material, he experienced this difficulty as an impossibility: he could not face his horror of and guilt for his internal world, created originally in his development. (I will not go into the details of this, but I think that the 'Dead Sea' had to do with his mother, a very ill woman, and his own deadening impulses.) These feelings were made worse in the analysis by his continuous use of as-if behaviour. His solution then was to destroy my sight by plucking my eyes out.

After this dream there was a slight shift in the patient's attitude: his behaviour became a little more genuine. This brought to the fore very intense anxieties, which brought about other defences.

D had had on and off in the analysis problems of hearing. At first I did not know if he had a hearing impediment. I raised my voice and called this hearing problem to his attention. He had the problem investigated and the results were inconclusive: the word used by the ENT doctor was 'borderline'! During this time the hearing problems increased, and, since his attempts to prevent my seeing what was going on had failed, a new symptom emerged. He complained of having something like a fog in front of his eyes. Ophthalmological examinations were as inconclusive as the audiological ones. Another new symptom appeared: intense itching over his whole body, which prevented him from listening or thinking.

The itching was sporadic and infrequent, while the sight problem was of long duration.

The analysis during and after the dream period had brought the patient closer to perceiving problems which he felt to be unbearable. This perception extended in some degree to the awareness of his use of reversible perspective, and the effects of this on the analysis. His dilemma was either to face and work through his problems, with all the horror, hatred and pain involved in this, or to resort temporarily to different methods.

Bion says that when the patient cannot reverse perspective at once, he can resort to altering his perceptions, which can be seen as a delusional attempt to maintain a static condition. According to Bion, this temporary altering of perceptions is done in order to re-establish the operation of reversible perspective.

In patient D the three symptoms involved alteration of perception. The itching was an irritating distraction for him, and was temporary. But the problems of hearing and seeing were more serious, longer lasting and potentially more damaging manoeuvres. They were destructive attacks on the perceptual apparatus itself, and their effects could result either in a shift back into reversible perspective, or further fragmentation and deterioration.

Patient D, in associating to the Corbeaux dream, spoke about 'Ravens that pluck your eyes out', and some time after the dream, when some insight was achieved and he was aware that my vision of the situation was not impaired, his sight problems began. This new symptom became an absorbing subject in the analysis, and it was extremely difficult to move beyond extended descriptions of his impaired sight and medical explorations, and his terror of blindness. As a result, the insight obtained up to the time of the onset of the symptom was blocked, and a new all-absorbing static situation established itself with great intensity. Due to this all my attempts to reach my patient were barred. This only diminished when the patient felt that he could re-establish his old methods of changing perspective. As can be seen, this attack on his perceptual apparatus brought a long cessation of the analytic work, and effectively destroyed the previous insight, therefore making any working through impossible.

In looking at the phenomena involved in reversible perspective I think one can detect several elements at the root of it.

In all the cases I have come across, certainly in the four mentioned in this paper, I have been struck by the balance between the maternal pathology and the patient's own envy. I will describe the latter under the heading of 'minus K'.

In his researches into learning, Bion picked up Klein's early and abandoned idea of an 'epistemophilic' instinct. He developed this idea by linking it to the operation of projective identification, which is for him the infant's first way of communicating his reality. Bion describes projective identification as the first link between baby and mother. The infant projects his feelings into his mother, who responds to them with what Bion called 'reverie', an activity which transforms the baby's raw sensations into tolerable feelings which can then be reintrojected. This early projective identification can be done in love or in hate, and those early emotions affect the baby's approach to his exploring and perceiving reality, which is the beginning of learning.

In learning, or what Bion calls 'K' activity, Bion brings together emotion and cognition, and he says this occurs always in a meaningful relationship between people, be it baby and parent in infancy, or patient and analyst in analysis. He differentiates 'K', or what he calls 'coming to know', from the acquisition of pieces of knowledge.

I will turn now to what Bion called 'minus K – or reversal of learning'. Bion says that 'in minus K meaning is abstracted, leaving a denuded representation'. All the four examples I have given have a striking characteristic in common, which is that by shifting the perspective, the interpretations have been denuded of meaning. Bion described the phenomenon of 'minus K' as not understanding or misunderstanding, and he linked it to primary envy. The infant, because of his excessive envy of the breast, does not experience mother's reverie as a relief. On the contrary, by projecting this envy into the mother, what might have relieved anxiety is experienced as mother taking his own value away.

As I said before, all four cases clearly share the presence both of severe maternal pathology, as well as of the patients' inborn intense destructive impulses (envy). The interplay of the two can exacerbate and potentiate each other. A mother who has difficulty in containing her baby's feelings is likely to find it more difficult to deal with his envious rejection of her attempts to ministrate to him, while destructiveness can be exacerbated by the absence of a maternal capacity to modulate it, thus increasing problems in development.

The point I am making in this paper is that slicing-splitting is the basis of reversible perspective, which leads to as-if behaviour in analysis, and it is the result of the operation of minus K.

In the same papers quoted earlier, Bion, when speaking about agreement and disagreement between patient and analyst, says 'The principle should be that clinical observation must determine where the intersection of analyst's and patient's views is'. It is my point that the patient, by slicing the interpretation, and thus changing the premises, makes sure that such an intersection does not take place. Patient and analyst, though appearing to be together, do not make contact. It is precisely the contacting link which is cut, leaving the interpretation useless, repetitious and empty.

As-if patients cannot tolerate the analyst's interpretations, which they do not perceive as relieving or as conducive to growth. They resent them, feel them to be demeaning, empty them of meaning, and use them only to maintain a status quo. This envious reaction, I think, was clearly illustrated in patient C's dream about the sliced cake. Her mother was certainly a disturbed person (as were the mothers of the other three patients). But in the analysis, when the patient could feel the analyst as a better and more helpful object, and feel the possibility of liking and enjoying what she could get in the analysis, she was stopped by the hatred that originated in the fact that the analyst could get satisfaction from her (the patient's) relief and improvement. In the dream she did not want to get the bun (though she liked it) because 'the woman will enjoy the cream'!

Patients who predominantly use reversible perspective do not expect the analysis to be helpful for what it is. They do not learn from the analysis. They repeat with great frequency an attack on learning by denudation of meaning. They use projective identification with the analyst to mimic an analytic personality, misusing the interpretations. These feel useful for what they are not, or for whoever they are not meant to be for, but for themselves they are useless and despised.

The repetitive use of minus K in analysis in my view not only repeats an early difficulty of the patient, but in the configuration of the 'as-if syndrome' is specifically designed to prevent the exploration of an internal situation. This situation is the consequence partially of an early operation of envy, partly of other developmental problems, and partly, too, connected with a specific maternal pathology, which in my experience has increased the child's early difficulties by stimulating a pseudo-adaptation.

In as-if patients there is a split between an ideal called 'The Analysis' and the actual analytic work. The ideal analysis is supposed to contain an unacknowledged disintegrated part, while the actual analytic work is felt to threaten this containment.

The slicing of the interpretations is, in my view, an attack on the dynamic link of the interpretation. It destroys the very meaning that the interpretation aims to convey. By severing this link, the patient ensures that the analyst's interpretations become repetitions of empty statements, which, when not disposed of immediately, are heard by the patients as some kind of moral pronouncement. It is difficult to grasp the subjective experience the patient has. Certainly, as I have just said, he often seems to betray a sense of being morally judged. Patients seem often to be conveying an incessant sense of activity or busyness. There very rarely appears to be a spontaneous emotional response.

The phenomenon of 'slicing-splitting' is clinically observable, but it leaves me with many unresolved theoretical questions. One of them is: how does this type of splitting establish itself as a primary way of functioning?

In all the cases I have seen in which this phenomenon predominates I have found a puzzling balance between severe maternal (and often also paternal) pathology and a high endowment of envy. This double affliction of envy and parental pathology seems to be more commonly present than in other kinds of patient with different types of defensive organisation.

Ross (1967) described a variety of as-if personalities. I prefer to call this an as-if analytical phenomenon, rather than an as-if personality. Certainly the four patients I have described had very different personalities. For instance, patient A was the most ill of the four, and was closer to psychosis proper, while patient D would easily fall in the category of severe narcissistic personality.

The destruction of the internal coherence of the interpretation by breaking the meaningful links is triggered both by the hatred of the analyst, when the latter is able to provide understanding and to bring new meaning, and also by a dread of obtaining insight into a terrifying internal world. In this sense the 'slicing phenomenon' is at one and the same time a result of and a defence against envy. The type of denudation to which I am referring allows for some of the qualities (minimal as can be seen in the cake dream) of the experience to remain protected from further envious attacks, which would result in a more minute fragmentation. But the problems are never faced up to enough to be modified. To do this the patients would have to face what they have done, and do, to their objects, and only then would they be able to repair and recognise the reality of their external objects. They fear on the one hand that their objects are beyond repair, and on the other they resent the help they need to allow them to repair the objects.

In this sense the as-if syndrome, with its specific type of splitting, is a defensive organisation formed to operate against awareness of and progress through the depressive position.

As-if patients experience the awareness of their internal world as a menace to their sanity. They feel that they have (and had historically) only one of two ways of coping with this situation. Either they disintegrate completely, or they remain 'as-if'. The experience of being in analysis and not learning offers these patients a *modus vivendi*.

Summary

In this paper I discuss a clinical problem presented by those patients who, instead of using analysis as an emotional learning experience, invest all their energies in keeping it in a static condition. Using the material of four patients, I illustrate how they have an underlying state of disintegration which is contained in a precarious enclosure. The patients experience great difficulty in facing this situation and preventing further disintegration. I describe a particular type of splitting, which I call 'slicing', by which they achieve an arrest of further disintegrative processes, and for which they need the continuous existence of a useless analysis. I link this situation with Bion's concept of 'minus K'.

8

Hyperbole in hysteria
'How can we know the dancer from the dance?'

> The body is not bruised to pleasure soul
> Nor beauty born out of its own despair
> O chestnut tree, great-rooted blossomer,
> Are you the leaf, the blossom or the bole?
> Labour is blossoming or dancing where
> O body swayed to music, O brightening glance,
> How can we know the dancer from the dance?
> W. B. Yeats, 'Among school children', in *The Tower* (1927)

In this paper I want to discuss histrionic behaviour, which I regard as specific to a particular type of the hysterical character. I have found that my understanding of histrionic behaviour has been greatly helped by Bion's notion of 'transformation in hyperbole'. I will examine the role of this type of transformation in histrionic behaviour, and I will describe the types of object relationship that I think are typical in histrionic behaviour.

Freud's discovery of the psychoanalytic method began with studying or treating hysteria, which in turn permitted the whole development of psychoanalysis. The aim of psychoanalysis is to provide a situation in which experiences can take place which reproduce old ways of being, but in which these old ways of being can be transformed into different ones that allow patients a more satisfactory and possibly less painful life. Psychoanalysis aims to integrate different mental elements through insight, that is, it aims to give an emotional awareness of meaning that is in itself an agent for psychogenic growth.

In the course of his development the individual experiences feelings,

---

This paper was first read to a Scientific Meeting of the British Psycho-Analytical Society in 1995 and was published in the *International Journal of Psycho-Analysis*, 77 (1996) Part 4.

thoughts, and relationships which are modified by other feelings and relationships, internal and external, resulting in new and different experiences. But in this development there are sometimes hurdles that cannot be overcome. When this occurs the transformation of emotional experiences does not result in new and further integrations. On the contrary, such transformations as occur tend to be in the direction of fragmentation and disintegration.

The reasons for such situations are manifold, lack of a receptive primary object and envy being two of the most important.

A more integrated and advanced state of functioning requires a conjunction of environmental and internal factors that allows a transformation of early experiences into what Klein called the 'depressive position'. This transformation results in more whole and realistic object relations with a greater degree of integration and a capacity for emotional learning from experience.

Sometimes, for many and different reasons, the depressive position is reached but not 'achieved', creating a clinical picture which we call personality or borderline disorders. In such cases, the patients resort to a variety of different defensive organisations, which on the one hand allow them a certain level of functioning, but on the other hand contain, and often maintain, a degree of pathology which partially cripples the patient and strongly affects the people with whom he lives. One such organisation is the histrionic character, which is an aspect of the hysteric personality as described by Freud.

In his early descriptions of cases of hysteria Freud portrays with great richness a symptomatology which belonged to a considerable degree to the culture of his time. Florid hysterical behaviour is unusual nowadays, although it is not unusual to encounter more subtle types of conversion and especially to encounter certain types of dramatic behaviour among all patients. But for some patients histrionic behaviour is more organised and becomes one of the patient's central symptomatic expressions and defensive manoeuvres. I have found Bion's ideas on what he calls 'transformation in hyperbole' useful in understanding such patients' behaviour.

Bion has developed a theory in which he describes different types of transformation and the conditions in which these occur, resulting in various types of mental phenomena, but I will not go into this here. Among his ideas is the view that when transformations in hyperbole take place, that is, when the main expressions of the patient are dramatised, the patient often needs to have an emotion recognised and resorts to exaggeration to achieve his aim. The problem is that the object seems to reject the emotion. I think that it is not just that unrecognised emotions are exaggerated. In my view, exaggeration itself gives a picture of how the patient experiences his internal objects and his relations with them.

Before proceeding further I will give a brief vignette from a case treated by a colleague from abroad whom I supervised, and to whom I am grateful for allowing me to use his material.

Mrs A, a married woman with three teenage children, had been in analysis for several years. At the time of this session she was going through some marital difficulties expressed mainly as a state of not-too-clear dissatisfaction exacerbated by the increasing independence of her children. She often had fantasies of having a 'fling', as a way out of her troubles, but these fantasies had never been acted upon. After an office party – where some alcohol had been consumed – she 'found' herself involved in heavy petting with a colleague. Nothing more happened and the relationship ended there, each returning to their respective homes in the early evening.

On her way home, her first thought was, 'What have I done to my husband?' This thought flitted away quickly, and she started to get more and more preoccupied with ideas of having contracted some venereal disease, and became progressively more frightened of actually having contracted AIDS. These anxieties lasted for some days. At times her fantasy ran away with her into all kinds of lurid images about the illness: her need to have an HIV test, thoughts about telling her husband what she had done so that he should be tested as well, etc. Eventually the whole episode petered out, partly thanks to the analytic work and partly on its own.

As can be seen, Mrs A's first thought went to her husband with a pang of intense guilt. This was rapidly suppressed, and replaced by a kind of pseudo-delusional persecutory preoccupation, which had some of the characteristics of obsessional fears and some of daydreaming. Apparently guilt, or any awareness of it, especially related to her husband, was too painful and so was replaced by the drama of thoughts which she at the same time knew were highly implausible. She reacted to the analysis by demanding reassurance, which, when she got a bit of it, was felt by her as intrusive. A more analytic stance was perceived by her as the analyst lacking empathy, being insensitive and therefore rejecting her predicament, and trying to push his own views on to her.

In *Studies on Hysteria*, when speaking about Fraulein Elizabeth von R, Freud says

> her love for her brother-in-law was present in her conscious life as a foreign body, without having entered into relationship with the rest of her ideational life. With regard to these feelings she was in a particular state of knowing and at the same time not knowing.
>
> (1893–5: 165)

Later he says: 'We may ask what is it that turns into physical pain here? A cautious reply would be: something that might have become, and should have become *mental* pain' (166).

The pain Mrs A actually dreaded was guilt. Because it could not be experienced as such, it got inflated in her mind, changing into the implausible drama of a physical illness, a drama which grew out of all proportion and enlarged into infinite dimensions.

Mrs A found it very difficult to get help from her analyst. The way she spoke about her fears, her repeated account of the events that had occurred and of her feelings had a quality of teasing the analyst, that is, of inviting him to help her with them while in one way or another she withdrew from his interventions. The aim of this seemed to be to immobilise analyst and analysis so as not to experience the guilt that she dreaded. With her dramatisation she tried to provoke her analyst to punish her and thus to create a sado-masochistic relationship which she believed would spare her from having to recognise and face guilt.

I understand psychic growth as resulting from different elements coming simultaneously and truthfully together. These elements are a mixture of feelings, thoughts and reactions in relationships. What I am talking about is an emotional experience which, by bringing together at one time different elements of a given situation, changes the situation into a more meaningful emotional category.

Hyperbole

In hyperbolic or dramatic behaviour the original experience is transformed into an exaggeration of itself: this behaviour generally expresses some real feelings of the patient, but genuine feelings are distorted by the manner in which they appear. This distortion often leads to other complications, but for the moment I will concentrate on the exaggeration.

In examining this problem of the patient's need to exaggerate, a need which is frequently met by rejection, one encounters a variety of causes, most often in combination. Imagine a baby who cannot get its emotions recognised. This may be because the mother is too depressed, or she is too narcissistic and or hostile to her baby. It may also be that the feelings of the baby are of such hostility that the mother cannot cope with them. In any such situation the baby might resort to exaggeration to try to rid itself of, or convey, something.

As in the examples I am describing, there can be many combinations with many factors intervening in them. The central point I want to make is that in the histrionic character hyperbole, that is, the use of exaggeration, aims at communicating to someone, or to get rid of emotions which are felt not to be received by the object and therefore impossible to manage in any other way.

Clinical example

Ms X, a woman in her early thirties, had been born in Scotland into a very religious aristocratic family. She was one of several children. There were always nannies and governesses to help educate and look after the children. Because of her father's occupation the family resided most of the time abroad. As soon as the children were old enough they were sent to boarding schools. They used to spend their holidays in their country estates in Scotland. There were many children, cousins and other relatives. Ms X was especially close to a male cousin of her own age, with whom she had a peculiar relationship. They called each other by a special name (the same name for each) and were involved in many provocative, dangerous and sometimes perverse activities. She is single, lives in and runs a farm near London. She has a degree in economics, and serves on the boards of some of the family-owned companies.

The relationship with her family was described as bad, and she reported herself as making frequent 'scenes' (for which she had a special name) in which she shouted, threw things around and threatened to kill herself or jump out of the window. These scenes seemed complex and difficult to judge. Often from her verbal description of them, they could be thought of as psychotic. Nevertheless, from the atmosphere in the session and the feelings she conveyed, they appeared to be more wilfully staged scenes than plainly mad. In her communications of those scenes I often thought them to be a peculiar mixture of madness and feigned madness, more dramatised than genuinely psychotic – though of course one can think of this tendency to melodrama as mad.

Session one

On a Monday Ms X arrived looking serious and melancholic. She sat down on the couch and remained silent for a few minutes, after which she whispered. She began to imitate me after what she correctly felt was my attempt to say something. Speaking fast and now loudly, she said 'She thinks that I am one of her regular analysands.' She paused to hum and keep the rhythm with her fingers. Then she continued, 'One of your compatriots, members of your Latin American clique.' She laughed loudly, not paying attention to my attempts to speak, apparently concentrating on her drumming. I finally said something about the weekend interruption and her feeling of exclusion. She seemed thoughtful for a few seconds and then mumbled in a very low voice: 'I'm not going to think.' (This was not a new reaction.) She became very dramatic, raised her voice, and, imitating a religious incantation, recited several biblical pieces, ending with 'I am the wound, I am the sword, I am the word – I am God!'

It is not easy to describe the atmosphere. Ms X repeated the same thing many times, occasionally chanting more biblical quotations, her speech fast and loud. I felt myself helplessly exposed to a third-rate dramatic performance. After various attempts to reach her, I decided to make myself heard and to take on the histrionics. Speaking a bit more loudly than usual, I said, 'You feel as if you were acting on stage and the representation that you find so exciting is the exaggeration of something real and painful. My words put you in contact with disagreeable thoughts about us not seeing each other for two days.' She murmured, 'This softens it,' and tried to begin the same thing again. But I carried on, saying that now she cut me short, just as she had probably felt that the contact with me had been cut off because of my weekend, and that this left her with a wound. Because of this she resorted to 'big drama', to give the impression of being omnipotent, of being God, and of being above the feelings of having been hurt.

We can see how in this complex situation, the patient needed me because she felt me to be good, but my unavailability made her more aware of her need of me. She hated to experience need, and because of this hatred she turned me into an exaggerated caricature of an analyst: the ridiculous God with whom she identified and enacted in her dramatisation.

She went back to a similar avalanche in the middle of which, like an aside that she could only slip in as if hidden from a part of herself, she murmured something about a 'storm of shit', and said that her cousin had telephoned her. This was said in a barely audible whisper.

I intervened again, interpreting her need to dramatise to be able to reject her feelings about my not being available by being worried about the telephone call. She calmed down, and in a low voice said 'You shouldn't hear this. I wanted to come yesterday.' I told her that she felt that her wanting to see me when I was not available was cruel and wounding, and that this provoked a storm of shit, in which she freed herself of these feelings by feeling powerful and independent of me. She said 'I had a dream,' but she did not recount it, provoking me with it, turning it into yet more theatricals, until I finally intervened and asked if she had or had not had a dream. She then recounted it:

She was in a dead and sterile desert, like a preservation zone, where many reptiles appeared. There were lizards, iguanas and lots of snakes. A man in a suit and tie walked by. She was standing on a rock that she believed to be firm, but the stone gave way and she was very frightened. Below, there was a rodent who said to her 'Don't worry, I'll catch you.' She felt very anxious and told him to go away because she would squash him and tear him to pieces. She woke up in a sweat.

Associating, she said that in her childhood her cousin and she had liked natural history and had studied prehistoric animals. They had loved nature passionately. Then they had lost their interest and had become addicted to ghost stories and stories of violence. She frequently had dreams in which she fell into a void and woke up screaming in a panic. The man she thought was a close relative of hers, the rodent a squirrel, sweet but very weak.

While she associated I got the impression of a very precarious atmosphere: I felt that if I was not exact, or if I was mistaken in any way I would bring on a stormy outbreak. I began to interpret that in the session today she had been representing an ancient and familiar story, that when she was hounded by horrible feelings she created a protection that she felt to be firm, as a rock. To do this she placed in me the horrible and biting feelings (I was a rodent). But when the so-called rock gave way she was left with me too weak to help her; this made her frightened for me, and also want to protect me. She said 'I have told you that you are too weak for me.' I said yes, and that when she was invaded by needs and impatience she felt helpless. I went on with more details about how this had occurred during the session, the storm of her dramatic speech, which she thought would protect her like a firm rock, but which in reality left her on an unsafe and crumbling base. She listened to me attentively and seemed thoughtful when I finished speaking. After a while she said 'I am thinking of a fork-tongued animal. Do you know what that means? *Falseness*.' I said then that she feared I was false and that I protected myself with a seductive attitude. I referred to the falseness of the beginning of the session, possibly similar to the pretence she resorted to when she felt lonely and under pressure. I told her that at that moment she felt and feared that I would do the same thing, that is, become seductive so as to feel big and powerful *vis-à-vis* her.

I shall break off the presentation of the session here so as to summarise what I believe to be the meaning of this material.

At the start of the session the patient expressed mainly through enactment the feelings she had in the session as well as during the weekend break. She seemed to have felt abandoned and exposed to both internal and external demands (e.g. the call from her cousin). She came looking melancholic, but she behaved in a superior, arrogant way in which she mocked and performed the role of someone indifferent and aloof (her finger-drumming and incantations). In this, as well as in the few mumbled direct verbal expressions, she showed how she perceived her object as well as her defences against those feelings. The defences were predominantly manic, reaching megalomania: she mocked, controlled, and was everything and everyone, God.

I think the performance expressed a partial identification with the caricature of a neglectful object as well as a faint hope of evoking some response. Corroboration of this hypothesis can be found in the content of the dream: the mammal, the squirrel not seen at first, and someone who walks by indifferently. The dream shows also that her solution did not work. To be this superior object she has to split off her weakness, which she projects into her object (myself in the analysis); and she constructs her so-called strength, as I said before, partly by identifying with the object, and partly through faecal omnipotence (the rock on which she stands in the dream). But the rock crumbles, and she is left with fear for herself and dread of the object's weakness and possible death.

The session also shows how mobile the patient was. As soon as a point of contact was established she distanced herself by an excursion to places from which it was difficult for me to reach her and from where it was difficult for her to return.

My first attempt to find her was heard. It threatened her with pain and she rejected it (she might also have perceived me as showing off), bringing forward a histrionic excursion. Fresh attempts to bring her back to analytical territory finally achieved a movement near to returning, as if she was smuggling the information through to me when she told me that her cousin had telephoned. For two-thirds of the session I tried steadily to make sense of what was going on and of what she was saying, and to communicate my thoughts to her. I believe that this slowly enabled her to introject both the meaning of my words, as well as the experience of me as a more benign and functioning object, thus resulting in a transformation of her internal situation, moving from hyperbolic behaviour towards some integration. Only when this transformation was achieved did we manage to establish enough analytic contact to allow *her* to work with me.

Once work with the dream was possible, the dramatisation diminished and gave place to a more direct communication which permitted some modification of the underlying anxieties, bringing relief and some integration. This newly created state stimulated other emotions such as greed, bringing with it further problems which I will describe in the material that follows.

Session two

In the next session we continued working in the way I have described. She complained directly about her parents and their lifestyle. She spoke of 'massacring a chocolate' and of voracious hunger. Overall, she was less dramatic.

Session three

I shall give only a short excerpt from this session to show a different aspect of how Ms X's material brought new dramatic complications. She came looking gloomy and told me about a board meeting she had attended. While she spoke she was playing with a tissue. I noticed she was making a boat; when she had finished it she crumpled it and put it into her mouth, chewing it vigorously. I interpreted that she felt the analysis and I could be like a boat in which she could be inside. She interrupted and asked, anxious and obviously not having heard properly, whether I had said with me or inside. I said 'Inside.' She relaxed and said 'Right,' with a sigh of relief. I said that being inside and united with me was the only way in which she felt protected from those ferocious and biting feelings which put her in such great danger and made her feel that I was very weak.

I want to make clear that all this is highly simplified, since all these processes were intermingled and complex in their presentation.

We can see from the material presented that many factors were involved, and the patient seemed to be expressing through her behaviour many different feelings, especially greed. When in the session her experience of me changed and once again I became more desirable, she felt greedy. This appeared more in acting than in speaking. Ms X dramatised her greed by overstating verbally that she could 'massacre a chocolate' and by the vigorous chewing of the paper boat, which I think represented me as a containing object. She desired to possess this containing object by being in it and ingesting it ferociously at one and the same time (see Brenman [1980], who remarks on the greed of hysteric patients).

Discussion

Hyperbolic or dramatic behaviour permits the patient to distance himself from the original significance of what goes on in his mind, and appears to bind together his different emotions and conflicts.

Dramatising patients show great difficulties in tolerating frustration, of which they seem to have had plenty, and when they are confronted with complex experiences which produce pain or are felt as painful, they react to them in a way that results in some sort of swelling of the total experience, which then gets inflated and exaggerated but in a way remains integrated. It is then separated from the self and deposited onto a 'stage' where the performance seems to take place and from which the person can distance himself without completely losing contact with it.

To discuss histrionic behaviour I will build a model in which I shall divide this behaviour into three parts:

1   the observing self;
2   the acting self;
3   the audience.

I will then proceed to examine each part.

The observing self

The observing self appears to be powerless, at least in the sense of being able to alter the situation. This could be seen in the first part of the session, when she did her stage performance, a performance in which she not only acted but seemed to be watching as well. I believe that a part of the patient capable of observing was present, but it was inactive and mute, unable to do anything about it. But this observing self appears as well to maintain the illusion that by being able to observe (albeit at a distance) it stays in control of the painful experiences and of the object that provokes them. This control can be felt as exciting. The fact that the observer cannot use the observation in an effective way derives, I think, from an identification with an object felt as incapable of taking in the patient's (infant's) projections and transforming them sufficiently for him. At the same time this object with whom the patient is identified appears at least to have perceived the infant's communications.

The object with whom the patient identifies later appears to be someone who could be saying: 'Yes, I heard what you said, but so what? I won't feel it.'

It seems to me that the object is also perceived by the infant as offering some hope by noticing the patient's/infant's communication. This aspect of the perceived object contributes to the fact that hysterics somehow seem to expect to be seen, heard and perhaps understood. This mixture of hope and disappointment is possibly felt by the infant as teasing, an aspect with which the infant may identify later.

The acting self

This aspect of the patient is totally identified with the action. It creates the acting, and at the same time is at one with it ('How can we know the dancer from the dance?'). I think this action originates in the need to get some feelings across to the object, while at the same time identifying with the object, perceived as rejecting and teasing. The patient cannot reject the totality of his experience without going mad. But he can distance himself from these experiences and exaggerate them into caricatures of themselves. This distancing and exaggerating alters the form of the experience and the place where it is supposed to be, as if the patient was saying with this action 'It is not in me, I am very busy, it is something out there and it is not too bad.'

The elements of the original experience are not lost; what does get lost and distorted are the links between those elements. If those links were permitted to exist the situation would be different and would allow the patient to transform the experience into a better and less painful state. The action aimed at keeping pain at a distance by exaggerated over-activity paradoxically renders the situation static and sterilises it. In my patient's material, her dream took place in a 'sterile desert'.

The dramatic performance affects and damages the process of symbolisation. Hanna Segal in her paper on symbolism (1957) describes the psychogenic development necessary for a differentiation to occur between the symbol and the thing that it symbolises. I think that in the dramatised action the patient oscillates very rapidly between this symbolic functioning and what Segal calls 'symbolic equation'. This rapid oscillation prevents the complete breakdown of symbolic functioning. But it also prevents the consolidation of symbolic functioning, which could result in a more depressive-position way of functioning. This rapid oscillation in my view creates a peculiar state of in-betweenness that is neither symbolisation nor symbolic equation. This state is one of the specific characteristics of hyperbolic behaviour.

The audience

In the hysteric's performance, one very important role of the audience is to render credible the scene that is being enacted. By credibility I mean the assurance that hyperbole is working. It can be checked against an outside other who responds and takes notice. This outside other is expected to respond, but his responses will be treated according to the feelings that predominate at that time and the situation will often remain unaltered.

The outside other generally has to be a specific person, the analyst in the session, and, as I could see in my example of Ms X, a specific relative of hers. But when specific people are not available, often anyone will do. The audience can also be temporarily a figure about whom the patient can fantasise and daydream. But I think that this daydream audience only works temporarily, because it threatens the precarious equilibrium the hyperbolic action aims to maintain, and for which, as I have just said, the patient needs a reassurance from an external presence.

The patient projects into his audience partly his observing self and partly his infantile helplessness. The audience/analyst is obliged to witness helplessly the cruelty and mocking with which he is being treated and to experience the hopeless despair, while the patient seems to be partially identified with a sadistic object, rejecting, cruel and contemptuous. This, as can be seen, occurred in the drama of the first part of session one. It is only through the analyst experiencing these projections, and conveying his experience and understanding to the patient, that he can hope that the situation can slowly begin to change.

To understand histrionic behaviour in analysis, the analyst must be aware of and follow the various splitting processes I have described, as well as the multiple projective identifications these splits result in. The analyst has to be alert to the shifts between different internal objects as expressed in the transference, since when the analyst addresses himself to one aspect of the patient he is often answered by another.

In my view the model I have described helps us to understand these patients. In understanding the divisions between relatively large areas of the patient's personality, we can explore them in greater detail and see how these divisions serve the purpose of defending the patient, at least temporarily, by encapsulating fragmenting processes which are very active and continually threaten him.

In studying human development one is concerned with the way mental phenomena are transformed in the mind. It is possible to think of a vast range of states, starting from the most normal ones in which different elements result in new and integrated experiences, to the most pathological ones in which the original elements are profoundly distorted and result in psychotic development (see Bion 1965). These patients oscillate between relatively 'normal' and the most pathogenic forms of transformations.

Bion's understanding of early projective identification of a normal communicative type, and his ideas about transformations in hyperbole, helped me to look afresh at the phenomenon of dramatisation and to think further about some of the identifications at the root of the hysteric patient's dramatising syndrome. This in turn made me more aware of the type of primary object these patients seem to have experienced, that is, an unresponsive object not totally closed to the infant's communications but incapable of modifying them enough to allow the infant to progress.

I am well aware that the phenomena one encounters in this type of hysteria are more complex and varied than those I have described in this paper. Though my model describes a triangular situation I have left out any exploration of Oedipal phenomena, which I think are very important in this group of patients. Because Oedipal issues are of such importance in hysteria they should be the subject of another paper.

The Oxford English Dictionary definition of hyperbole is 'A figure of speech consisting in exaggerated or extravagant statement used to express strong feelings or to produce a strong impression and not intended to be understood literally'. The patients that I have been speaking about resort to exaggerated behaviour both to express strong feelings and to produce a strong impression which might help us to understand them better.

---- 9 ----

Pain, sorrow and resolution

In this paper I shall focus on the difficulty some patients encounter in analysis in becoming aware of their separateness from their objects, and I will link these difficulties to the patients' experience of psychic pain. I understand psychic pain to occur when the patient is faced with having to undo a particular type of relationship which ties him to his object – a phantasy of oneness with the object. I will use examples from the analysis of three different patients to illustrate the way their difficulties manifested themselves in the transference. I shall also expand on the types of pain these problems brought to the patients.

In her paper 'Towards the experiencing of psychic pain', Betty Joseph (1989) movingly describes a kind of pain that certain people have when a particular type of mental equilibrium is disturbed. She describes it as pain felt somatically, generally located in the chest; she says it is not yet a 'heartache' and it appears not to have a name, it is 'just pain'. Joseph speaks of it as a 'borderline phenomenon', that is, something that is experienced in the border between body and mind. Joseph relates this pain to the breakdown of certain types of projective identification which had allowed the patient to keep a kind of balance that permitted him to get on in life, albeit in a precarious way. Such a breakdown, she says, can be one of the factors that makes the patient seek analysis. I would add that when he does not look for treatment, he will try to use again and perhaps more drastically these forms of splitting and projective identification to re-establish some kind of balance.

Freud was concerned with a similar problems; he asked: 'When does a

This paper was first read in a Public Lectures Day of the British Psycho-Analytical Society for Betty Joseph in March 1987. It is published for the first time in this volume.

separation from an object produce anxiety, when does it produce mourning and when does it produce, maybe, only pain' (1926: 171). He then described different reactions experienced by the person when separating from the object, and he linked it with the nature of mental pain, which he considered to be a reaction to the loss of an object. He referred to mental pain as an equivalent to a person's physical pain, and he said that 'the transition from physical to mental pain corresponds to a change from narcissistic cathexes to object cathexes' (*ibid.*).

Klein saw the paranoid-schizoid position as dominated by the infant's need to ward off anxieties and impulses by splitting both the object, originally the mother, and the self, and projecting these split-off parts into an object which will then be felt to be like, or identified with, the split-off parts, so colouring the infant's perception of the object and its subsequent introjection. In 'On projective identification', Joseph says 'The infant and adult who goes on using such mechanisms *powerfully* can avoid any awareness of separateness' (1989: 169, my emphasis).

Pain

Some patients who seem to function predominantly in a paranoid-schizoid mode appear to be living in a cloak-and-dagger world, dominated by feelings of persecution. People who operate in this way project themselves into their objects so massively and with such intensity that the object seems not to exist outside the subject's perception of it. Object and subject are often felt as fused or confused: the object is perceived as reacting only to what has been projected into it.

When through the analysis the patient begins the process of withdrawing projections from the object, he starts to feel more separated from it and more aware of his own self. This process is often very painful to him, pain which to begin with he experiences as undefinable, non-specific and undirected – it is 'just pain'. It often indicates a movement from narcissistic fusion towards object relations, the first step towards a more depressive mode of functioning, and the patient reports the pain with some relief. I will bring now some clinical material to illustrate such a situation.

Ms A is thirty-five, an ambitious lawyer who works in an international corporation where she holds a responsible and demanding job. The material I shall present is from the second year of her analysis, when she was often assailed by persecutory anxieties. She felt she was being unfairly treated and 'got at' both by her work and often by me as well. From the beginning of her analysis she had spoken with interest and hope of getting a promotion in her own department which would carry greater responsibilities, including some teaching and higher pay. When eventually this was offered to her, almost immediately she became assailed by doubts.

Prior to the session I will present, there were two very heavy weeks in the analysis. The patient felt either got at by me, or very pressurised by what she called 'demands', especially at work. I felt it was almost impossible to reach her. She spoke in a remarkably cold and cruel way, her speech was obsessional and repetitive. She called it her 'legal reasoning'. She complained about being pressurised by demands from work. These 'demands' she felt to be incessant and peremptory, and they were created by 'the nature of her job', which she spoke of as 'impossible'. I had the impression of being with someone passively exposed to a situation in which an object seemed to order her continually to take responsibility for one chore or another, while at the same time the object was never satisfied, leaving her feeling near-paralysis and very criticised. In these sessions I felt myself to be in a similar position: she brought multiple and endless complaints, about which I felt that I could do very little. She kept saying that she had no faith in analysis. When she spoke about the analysis she referred to it in such a way that she made me think of a kind of 'state that ruled us both', and we, both of us, appeared to me to be flooded by 'the demands' – helpless and imprisoned by them, she from her work and I from her. At times I found it very difficult to find something in her which I could contact. I felt and thought that something cruel was going on, but that to address myself to this would have been to bypass the fact that she was so thoroughly identified with the cruel work, and so quickly projected her paralysing helplessness into me, that to talk about this process would have been like blaming her. She blamed me for not helping her either with her job or her bad feelings. I felt oppressed and exposed to a tyrannical situation.

Very slowly I started to describe what I thought was happening. After a while, on a Wednesday session she came with something new. Instead of starting as usual with her list of complaints, she was quiet, seemed thoughtful, a little uncomfortable, as if uncertain of herself, and spoke about having some difficulty in starting. Then she said that she could *choose* to start the session by talking directly to me but, she added, if she did this she feared it could make her vulnerable. Or she could report the usual unpleasant events. With some effort she said that she would just start speaking. This she did by talking in a slightly different way about her doubts concerning taking the new job, emphasising that she was expected to make a decision. She described the potential difficulties this new venture would involve. She spoke in an obsessional way and said she felt worried about it all. Finally she said that she did not know how she could think of taking on these kinds of responsibility since she did not even understand her own analysis. After a short pause she moved on to say that she had read an article in the *New York Review of Books*. It was extremely scathing about

Freud, questioning the very basis of psychoanalysis, and she added 'You must have read it, I wonder what you made of it. It was really anti-analysis.' This was said with obvious satisfaction.

At some point as she talked it came into my mind how paralysed and vulnerable I had often felt in her sessions, and that I was feeling different in this one, as if weeks of analytical work had loosened the grip that a very hostile internal object had on her, a change which I sensed in my own responses to her. I thought that by feeling myself freer I could risk interpreting directly her fears about feeling vulnerable, which I did. I reminded her of the way she had spoken to me in previous sessions. I said that when she acted in that cold and rigid way she believed that the 'vulnerable' her could be disposed of, separated from her and inserted in me, and that this in turn made her feel that we both were in the same position: helpless and exposed to cruelty. While she listened to this her eyes filled with tears which rolled down her cheeks. She was silent for a little while, then she started describing a sudden pain in her chest, pointing to her heart, and saying that it was very intense, but saying it did not worry her since she did not think it was an illness — just as Joseph describes, and which can be seen in Freud's terms as a transition from physical to mental pain.

When at the beginning of the session she had spoken about having a 'choice', I could sense that something new was emerging, like a ray of light coming from a tiny opening in a window. I felt less constricted and felt the possibility of taking the risk of speaking directly of something feared and painful, without her experiencing it as my pushing back her projections into her. I also had a choice now. I interpreted to her that when she sees me as someone who cannot understand that she needs time to find out what she wants to do, she is frightened of me and feels me to be harrying her and demanding. I expanded on the theme of how it was *this* her, lodged in me, which made her experience me as impatient and demanding. And I linked it with something inside her that seems continually to demand more and quicker responses and solutions. She associated some more about the job in an increasingly realistic way. Then she spoke about how different she felt in this session from before. She looked more relaxed and warm. She talked about how beautiful she felt Hampstead to be, attractive and uplifting.

For a long time in the analysis Ms A had been dominated by a merciless internal condition, which she projected both into her work and into me in the analysis. She rarely complained of or felt pain, but felt persecuted by demands at work and continually misunderstood by me. I was submitted to cruel and endless complaints, and I often felt paralysed and incapacitated and sometimes quite hopeless. In other words I felt I was having to be both the helpless infant her, and also the cruel denying object, while she similarly felt helpless but also behaved cruelly. From whichever point of view one looked at what was going on it did not seem possible to see a different view. It seemed as if we were on a rotating platform which kept reversing the perspective. There was no outside viewpoint. The intensity of her projections kept erasing the space between us, and everything remained static.

Her emergence from this enmeshment with me (as her internal object) changed her view of me into one in which we were different from each other. We could talk to each other in a friendlier and more direct way. I am not talking of a state of continuous 'agreement'; in fact her awareness of her own criticism and hatred become sharper, as expressed through her account of the article she had read, but there was a clearer sense of her identity and mine. Her growing capacity to separate from me as her object brought a different kind of experience to her, and she did not feel so intensely 'got at'. She just felt 'pain', and with this pain came relief and hope; she felt moved.

I have described a period in the analysis of a patient whose massive use of projective identification created a situation in which both of us seemed to be the same, both of us were persecuting and persecuted; I described a shift in the session I presented which indicated that more than one position existed. She began to become aware of a differentiation between herself and me, while I felt freer. I was helped in assessing this situation by being aware that my own feelings had changed, and we could begin to explore this new situation.

Change like this lasts a moment – brings a possibility of further change – but will of course be threatened by inevitable situations of anxiety, so the patient will retreat to a state of non-differentiation. This patient is only at the beginning of real change.

Sorrow

To progress into a further and more consolidated use of a depressive mode of functioning, a much greater capacity to tolerate psychic pain is indispensable. The anxieties brought forward by depressive-position functioning are felt both for one's self and for one's objects, internal and external. The awareness of separateness increases these anxieties, since it sharpens feelings of love and longing for the object as well as hatred towards it. When in some cases anxieties are too painful, patients retreat from them. One way of doing this is to have a phantasy of a state of oneness with the object through projective identification (Ms A). Sometimes progressing slightly from there, the subject may alternate between phantasies of oneness and phantasies of owning the object. These patients experience being separate as immensely painful, but the pain is not projected or nameless, it acquires a name: 'sorrow' (or grief), indicating that 'just pain' has turned into 'heartache'. This is a very difficult problem in the analysis. It can be a turning point towards further progress; it can also turn into a stumbling block. Sorrow comes from pain and concern for the internal object and the self. It is a lasting pain. Sorrow derives from awareness of being separate, which brings with it awareness of need and dependency, loss and guilt; and this awareness leads to resentment of feelings such as envy, jealousy, awareness of time, being left out. In the patients I am speaking of, these feelings are so strong and produce such hostility that they fear that in their omnipotent attacks they have destroyed and lost their good object. This in turn brings intolerable guilt and grief.

I will speak now of Mr B, who felt intense and intolerable pain when he experienced awareness of being separate from his object. He felt he could not bear this.

Mr B, a married man in his thirties, has three children and is separated from his wife. He previously worked for a time as a philosophy lecturer in a university, but presently works in finance in the City. Mr B came to analysis because he felt he was incapable of loving, and suffered continuous intense anxieties and depression.

The material I will present is from a very difficult time in his analysis. I will speak about a time immediately after a summer break, but first I wish to mention a recurrent episode in his analysis. For quite some time he kept repeating something I could not understand. He spoke in many dismissive ways of the analysis, often interrupting what he had been talking about by saying that the analysis did not amount to anything, it did not count and it was not real. I felt very puzzled by this since it kept coming back with considerable intensity, until finally I came upon the idea that for him reality related to counting, that his not seeing that there were two of us and not one, a him and a me, and maintaining instead the 'not counting', allowed him to stay in the unreality of oneness with me. This I interpreted to him, and he accepted it, and it brought a marked shift in the session, which led to further movement in the analysis. At that time he also became aware of being able to experience very tender, loving feelings (mainly in relation to his analyst and his children), and became troubled by feelings of craving.

After the summer holidays Mr B came back punctually, but after a few days he stopped coming for nearly three weeks. On his return he said that he had been giving himself an induction course of how to do without the analysis. Eventually it emerged that he left the office every day as if coming to analysis, and spent the time he should have been in his session in bookshops or libraries reading philosophy. After his return a lot of what we spoke about was his wish and determination to keep me useless or dead so as not to have feelings for me when we were away from each other. He stated in different and repeated ways that he could not stand my seeing other people, so he had to quit. The situation between us was very intense and fraught. In different ways (supported by dreams) it indicated his wish to do away with me. Murder and violence were very much to the fore. Skinheads and criminals populated his associations.

On a Monday he came to his session, and after a pause said 'I have nothing to say.' He teased me a bit with this, then became silent. I pointed out that 'nothing to say' seemed to mean not having a speech prepared and that this seemed to make him frightened of what might come into his mind. He nodded affirmatively. I said that when feeling troubled him, his immediate recourse was teasing and flirting. I described this to him and said that with this behaviour he was preventing me from doing the right thing by him. (Somewhere I linked it to the weekend.) He smiled and remained silent. After a longish pause I spoke again, saying that when he and I talk to each other, he feels that I can function as his analyst, and this makes him feel love, desire and hatred. He feels that he can avoid the conflict by giving himself almost completely to the hating him, and I linked it to the previous weeks when he had spent his sessions reading philosophy. My interpretation brought some interchange between us, and a dream of his of the previous week floated into my mind. In the dream he had gone shooting and had killed three ducks; we had understood the dream as his turning to murder when he feels he cannot own me. I reminded him of this dream and said that by attacking himself, me and our talk he believed he could make the pain disappear. I added that when he felt he did not possess the loved and needed analyst, his pain was so intense that it was not *felt* as unbearable to him, it *was* unbearable.

The point I want to emphasise is the intense difficulty this patient felt in tolerating his own experiences. The experience of love and tenderness was especially difficult for him, and as I have already mentioned, it was one of the reasons for his coming to analysis. A loved object, myself in the transference, is a needed object, and this made him aware of separateness and triggered intense possessiveness. Feeling so possessive left him feeling frustrated and exposed to (ordinary) feelings of envy, jealousy, being rejected or feeling left out, which stimulated further hatred. These feelings were for him impossible to experience, they were intolerable. In the period I have been speaking about, he tried to establish or re-establish a fusion with me. When he felt he could not maintain it in the sessions, he dramatically stopped coming. In this way he felt he could control me and be independent of me, while I was left waiting and worrying about him. He was very surprised to discover painfully that he became progressively more anxious, and that his feelings of need and desire for the analysis were there in spite of his acting out the phantasy of cutting off those feelings and leaving them in me.

I will return now to the session, that is, our talking about his not being either at one with me or owning me. Mr B expanded in a familiar way, by saying 'I want you to exist only for myself, otherwise I don't want you at all.' I commented that this idea of ownership stifles us into one being with no feelings. I referred to his fear of the coexistence of conflicting feelings and I linked it to his behaviour in the previous weeks. Mr B looked sombre, and explained that while reading philosophy, he had glanced through Plato's *Symposium* and that what we were speaking about reminded him that in the *Symposium* Plato says 'that first there was one, this was divided and separated into two, then there was a relationship and this was sorrow.' (I found his way of saying this very moving.)[1]

After a while I interpreted to him that he wished us to be a pair of Siamese twins, and that the sorrow he experiences is in realising that he is in a relationship with me and that we are not Siamese twins. He responded by saying he could not stand this. 'It is too painful,' he said, and it felt so to me. I interpreted that he felt it very painful to be in a relationship to me as a baby to a parent, that when there are others he gets invaded by jealousy and bad feelings. I linked it to the impulse to bypass all this as he did in childhood in his relationship with Bill. (Bill is a close friend; they were together at prep school, boarding school and university, where they both read philosophy, and in their adolescence they believed that they thought and felt exactly the same.) I said that now he wished that he and I should be like Bill and him. He looked very serious and said that what came to mind was the time Bill came back from abroad where he had been teaching. By then Mr B had already married and had his first daughter and had changed jobs. Bill visited them, and when Mr B was helping his child, who was learning to walk, to keep on her feet, Bill had laughed and mocked the child. Mr B had felt confused by what Bill was doing. I interpreted that when he experiences love in the analysis, it is a new feeling, fresh and growing, then another part of him laughs at him and mocks him. The 'him' who has love feels guilty for not standing up to the attacking him. To avoid these awful feelings he resorts to all kind of devices – such as attacking his own mind so as not to feel guilty towards the analyst he loves. After a short pause, he said that on Saturday he had felt very anxious and kept thinking about skinheads again, and had wanted to shave his head, but did not. I interpreted that when he felt pained by our absence from each other over the weekend, he felt a pull of hatred and mockery as he saw the skinheads. He also felt very criticised by me, who he feels accuses him of being a 'criminal' for wanting me all for himself. All this made him feel confused and impelled him to cut it all out – shave it all off – no feelings, no mind, just out. With a faint smile he said, 'I like you, but I hate to need you.' After a while he said that his eldest daughter came to mind. When she was born his wife had a very difficult and lengthy delivery, and he has always feared that Fiona, his daughter, might be brain damaged. He sounded very pained. I said that when he is frightened of things being beyond repair in that he has destroyed them omnipotently, he then imagines that he can cut everything out, his feelings of guilt, his worries about Fiona, our separation through an illusion of freeing himself from it and leaving it in me. He grunted, paused, then said 'Yes,' and seemed thoughtful.

In the analysis, when he became aware of a him and a me as separate, positive feelings to me as his analyst came to the fore and he expressed them. Those feelings immediately triggered an intense and intolerable possessiveness which in turn, when inevitably unsatisfied, flooded him with acute desires which quickly turned into hatred. Only very occasionally could he experience this as ambivalence. Much more often he was split between a loving him and a hating him, and tried to dispose of either in me, so as to avoid any perception of conflict. Mr B was just venturing towards a depressive position mode; his 'sorrow' was experienced when he was aware of separateness, and he felt he could not stand the mixed feelings it threatened him with.

The difference between the two patients described so far is that Ms A at first just felt 'persecuted', and when we worked through this state of persecutory feelings she experienced just pain, while Mr B seemed to feel sorrow, an unceasing heartache.

So far I have been speaking of pain as experienced by two patients, one Ms A, early on in her analysis when she became more aware of separateness from her object, and the second a man struggling against awareness of separateness, which continually threatened him with having to resort to drastic defences to avoid unbearable heartache. 'Just pain' brought relief to Ms A. 'Sorrow' was a continuous agony for Mr B.

Resolution

Finally I will consider those patients whose development in analysis has led to diminished use of a pathological kind of projective identification. Such patients can recognise differences between themselves and their objects. They can also more easily recognise their feelings and actions as their own, and take responsibility for them. This changes the structure of their internal world. Good objects and their relationship with them have become more established, and their whole way of functioning denotes a more mature depressive-position mode.

I shall now speak of Ms C, a patient nearing the end of her analysis, and I will describe an example of the internal oscillations and her own picture of an eventual resolution of some of her conflicts about separateness and separation. For many years in her analysis Ms C had tried to fend off feelings of exclusion and jealousy by splitting herself and depositing the her that felt such feelings into me or into her husband or colleagues, thus allowing herself to feel very close to me, or sometimes at one with me. We had done considerable work on this problem, which had led to progress and integration. By the time of the material I will describe we had fixed the date for the end of the analysis, and though old defensive patterns tended to recur, the patient had considerable insight into them.

Ms C started a Monday session saying that she had had a hectic weekend, which she described. She and her family had visited her mother-in-law in the country for her sister-in-law's birthday. She had also attended a meeting of her profession. We spent some time on these subjects and then she brought a dream.

In the dream she was very busy; she was eating her lunch while at the same time she was cooking and doing something for James (her husband) and the children. The bell rang and she went to the door. A man was at the door; she kept thinking that the man was James but he wasn't, he did not look like James, but she thought him to be James. He had some children with him. The man wanted something from her. He asked something about 'the environment', after which he asked her if she did not agree that each person had to have a bit of neurosis, and that this was OK. She did not agree. He looked as if he wanted to be loved; she felt she should do something for the man, but she did not feel like it. The scene seemed to change and a waitress started serving food. Apparently all this was taking place at the door. She was a pretty girl but did not know how to be a proper waitress. The patient was behaving like a 'grand lady' towards her.

While she narrated the dream the atmosphere in the session was unclear and there were oscillations of mood. Immediately after she told the dream she said that she had been very angry with James. He had been in Berlin and came home late on Friday, and then they had to go to his mother early on Saturday. She felt that if they had a day together just for themselves, they might have been closer, but she just felt angry. James was restless in his sleep and woke her up. She got furious, so she thought of going to sleep somewhere else but did not. After she spoke some more about all this, I asked if she had any thoughts about 'the environment'. She said that it is one of James' main interests. She laughed and said that of course all that stuff about neurosis was nonsense. I interpreted that when she was away from him as well as from the analysis, she experienced problems of a very specific nature. As she knows, she tried to keep the awareness of these problems (for instance missing and wanting him) out of herself. She responded very quickly, saying 'But I did not feel it.' To which I replied 'You believed they were in him.' But I added that the dream suggested she knew better and knew what it was about, since in her dream the man at the door wanted to be loved and did not quite look like James. 'Maybe,' I said in a lighter tone, 'a James mixed with Anne' (her name). She laughed. I continued, saying that she wished to maintain that she does not know how to wait (the waitress who does not know her job) by pretending to be the 'grand lady'. She laughed and interrupted, saying 'Propaganda for neurosis.'

She was thoughtful for a while and eventually went on to speak about the previous day's activities. With James and the children she had gone to James' mother's house in the country. Mary, her sister-in-law, had expressed a wish for her parents' house not to change at all forever. In this Mary was like Emil, the patient's brother, who said only a couple of weeks ago that their parents' house should be kept as it is now, and maybe eventually some of the children would live there. The patient did not agree with Mary and Emil's view. She felt that things and places should reflect life and should change. What she would like, and hoped to do, was that next time she visited her parents, she would make drawings of the house. In this way she would remember and keep it for ever in her mind in a better way. In this session Ms C knew and remembered that we had worked on similar anxieties. I interpreted that she was acknowledging that there was a better way, that is, to keep in mind what she knows and loves and to know her own reactions and thus to be able to allow change, contrary to what she seemed to say in the early part of the dream. She agreed.

This material shows the patient's increased capacity to use her experiences to understand the problems she has had, and still has to a lesser degree, about separation. It also shows her increased understanding of what goes on in her mind as well as in her behaviour. In the dream she expressed her awareness of disowning her own feelings and projecting them into James. The manifest content of the dream suggested that she does not know how to wait (the figure of the waitress) but also that she knows that this is not so, a pretence, and that this is not healthy but neurotic. Our work on the dream helped her to re-establish and strengthen her own understanding. She felt moved by this analytic work, and also felt aware of what she would miss when the analysis ended, which it soon would. Her thoughts went to how she could hold in her mind what she loved without having to possess it for ever. Furthermore, she had hope for the future in her view that 'things and places could be alive and change'.

I have used Ms C's material to describe what I call 'resolution'. Of course the idea of resolution does not mean a permanent state. The human mind is never quiescent. The impact of life events brings further or new anxieties, which in turn calls for defences. To my mind, resolution is a dynamic state acquired in analysis through insight. It permits the patient to experience and face life events in a more constructive way. It is by no means a painless state, but the nature of the pain is tolerable and often instrumental toward further progress.

Discussion

In this paper I have used the experience of pain as a central pivot to describe three stages in the process of individuation, that is, in achieving awareness of separateness between subject and object. The lack of a sense of separateness, as well as the steps needed to achieve this sense, depends on the operation of projective identification and its modification in analysis. This in turn depends on the person's capacity to tolerate pain, and on the nature of the pain. The taking back of projections into the self (undoing projective identification) increases the strength of the ego, which in turn increases the person's capacity to deal with painful states.

Bion's (1962) theory of container and contained has helped me to understand how the analyst receives and transforms the patient's communications so as to render them comprehensible and able to be presented to the patient in a way that conveys meaning to him. The analyst's attitude and the meaning conveyed permit the patient to introject a better object and a better functioning of this object as well as the content expressed in the interpretations. This introjection of course is very gradual, taking place in small doses and continuously impaired by conflict, anxieties and defences. I believe that the entire evolutionary change takes place in stages, such as the ones I have described in this paper.

My description of these three stages is closely linked to John Steiner's ideas (1993: 54–63). Steiner describes the recovery by the patient of projected aspects of the self as occurring in two stages. The first, which he calls the 'phase of containment', requires the presence of the analyst to maintain the withdrawal of projections, with the resulting integration and relief provided by it. He calls the second phase the 'phase of relinquishment', which he associates directly with processes of mourning. This last phase can be excruciatingly painful, for the patient needs to let go of the object, and defends himself from this pain with all the means at his disposal. Steiner expands on some of the factors that make this process so difficult, and describes possible outcomes, especially pathological ones.

What I described as the first stage, that is, 'pain', corresponds to Steiner's phase of containment, while 'sorrow' and 'resolution' can be thought of as pertaining to the two opposite ends of what Steiner calls the phase of relinquishment.

Ms A's paranoid anxieties kept her at first stuck to an object felt to be bad, but from which she could not detach herself. This painful situation could only be relieved when the nature of the pain resulting from paranoid processes changed into 'just pain', that is, when she became aware of separateness from the object and could feel more herself. Her feeling 'just pain' brought relief, but necessitated my presence to accept further projections from her and help her deal with them again and again.

Mr B had to experience unbearably painful anxieties to relinquish his object, his grief was horrendous and he resorted again and again to a borderline position (see Steiner 1993: 39) which encompassed his feelings of being at one with an idealised version of me, or in total possession of such a me, or exposed to the pull of murderous impulses.

Ms C was struggling with the mourning brought about by our preparation to end her analysis. Having to let go of analysis altogether accentuated the old projective defences by which she tried to rid herself of painful feelings about being left out or missing her object. Ms C, further advanced in her capacity to deal with such anxieties, was able to bring all those feelings into her mind as her own and was able then to think about what she felt and did.

PART III

Theoretical refinements

Introduction
Priscilla Roth

The two papers in this section focus on theory and technique. They are among the most recent of Riesenberg-Malcolm's papers, and demonstrate her understanding of the way in which theory influences what we see and how we respond to what we see. She is concerned with the analyst's theory of mind, and with how his theory of mental functioning influences his perception and response to his patients.

The first paper in this section, 'The three Ws: what, where and when: the rationale of interpretation', focuses on technique: how do we interpret to our patients? Reiterating her conviction, following Strachey and along with all Kleinian analysts, that mutative work is work done within the here-and-now of the transference relationship, Riesenberg-Malcolm here explores the constituent parts of the transference interpretation. She describes *what* we interpret as that configuration of the patient's internal object relations which is being communicated within the session; she describes the way proper use of the counter-transference enables the analyst to perceive and understand often confusing and chaotic communications from his patient. Here she is elaborating and further exploring the work of Wilfred Bion and Betty Joseph, particularly Bion's description of projective identification and how it works as communication, and Joseph's understanding of Klein's concept of the 'total transference'. She works firmly within the Kleinian tradition. What she experiences with her patient are counter-transference affects: confusion, annoyance, relief, friendliness, exclusion. Her understanding of these experiences in herself and as communication from her patient is, she tells us, structured by her theoretical background, her 'theory of mind'. This enables her to understand the way splitting and projection are used by the patient as defences against both the pain of the weekend separation, and the patient's anxiety about feelings of anger towards his analyst.

The second factor Riesenberg-Malcolm considers, *where*, is the orientation of the interpretation. Assuming the analyst arrives at some understanding of the transference relationship as it is being experienced in the session, how can the interpretation be formulated? Here she makes a clear distinction, based on John Steiner's (1993) paper on patient-centred v. analyst-centred interpretations. She says that when the patient is largely operating in the paranoid-schizoid mode, so that he has projected many of his unwanted impulses into his object (the analyst), it is vital that the interpretation be directed at his view of his analyst, along the lines of 'You feel I am...' When, however, the patient has moved more into a depressive-position mode of functioning, where he is able to contain more of his own feelings and impulses, the interpretation should be centred on his perceptions of himself. Of course, movements between one position and the other take place both within and between sessions and periods in the analysis. In other words, the point about *where* is that it addresses itself to the question: where are the patient's impulses felt to be located — in himself or in his object?

The concept of *when*, Malcolm makes clear, is not to do with timing of interpretations, but with what factors affect the sequence of events within the session whereby the analyst hears, perceives, internally monitors, contains and thinks about the patient's material until, at some point, his perceptions and thoughts clarify and formulate themselves into what he believes is a truthful understanding. She discusses this in relation to Bion's (1962) 'selected fact' and Britton and Steiner's (1994) 'over-valued idea'.

This exploration of developing Kleinian theory is discussed in relation to a complete session of a patient in analysis, so that the reader is made aware of the way theory, as it develops, can lead to an expansion and a clarification of analytic work.

In 'Conceptualisation of clinical facts in the analytic process', she specifically addresses the way theory inevitably and necessarily influences and affects what become 'clinical facts', that is, the analyst's understanding and interpretation of the patient's transference relationship. She demonstrates how Kleinian concepts of the paranoid-schizoid and depressive positions — with their different anxieties and defences — structure her thinking and allow her to understand the disturbing material of her very ill patient, Ms A. She sees the patient as moving rapidly back and forth in the session between paranoid-schizoid and depressive states of mind, as Ms A feels first hopeful and relieved about being helped, and then assailed by intolerable impulses. Riesenberg-Malcolm shows clearly here the way her own understanding of theory enables her to follow these rapid shifts in the patient's mental state, and she differentiates the work that can be done within the session and the important reconsideration that must be done after the session.

Two other points are worth remarking on here. The first is the distinction she makes between clinical facts, which she sees as arising only within an analytic session, and everything else that happens in the patient's life: his history, his current relationships, even the place of the analyst in his mind outside sessions. In this paper, as in earlier ones, she is extremely sensitive to what the patient tells her about his life outside his session, but she uses this information to inform her perception of what is going on between analyst and patient within the session. In this sense she is true to her conviction that it is within the analytic relationship itself that the patient's internal world with all its conflicts is played out.

My second point, which follows from the first but is more specific to this paper, is to note her description of the way a first session can reveal the 'genetic coding' – the DNA one might say – of the patient's archaic object relations which reappear, to be explored and understood, over the course of the analysis.

10

The three Ws: what, where and when
The rationale of interpretation

Interpretation is the very stuff of analytic work. In the session the analyst listens and tries to feel what the patient is saying, and observes how is he saying it, the language he uses, the expressions which are usual and unusual (for him) and the emotional tone, as well as the patient's movements, posture, changes of mien, etc.; in fact, anything that can be observed.

The analyst also observes his own reactions, as well as the feelings that the patient elicits in him, and tries to differentiate which come from himself and which are direct expressions of the patient's dynamics. Using all this material he reaches a view of what is going on, not only in the patient and himself, but most importantly in the relationship between them. This he presents to the patient as an interpretation. The interpretative work is a continuous diagnostic activity, aimed at reaching hypotheses about what goes on between patient and analyst; the analyst hopes that these hypotheses will affect the patient in some way, preferably in such a way as to produce insight and promote further analytic understanding. To continue the analytic work the analyst has to observe all the patient's responses, whether they are insightful or not, so as be able to assess the situations brought about by his interpretation and formulate in his mind a new interpretation, which he eventually might give to his patient.

Interpretative work is thus a mixture of emotional and intellectual activity, both of which have to be present. The emotional understanding by the analyst of his patient has to be processed by thought to be able to form an interpretation.

In this paper I wish to speak of three factors which together form a

This paper was first presented to the Anglo-Chilean Conference of Psycho-Analysis in Santiago, Chile, 1994. It was published in the *International Journal of Psycho-Analysis*, 76 (1994) part 3, and in Spanish in the *Libro Anual de Psicoanálisis*, volume XI (1994).

framework in the mind of the analyst when making interpretations. I hope to make it clear later that I am speaking of how the material takes shape in the analyst's mind before he formulates the interpretation to the patient.

In *what* we interpret, I shall speak about the transference relationship, understood as an expression of the internal world of the patient, that is, the present relationship of the patient to his analyst as an expression of past internal object relationships which for some reason could not evolve. The nature and the cause of the lack of development or faulty development as expressed in the transference come into what we interpret. In other words this is a *why* things express themselves as they do in the analysis that also constitutes part of *what*.

In *where* I will refer to levels of functioning of the patient as reflected especially in the movement between the paranoid-schizoid position and the depressive position (PS↔D) which results in the predominance of either projective or introjective processes. Excessive projection results in the patient feeling that the cause and responsibility for the situation as expressed in the transference lie with the analyst. Less projection and an increase of introjective activities allows for recognition and eventually responsibility for the feelings being the patient's own. The analyst's assessment of this situation will determine the orientation of the interpretation.

Finally, in *when* I shall address the factor(s) that help the analyst to integrate at a given time the different elements of the patient's communication into a new formulation that can then be verbalised to the patient. I want to make it clear that I am referring not to what is often called 'timing' of the interpretation (that is to say when should it be given to the patient) but to the moment when something comes together in a particular way in the analyst's mind.

What, *where* and *when* are factors in the formulation of every interpretation and therefore are essential for the development of the analysis.

Most analysts will perceive emotionally what is going on, but each analyst will understand what he perceives according his own theoretical background. It is our theory that makes us understand the patient's material and interpret it to him one way and not another. For instance, some analysts believe that the most important work in the analysis is the reconstruction of the patient's past. My view is very different. I believe that the patient's early conflicts (that have not evolved into more mature states) remain alive in his mind and express themselves in the present relationship between patient and analyst, that is, the transference; therefore I emphasise the interpreting of transference. In this sense my view is closer to that of Sandler and Sandler (1984) concerning what they call 'the present unconscious', that is, those unconscious expressions of the patient which are available and can be reached only in the here-and-now of the analytic session.

My position also differs from those analysts who believe that extra-transference interpretations can be mutative, that is to say, interpretations of situations or relationships that the patient narrates in the analysis and which are interpreted in the 'there-and-then', in relation to wherever or whenever they happened. I consider that changes in the patient's mental operations and structure are achieved primarily through an alive experience of the here-and-now in the transference situation, and I therefore make this central, although I integrate it with what is going in the patient's external life and his past history.

I believe that all analysts will make transference interpretations related to the patient's life (past and present), but that the understanding of these phenomena will depend on each individual's theory of mind as the basis for understanding human behaviour.

I shall now discuss the subject of the paper itself and try to clarify each of the points I have listed in the light of clinical material, and to link it with the theory I use.

I shall present a session of a patient, Mrs A, who at the time of the session had been in analysis with me for about five years. She comes from a northern European country, where she was in analysis before marrying and moving with her husband to England. She is in her late thirties and has three small children.

Mrs A is the fourth of six children, born into a Catholic family. One of her brothers lives in Italy, while the others remain in their country of origin. They are a united family and she goes often to visit her parents and siblings for weekends. Sometimes they all spend holidays together. Starting in late adolescence and until the birth of her first child she was a severe bulimic. She binged regularly and made herself vomit. (This she did at least daily, but more often several times a day.) She very proudly told me at the start of the analysis that she had perfect control of her weight, never losing or gaining a single gram. She objected to the word bulimia, and her own expression was 'eating and vomiting'.

Mrs A is intelligent, educated and cultured. She has a good capacity for love, but she also has a very hostile, envious streak. For years during the analysis she had been very protective of her mother, who emerged in the transference as caring, perhaps overwhelmed by so many children, and rather unavailable. Mrs A felt very hostile to her father, apparently since childhood, but lately he is beginning to emerge in a different light, and she is more friendly to him. Feelings of jealousy are very strong in her, and are especially directed at her eldest sister and younger siblings.

At first she took to analysis like a fish to water; she brought abundant dreams and seemed very accessible. Nevertheless after some time I realised that often in her sessions I became drowsy and somewhat bored. I liked her, and never felt I wanted her not to come, but during the sessions I often found my mind wandering. Slowly I came to realise that a subtle but very tight control was being maintained so that nothing much should change; interpretations seemed to be taken in but to be quickly partially rejected. She seemed to feel that some problems were insurmountable and that she was trying in the analysis to impose the same *modus vivendi* she had developed in her life through eating and vomiting. This so far had been understood as an expression of control aimed at maintaining a certain equilibrium. There were lots of associations and dreams, but the way in which she spoke had a certain dreamy quality. When I was able to understand this a little, and to describe it to the patient, it became clearer that her aim was to achieve a kind of 'suspended animation', that is, to control the session in such a way that nothing much would happen. She often felt triumphant when she felt that she had achieved this control.

Work in this area took a long and painful course. She dreaded confusion, which she often experienced. No sooner had Oedipal material and feelings come to the fore than she became very confused, and afraid of losing that bit of understanding she had acquired. This immediately drove her to the paralysing control I have just described, which usually resulted in calming her down.

By the time of the session I will present she had gained considerable insight into her controlling behaviour, that is, her 'analytic bulimia' (her actual bulimia was not in evidence by the time we started). My drowsiness had nearly gone, reappearing only as a specific reaction to a particular defensive stance in the patient.

In the Saturday session previous to the one I will present, she was very upset and agitated about some news she had received from her family. Just before that session she had received a phone call from her sister who told her that their brother Bill (Bill is the brother who immediately precedes her; he lives in their place of origin) was in severe financial trouble because of some business irregularities. She was so upset by this news that she shivered during most of the session. She referred repeatedly to the fact that her parents had been so demanding about everybody being honest; she remembered how they used to scold her when she lied; but, she added, 'They had accounts in banks in other countries, presumably to avoid tax.' She also expressed worries about paying for the analysis with what she called 'contaminated money', since her personal money came from her family.

On Monday she begun by saying that she thought she had a cold, but she did not want to tell me because I might say something about it which would be wrong. On Saturday she had not been able to stop the shivering but somehow, just barely, she managed to cope. Tom (her eldest brother) had phoned her and it was awful. She then proceeded in a rapid and muddled way to narrate the telephone conversation with Tom, who had phoned from Italy. They discussed a possible meeting of the whole family, since their mother wanted to inform them about some final decisions she had reached, affecting them all, and Tom very much wanted this meeting to take place in his house in Italy. She reported the conversation with her brother in a way which suggested that they disagreed about almost everything, and she described him as hectoring and bullying, and contemptuous of the other siblings. He also wanted her to send her children with his son (who was a boarder in England) to Italy for half-term. She refused. He grew angry and insisted, and she eventually told him that she was not going to comply, since his son was very cruel and her children were too young. He continued to demand that the family meeting take place in Italy, while she held that the distance made it impossible, and suggested a more equidistant point for them all.

All this came out in gushes of words and emotions. Within her there seemed to be a great number of characters, each with a distinct point of view, and she conveyed a sense of being split in many parts. She continued to tell me how awful it was, and finally told me about having phoned some other of her siblings.

While she spoke I was very impressed by two things: first, that my mind was focusing on a feeling of the presence of someone absolutely selfish and self-centred (Tom in her associations); and second, that I also felt myself getting confused, with my mind moving in different directions at the same time. I thought of intervening here, but I had no opportunity to say anything, as she continued by telling me that on Saturday her husband had returned from a business trip and that she was able to tell him the whole story concerning Bill's problems. She once again brought up the fear of paying for her analysis with dirty money, and appeared to be very troubled by this.

Before presenting my interpretation, I shall discuss what I thought was going on in the session. On arrival Mrs A appeared persecuted and split in many parts, and she projected a lot of these parts into me when she spoke in a confusing way: I felt a little confused. She felt criticised by a misunderstanding object, whom she had to keep at bay: she had said that she could not tell me that she had a cold because I would take it wrongly. During the weekend Mrs A felt rejected by me because I had left her (especially in the difficult family situation); she felt me to be cruel and selfish. My impression is that she split this experience with the bad (transference) object-me and tried to free herself by expelling and scattering the fragments into her brother Tom and his son, while her own children represented the cruelly treated her. This action seemed aimed partly to spare her from feeling rejected during the weekend, but it left her feeling 'got at' from outside and not knowing why. She appeared frightened of being invaded. The apparently selfish behaviour of her brother facilitated these projections into him.

In an early period of her analysis Mrs A had very frequently used splitting mechanisms, which often resulted in states of fragmentation. Her use of fragmentative manoeuvres was mainly defensive, and as a consequence she often felt weak and flat and complained of difficulties in keeping things in mind. At this time in the analysis Mrs A had achieved considerable insight into her hostility and splitting mechanisms. She was on the whole more integrated and was struggling with mixed feelings towards me, representing her primary object. In the session I am presenting, the pain of the weekend separation and her difficulties with her family made her resort again to multiple splitting and projection, which left her feeling depleted, shaken and guilty. I seemed to have become a dubious figure in her mind, not only bad for having left her, but also, she felt, for being critical of the method she had used (splitting and projecting) to deal with my having left her. Possibly she felt that I would only see its negative aspect, that is, the hostility spurred by the separation, and that I would not discern her wish to protect her good feelings towards the analysis and myself.

I think that in going back to such considerable use of multiple splitting, she aimed mainly at preventing herself from being aware of how ambivalent she felt, for awareness of this was very painful to her. Her mixed feelings and her projection of some of those feelings into me threatened her with experiencing me as a 'contaminated object', good and bad at the same time. As I said before, she tried to protect me by scattering her bad feelings into her family, but when this did not work she felt endangered by being left with a 'bad me' and she feared that as a bad object I would misunderstand her.

Now I will bring my interpretation: I began by saying that she seemed very invaded by many problems and people and unable to think. She immediately said, sounding slightly calmer, almost interrupting, 'This is very true,' and spoke in more detail about how when she was twenty she had refused to take money from her parents (this was known in the analysis). Now, she added, this shows that she had been right: it all turns dirty. My speaking seemed to have brought an immediate relief. Before I spoke she had felt me to be endangered by her phantasies; seeing me willing and able to work relieved her.

I continued my interpretation by saying that she seemed very frightened of me, and that she felt me to be unfriendly and unconcerned and ready to misjudge her. (This was based on my understanding that my absence was painful to her, and the feeling created by it had stimulated her projection of bad feelings into me, making her perceive me as unfriendly and ready to misjudge her.) I said that when she was accosted by so many feelings and problems, she felt me to be very selfish in that I took my weekend and left her. She had probably felt furious, very vulnerable and alone. I continued, saying that so as not to feel like that, she divided herself and lodged different parts of herself into her different siblings, in doing so resorting to a frantic activity.

My interpretation was based on what I was thinking about, but only drew my patient's attention to the points I have just mentioned. I spoke mainly about two things: her perception of me and her defences. *What* I interpreted was that I had become (in the transference) a bad object, and how she had felt and what she had done to create this. I described the defences she used against the resulting situation as well as the way she acted them out with her family. In considering *where*, it was I who was felt to be bad, containing her mixed feelings. The interpretation was oriented to the analyst because that was *where* the problem seemed to be; I was experienced by her in that particular way partly because of the separation and partly because of her projections. After verbalising this, I moved directly to her own actions. By addressing myself directly to her feelings, I was assuming that they were located in her. And as for *when*, it was only when those factors I spoke of above (the very selfish object and the fragmentation) came together in my mind that it was it possible to clarify the situation and make the interpretation, which made sense of my confusion and of the prevalent feeling of there being someone around who was very selfish.

To return to the session: after my intervention there was a change in Mrs A. She first relaxed and was silent for a while, apparently thoughtful. After some minutes, as if reacting to something, she said that she also would like to go to Tom's: all the siblings together, that part of Italy is so beautiful, walking on the red leaves in the countryside....Her voice sounded sugary (which is not characteristic of her) and provocative. She also seemed to be speaking as if someone was preventing her from going or forbidding her to go. While she spoke I felt that my sense of working together with her was disappearing, as if she had left me behind while she floated off into beautiful Italy. I pointed out that she seemed to be embarking on some peculiar provocation, reminding her that the last time all of her family had been together the picture she presented of the event was not so rosy, and I remarked that she seemed to experience me as not wanting her to go. To this she responded with a mixture of belligerence and a smile in her voice, expanding on how nice it is and how much she likes it when the whole family is together.

Her response was puzzling, and I felt that my interpretation had not been right and that most probably I had missed something important, possibly the contaminated money, and the idealisation with which she had reacted to my previous interpretation, which she had experienced as helpful in gathering herself together. Following those thoughts, I told her that during the weekend she had felt abandoned by me and had felt me to be cold, and that she had had to scatter aspects of herself into her siblings, but now she felt understood by me she not only felt me to be good, she idealised me. She identified with this me in creating this ideal picture of togetherness which left her feeling that we were very close, but she experienced me as not wanting her to go. The relief created by the analytic work, I think, made the patient wish to be at one with me and to take me over for this purpose. In this sense she identified with an idealised version of me. What I am speaking about is a type of projective identification in which the patient projected the her that feels so possessive, resulting in her feeling trapped in me. The way I see what happened is that she split me into an idealised object with whom she wanted to be and whom she took over, and a me left empty, abandoned and angry. I think that this latter version of me contained and reflected the feelings she had experienced during the weekend, from which she had to get away.

After a short pause and some comment of hers, I added that this view of me and our relationship and spreading her bad feelings around created a false picture, aimed apparently at protecting her from knowing how angry she had been with me since she also felt that I understood her. She felt that to have contradictory feelings towards me was very dangerous, as these threatened her with feeling muddled by experiencing me as dirty, like the dirty money I was contaminated by.

Mrs A said at first 'Mmm,' then added 'This is true,' and after a short pause said that what I had said reminded her of a dream she had had last night. It was again a dream about packing. (Mrs A has had throughout her analysis dreams in which all her belongings are scattered around and she is not able to pack them together, sometimes having to leave them behind, at other times getting stuck.)

In this dream she was somewhere and all her things were spread around. She found it difficult to gather them so as to put them in her valise, and there was not enough time to catch the first boat. But then she realised that she did not have to catch the first boat since there was another one soon after that, and she managed to gather her things. She sounded pleased when saying this.

I interpreted that our work today and my previous interpretation had helped her to understand and deal with what she was experiencing, and that only then could she remember the dream. The dream showed clearly one aspect of what we had been talking about: what results from the situation in which she tries to free herself from her bad feelings by scattering them around so that she would not feel me as bad or even a mixed kind of person, nor should she feel too angry with me. I said that I thought that she had retained some contact with a good me inside her, but that she had felt pulled by contradictory feelings which made this contact precarious, and that she needed me to help her.

Mrs A was silent and rather pensive. Then she said something that I found totally incomprehensible, almost as if spoken in another language. She referred to something like 'my husband's "baby"', and how uncomfortable she felt when he played with all his toys in the drawer. She said this with great resentment. At first I felt enormously puzzled, as I had no idea what she was talking about. I made a lame attempt to get some more information, but she volunteered none. Then, still not knowing about her husband's activities, my mind centred on the impression that my interpretation was heard and agreed with by her but that it had made her feel resentful. (I want to call attention here to the fact that in spite of the content of what she said being so unclear, it had a profound impact on my mind, which permitted me to make sense of the involved emotions. I will return to this below.)

Returning now to the session: I interpreted that she had felt understood by me and did understand my last interpretation, but then she had felt sharply resentful and experienced me as egoistic, showing off how superior I was for being able to keep my thoughts in my mind (the drawer), that this was all 'play' for me, and coming back on Monday just an easy game. She answered directly to this, saying 'Yes,' and began telling me details about her difficult weekend and her work with her children. At the very end of the session, she said that she had recovered a credit card she had lost on Saturday. It had been rather easy; she had phoned Safeway (a supermarket) and they had kept it for her. This indicated to me that now a better relationship between us had been recovered; credibility had been restored and established in a safe place.

The work of interpreting is done by the analyst on the communications of his patient, as expressed in their relationship, about the relationship itself. As I said before, the way the analyst understands the patient's material depends on the analyst's theory of mind. My own thinking is rooted in Klein's theories as well as in further developments in Kleinian thinking.

In assessing the communications of the patient in a session, the analyst is alert and centred on the affects, anxieties and defences as they are experienced in relation to the object. In order to understand the patient's communications the analyst has to be alert to the continuous changes in the patient's state of mind as expressed in his total behaviour, verbal and non-verbal, in the session. These changes can be big or minute, but in observing them the analyst tries to make sure that he is addressing himself to the right aspect of the patient. As I said before, in order to do this the analyst not only has to be alert to the patient's verbal and non-verbal communications, but also to those emotions the patient elicits in the analyst. This is the countertransference, which can be used as a kind of sense organ to perceive certain aspects of the patient's feelings, which the patient either cannot express in any other way, for whatever reason, or which complement a more direct discourse. In order to understand and use counter-transference phenomena in assessing the patient's material, the concept of projective identification is indispensable. As is well known, projective identification was discovered by Klein in 1946; she understood it at that time especially as a projection of parts of the self into the object with which the object is felt to become identified, the main aim being to control the object.

This concept continued to develop and expand, and it was Bion (1962) who brought out its primary importance in the development of mental life. Bion described how the mother's reception and perception of her child's projections helps or hinders the infant's development. Thanks especially to Bion's, Rosenfeld's and Joseph's emphasis on the use of projective identification as a means of communication by the patient in the session, analysts have developed and refined the use of the counter-transference in understanding the transference and the nature of the patient's internal object relationships, the affects and anxieties that predominate, and therefore the various ways in which the patient defends himself. All this forms the core of analytic interpretations, the *what* of the interpretation.

I want now to look conceptually at the interpretations given in the material used for this paper. In my view, at this point in the analysis the patient had reached the depressive position; she was struggling to preserve a good relationship with me standing for her mother, especially when exposed to separation which stimulated hostility. The mixture of hostility and love for the object resulted in disturbing ambivalence which threatened her with confusion. To protect herself from this situation and maintain a good relationship with me in her internal world against the impact of hostile feelings elicited by the separation, she regressed to defences more appropriate to the paranoid-schizoid position, predominantly splitting, sometimes of a fragmentative nature, and projective identification, both into her internal and external objects, that is, into her siblings and children. But these defences worked only partially, and the object was felt to be contaminated. She felt me to be selfish and hostile for having left her, as well as because of her projections into me; but she also was aware of a different version of me. When these dynamics were interpreted and she felt more integrated, her first reaction was of an 'exaggerated' relief, that is, she idealised me as her object and identified with this idealised object, by taking over this ideal me. This resulted in a double situation of falsification and of feeling stuck in this 'gooey' object.

When we could work on this situation so that she felt a better relationship between us had been established, she could remember her dream. The dream showed that there was a reasonably good relationship with her object in her internal world, but that it was not reliable and solid enough. She felt it to be threatened by the reactions provoked in her by the analytic weekend separation, and she resorted again to splitting and fragmentation;

when she came back after the weekend, she needed to test and explore her object, myself in the analysis (containing part of her projections), to be able to establish more solidly the gains of integration. This better relation to myself in the transference did not bring out only relief and positive feelings, but also stimulated her envy and rivalry with me as representing her primary object. She experienced me as someone who could understand her, while being able to use my own mind with ease. She seemed to experience this facility as my feeling that the analysis was 'just a game'. Understanding and interpreting to the patient her envy and the way she perceived me because of it, allowed her to recognise her own feelings, and this in turn permitted her to establish a positive relationship to her object in a safer and more secure way. In other words, a positive transference predominated, which felt firmer and more genuine.

The understanding of the movement that takes place in the analysis between the paranoid-schizoid position and the depressive position permits the analyst to assess at what level the patient is functioning at any given time in the session. A patient functioning predominantly in a paranoid-schizoid mode will resort excessively to projective manoeuvres. In this case the object, the analyst in the session, will be perceived as having the feelings the patient has dislodged into him, and the patient will feel that the analyst is behaving towards the patient in a way that expresses those feelings. In that sense, because of the projection of his own feelings, the problem for the patient is then the perception he has of his analyst; the interpretation should then be centred on the analyst (Steiner 1993). In the material presented this can be seen especially when I interpreted at the beginning how selfish and against her she felt me to be, and again later on when I interpreted her picture of me as self-satisfied (analysis was a 'game' for me). That is to say, the *where* of the interpretation was momentarily placed in the analyst.

In moments during the session, or in particular periods of the analysis, when the patient is capable of more integrated functioning by containing in himself his own conflicting problems, that is, when the patient functions in a predominantly depressive-position mode, the orientation of the interpretation can point towards the patient. The *where* is judged by the analyst at such moments to be in the patient. By being more integrated, the patient is able to recognise and take responsibility for his own feelings. This can be seen in most of the interpretations given in the session I presented. I think it can also be seen that interpretations are often directed to both aspects of the place the feelings occupy, the perception of the analyst and the awareness of the patient's own feelings, in a kind of rapid oscillation, as for instance in 'You feel me in such-and-such a way because of this or that in you'. When projections are not excessive and introjection is possible, the interpretative work helps the patient to retrieve what belongs to himself and to further his own integration.

The three Ws: what, where and when

Let me turn now to the *when* of the interpretations. As can be seen in the material presented, when I speak about *when*, I am referring to the time when the ideas for the interpretation come together in the analyst's mind, before being verbalised to the patient.

Through listening with an open mind to the diverse ways in which the patient communicates to his analyst, eventually something happens that results in the formation in the mind of the analyst of a pattern that brings emotional sense to the many elements of the information. It is when this emotional discovery and configuration takes place that the analyst is in a position to formulate an interpretative hypothesis to himself and then to his patient. This event was called by Bion, following Poincaré's work in mathematics, the 'selected fact'. This is that element of the material that integrates the different aspects that are being expressed into a meaningful whole, a new formulation.

In most cases when the analyst is well tuned to his patient, the right element impinges on his mind and an appropriate integration takes place, an integration that corresponds to the dynamics of the patient as perceived by the analyst. I think this can be seen clearly in the material when the patient spoke about her husband 'playing with his toys'. Though I had no idea what she was specifically referring to, it made sense to me in clarifying her reaction to my working with her, and this allowed me to interpret as I did, and the patient could then move towards further insight. It is interesting to note that it could have been quite easy to speculate about the meaning of the unconscious phantasies in the expression of her husband's 'babies', his 'toys in the drawer', which at an intellectual level might have appeared correct, but this was not what imposed itself in my mind. What I did register was an envious reaction expressed in a biting remark. This was the selected fact, and when I interpreted it, it proved to be right.

But what the analyst conceives of as the selected fact is not always correct. Sometimes it may correspond to some personal reaction or interest of the analyst that refers more to his own dynamics than to assessing the patient's material. Britton and Steiner (1994) have spoken of an 'overvalued idea' instead of the selected fact. In the example described by them, this overvalued idea, originally overvalued by the analyst, is latched onto by the patient for reasons of his own. I have often observed that certain patients, when exposed to painful states of incomprehension, will try to latch on to anything, regardless of whether it is correct or not, in an attempt to bring some meaning to these frightening and painful states. There are many instances in which the selected fact can bring together the wrong elements, corresponding then to some interference in the analyst's mind, a problem in his use of his counter-transference; it is the role of the analyst to notice this and correct it.

An instance of such a situation in the clinical example I am using was when I questioned Mrs A about her views on the niceness of the family meeting in such idyllic grounds. I was aware of something being false and up to a point I sensed her idealisation of myself. But I was too much affected by the sugariness of her remark and the note of protest emanating from her feeling that I was preventing her from going. I now think that what might have happened is that what had focused my mind was *my* dislike of sugariness, which probably did not allow me at first to understand that the sugary, idealised object was myself.

A selected fact when correct often brings a sense of discovery and clarity to the analyst, even if not everything is understood. I believe also that this event corresponds in some measure to a state in the patient in which it appears to be more possible to present him with an interpretation. This of course does not mean that the patient will be ready to accept it, since his reaction will depend mainly on the anxieties that will be stirred up, but he will be affected by the interpretation one way or another. In essence, what I am talking about is *when* the analyst perceives in himself a new understanding of his patient's material that brings together different aspects of the here-and-now of the session.

Summary

In this paper I have been speaking about the main elements that converge in the analyst's mind when making interpretations. In *what*, I have described mainly the dynamic content of the patient's communications; that is, those aspects of his internal object relationships with their inherent anxieties and defences as expressed in the transference. When dealing with this aspect of making interpretations, the analyst is aware of a fourth W, that is, *why*. The *why* in the understanding of the material refers to how the patient came to be as he is, which includes some understanding of the interplay in his development between the role played by the patient's drives and the role played by the environment.

In understanding *where*, the analyst is continuously assessing the patient's responses, which indicate the level at which he is functioning, as given by the oscillation between the paranoid-schizoid and depressive positions and the predominance either of projective or introjective procedures; in this way he is defining *where* the interpretation should be formed.

The time when the *what* and the *where* become connected in the analyst's mind by a specific factor of the total communication, is when the analyst reaches the *when*, that is, the moment in which the interpretation can be formulated in his own mind.

11
Conceptualisation of clinical facts in the analytic process

The analyst's perception and understanding of his patient is greatly influenced by his analytic theory. It is his theory that makes the analyst view issues in the consulting room one way or another, and it is his theory that determines that which he believes to be clinical facts. Theory acts as a lens through which the events of the analytic encounter are judged and dealt with, and through which their kaleidoscopic presentations in a session acquire shape and meaning, forming themselves into clinical facts.

In this paper I describe the elements that converge to make clinical facts and I describe the way I conceptualise a fact. For the purpose of this paper I define 'clinical facts' as events that happen in the enclosure of the analytic session and are expressed in the relationship between analyst and patient. In my view it is in this relationship, when both patient and analyst are present, that these problems can be worked with analytically. In this sense one could say that clinical facts are those problems of the patient that express themselves in the transference in the presence of the analyst so that they can be explored analytically by both analyst and patient.

From my theoretical position I see the patient's way of relating in the analysis to his analyst as an expression of his experiences with his internal objects. These experiences are of old object relationships, which for certain reasons could not develop in a mature way and which contain and maintain within them active infantile conflicts that tend to repeat themselves in all the patient's relationships and behaviour. In the analysis, the patient relives these old conflicts in the relationship with the analyst, and the analyst can understand them in a living way and interpret them to the patient. I think this corresponds to what Sandler and Sandler (1984) call the 'present

This paper was first published in the *International Journal of Psycho-Analysis*, 75 (1994) parts 5–6, and in Spanish in the *Libro Anual de Psicoanálisis*, volume X (1994).

unconscious', present as accessible and expressed in the here-and-now of the session. I wish to emphasise that this here-and-now is for me always an expression of the relationship between analyst and patient as representing internal object relationships. These are internal structures, expressed in the analysis bit by bit, following their own dynamics, which become affected by the interventions of the analyst in the moment-to-moment work of the analysis.

The fact that the analyst works from a central theory does not preclude other lines of thought influencing his views. Other theoretical systems influence our own theories; the extent to which this occurs depends on how close or distant they are from our own set of beliefs. The further they are from our views their influence is lesser, provoking more resistance in us and probably occurring more unconsciously than consciously. The degree of wideness, flexibility and firmness of our own theories determines our clinical judgement, and especially the technique we use to deal with clinical facts. To understand what one is doing in one's clinical practice one has to have a solid central core of ideas, a theory, since our theory is the base from which we perceive analytically; from this central theory it is possible to pursue many often apparently unrelated experiences so as to be able eventually to make sense of them in the light of our central ideas. In doing so we must continuously shape and reshape our central body of ideas, and occasionally we even may add something new to it.

In analytic work we use theory in two principal ways. First, when we are with our patients theory operates on our perceptions mainly, though not exclusively, unconsciously. This central unconscious work is interspersed by quick, more conscious thinking aimed at making sense of what we observe in the patient, in ourselves, and especially of the interaction between patient and ourselves. It is this rapid conscious awareness of what goes on which permits us to judge these events so as to select what we make explicit to the patient.

Second, when we are away from our patients and we think about what has actually happened, our theoretical notions become central to our thinking. They show us what we understood and what we failed to understand; they impel us to think again or to look at the material in a different way. To do this we detach ourselves from the emotional involvement of the session, and we try to understand this involvement as a crucial aspect of the session. We examine what we see by using the main concepts we believe provide us with the understanding of the workings of the patient's mind; we operate from our own psychoanalytic theory of mind. It is important to keep in mind the differentiation I have just described concerning how we use theory in analytic work, to prevent both an excess of intellectualisation during the session and the loss of the necessary level of abstraction when we do our homework away from the patient.

When we conceive our theories clearly, we feel secure enough to tolerate the frequent difficulty in understanding what is going on, and to extend our analytic senses in all possible directions without superimposing our theory on material because we cannot understand it.

Holding on to a partial and often unclear understanding of the new phenomena which emerge in the analysis is often as difficult as tolerating not knowing, and both carry the danger of pushing the analyst into a defensive position of relying too much on theoretical constructs. The imposition of theory can result in the creation of pseudo-facts instead of the observation of clinical facts, and these pseudo-facts are fabrications of the analyst rather than an evolution of analytic facts in the process of the analysis.

I shall now present some sessions with a patient to show how I actually conceptualised her material. I shall start with her first session and then continue with material from some years later. I have singled out the experience of hope as the linking point between both pieces of material.

Ms A

I saw this patient twice before starting the analysis. She was in her mid-thirties, had a degree in economics and had been working for some time as a financial consultant to her family's companies. I formed the impression that she was a very ill woman. She is single. She comes from a landed family, and runs a farm which belongs to them, close to London, where she spends a lot of time devoted to animals – dogs, cats, birds and some horses and ponies. Her animals are not kept for profit. From what she said I deduced that her training in economics allowed her to manage her farm very well, but her description of her work made me think that she was probably living out obsessional defences which appeared most strikingly when she spoke about her animals. The family was often abroad, and sometimes as a child she was separated from her parents. She went to boarding school from her early years. She was knowledgeable about analysis and seemed to have read extensively.

She was not forthcoming about her reasons for seeking analysis, but said she had been advised by a friend of the family. Her principal complaints were a total lack of friends and her intense involvement with her animals. There was something evasive and secretive when she spoke about her animals, even though she gave details about her riding. I remember thinking about a possible perversion, though I inferred it more from tone and nuance than from facts explicitly narrated. She expressed a strong desire to be 'like other people', and she repeated this several times in a way that conveyed considerable despair.

On entering the room for the first session, Ms A impressed me by her elegance and gracefulness. She was two minutes late, saying immediately that she was late because 'she' was not like those 'eager people', making it clear how much she despised those 'eager people'. She knew about using the couch and lay down on it with what appeared great difficulty and discomfort, moving continuously, sitting up, lying back again, putting one and then the other foot down on the floor, and so on.

She began speaking in a tense, hoarse voice that conveyed intense anxiety. She said (in brief) that she was very frightened that I would not understand her need for her 'routine': if she did not follow her routine she would collapse. Vaguely, she described her routine as having to do with her work on the farm and especially the animals there, and more precisely and with considerable detail she described her need to ride an exact number of hours a day. She repeated several times, with what seemed considerable urgency, her need for her routine and especially her fear that I would not understand this. She said emphatically more than once, that without her routine she would collapse. While she was speaking or soon after she stopped, I coughed.

Intensely, as if frightened, she immediately said 'She is ill,' remarking that she had noticed cough pastilles and a glass of water on my table. In a rather puzzling way, in which intense worry seemed to predominate, she said that I was weak like her grandmother. With some effort, she told me that the grandmother was weak and old, but also extremely dictatorial and very critical of Ms A's way of life. She sounded bitter and resentful. She added that her father was also weak, and expanded a bit about this, in a mixed tone of voice, containing both pain and superiority. After a while she went back to emphasise the importance of her routine.

My interpretation referred to her fear that as well as being weak, I would be very critical and domineering, wanting to impose my views without taking into consideration her own ways of dealing with her problems, 'her routine'. I reminded her of the difficulties we had in fixing the timetable (in fact I had very little flexibility). She said 'I had a dream.'

She had taken some of her animals to Austria because one of them, a horse, 'my Jon', was unwell and fresh air would be good for him. She bedded him and went skiing. She saw a man riding her horse. She stopped to tell me that under certain conditions, when a horse is not well, it is bad to ride it. She then returned to the dream: *the horse was being ridden into a half frozen lake, where he was about to be hit by an iceberg*. She finished narrating the dream here, and was silent.

After a pause I asked her if she had any thoughts about the dream. With a voice that sounded strangled by anxiety, she said firmly that she did not think the horse was herself. After this she fell silent.

To consider what has taken place in the session so far, I first observed an elegant and graceful young woman who expressed with some haughtiness her superiority to other people while at the same time conveying a high level of anxiety. I noted how proper and careful she was in her speech, while at the same time her playing with her feet seemed to express something very different. Though she was careful in telling me about the importance of her routine and her doubts about me, she took a risk in doing so. But my coughing frightened her, reminded her of what she had already noticed, and I became a transference object whom she felt to be bad, weak, critical and dictatorial: I became in her mind an analyst who would not understand the importance of her symptom and was possibly too weak to take it on board. In other words a negative transference came to predominate over what at the beginning seemed a more mixed or oscillating one.

After my interpretation, two very important feelings came to the fore: hopefulness and fear of coldness. In the dream, and by bringing it, she was expressing hope. My first interpretation made her feel me to be less dictatorial, which in turn felt a bit more hopeful, but she had already expressed first her doubts and then her bad feelings about me. These feelings linked in my mind with her fears of coldness, the iceberg in the dream. Already her hopes were shown by her bringing herself to the analysis, and taking the horse in the dream to Austria. Yet the way she had pronounced part of my name on the telephone (Mrs R*ic*enberg) indicated her fear of encountering here not just a cold person, but someone possibly even more dangerous than that, a dictatorial me. In the dream, the horse who is unwell and has been taken to Austria to be made better is in danger of being hit by an iceberg. What I am describing is rather rapid movements of states of mind, resulting from splitting between objects and her relationships with these objects. Thus through her projective identifications, I became for her one or the other side of the split.

I have reported her reactions to me and how she seemed to experience me. I will now turn to observations that impinged on my mind, such as the disparity between her appearance and articulateness on the one hand, and what I would call her 'feet language', a disparity that at that time made me sense that though she tried to look very well behaved, she probably was rebellious, provocative or something else quite contradictory to her genteel behaviour. While aware of all this, I was also aware of the intensity of her feelings about what she called her routine. With the routine on the one side and her responsiveness to my intervention on the other I thought that another type of split was operating as well: a split between her as a functioning woman (the competent economist) and something much less integrated, probably held together by her routine. With not much evidence other than my intuition, I also kept thinking of something perverse, linked to her animals. As can be seen, I have been treating her dream and her behaviour as interrelated, and thinking about this first dream in the analysis as a scenario of her internal world. It should be noted that I could get no associations to the dream, and I felt that she was depositing it in my lap. (I will return to this below.)

I will now return to the session. My interpretation referred mainly to her hope in coming to analysis – Austria in the dream – and her fear of encountering someone cold (the iceberg). After my intervention she was silent, and then said, 'I can deal with what you said, but my animals, especially my horses, are most important to me, I call them "my boys".' At this point I felt quite puzzled. After a pause she said that I probably knew that Austria was where the Vienna Riding School is. Again after a pause, and appearing very uncomfortable, she said that when she was a child at boarding school, where she felt lost and lonely, she had an imaginary horse whom she called Lucifer, and whom she would summon to mind at any time, especially at night in bed, and this gave her immediate relief. I will stop here for we were near the end of the session.

I think that several things emerged from this material. My interpretation seemed to bring a shift and she felt hopeful, but very quickly she appeared to become disappointed, as if feeling that another aspect of herself was being neglected. She said she 'could deal' with what I said, that is, she appeared to understand it, and that I had understood part of her dream, but she seemed rapidly to put it aside and to feel that I had neglected something else, represented by her beloved horses. My conjecture was that she seemed to feel that my neglect of some aspect of her was so important and intensely disappointing that it turned me again into someone different, this time not cold and dictatorial, but an object not really interested in her and her feelings, more concerned with imposing norms of good behaviour and achievement: the prancing horses of the Vienna Riding School. Thus another aspect of her internal objects emerged.

Third, I thought that Lucifer was important, for he expressed a need or belief in someone magical and exciting who could provide an immediate gratification. Of course Lucifer could be thought of in different ways, but at this point it linked in my mind with her having deposited her dream on my lap. I thought she had a desire for an object that could provide, by itself and at once, what she needed. I thought this was linked with the issue of frustration: I wondered about her capacity to tolerate frustration, as I knew from her history that she had probably suffered much of it. In this context I thought about impatience, and whether it would prove to be a problem. I thought that she felt the dream should be dealt with at once by me, in the same way as Lucifer made her feel well at once.

A first session is a unique situation, which in itself could be thought of as a special 'clinical fact'. It is a new situation for both participants, each of whom brings a different set of expectations, both conscious and unconscious. An important aspect is that by the first session a decision has been taken implying that a commitment has been made by both patient and analyst. This is true even if the analysis does not last more than one session. This commitment precipitates, especially in borderline patients, an intense involvement with the analyst from the very beginning.

In the first session, with the kind of patient I am speaking about and to a lesser extent with all patients, this commitment often telescopes into something like a tableau or moving picture in which much of the patient's internal world appears at once or in quick succession, thus providing vivid information about the patient's way of relating and functioning. I think this can be seen in the material I have presented: there was in her responses to me a quick movement that seemed to indicate a continuous oscillation in the way she experienced her objects. She felt me to be someone who could listen, and in spite of her doubts she felt hopeful that eventually I might understand her and her routine. But almost immediately she felt me to be a bad and critical object. When I spoke, this experience of me seemed to change again and she could bring the dream. As I interpreted her dream, she felt I understood her and she could 'deal' with (take in?) what I said; but very rapidly she was assailed by doubts, experiencing me as being a bad object who acted superficially and ignored important feelings. She seemed to wish to encounter in me an omnipotent object, able to deal quickly with what she had reported as one of her main problems, loneliness. Hope and disappointment seemed to come to her in quick succession; she desired a good object, but no sooner had she allowed herself this feeling than she felt disappointed, and the object became bad.

Underlying my understanding of this material are Melanie Klein's (1935, 1940, 1946) concepts about the phenomena of the depressive and paranoid-schizoid positions, Bion's (1963) movements between PS↔D, and Joseph's (1989) work in bringing together theory and technique in following these movements in detail. As I conceptualise the clinical situation, Ms A moved from depressive feelings of hope and optimism to more paranoid feelings of suspicion. In these movements I, as the emerging transference object, kept changing. I interpreted the transference from the moment I began to understand it.

The following clinical material is from the fourth year of Ms A's analysis. During these years the analysis has been stormy and difficult. Soon after the beginning the patient stopped lying down; she sat on the couch, mainly facing the wall. There were intense swings between mania and depression in the sessions; she was histrionic and communicated a great deal by action.

At the time of the sessions I will now consider, she had decided to delegate the running of the farm and to give up her activities as financial consultant so as to go back to university to take a further degree in a specialised branch of economics. I had learned that there were considerable difficulties in her relationship with her family, and that she felt very lonely. She suffered from severe insomnia, and was in constant fear that she would not be able to sleep. She was addicted to all kinds of devices, some very bizarre, to make herself sleep (but would not take prescribed medication). It also emerged that she practised a perverse kind of masturbation which took place in relation to her animals and that she felt very ashamed and abnormal because of it. The masturbation occurred mainly when she was very anxious and afraid that her mind was fragmenting, which she referred to as her brain being 'mashed'. Also important during these three years were her intense problems in separation; weekends were especially difficult for her and holidays a major problem. She tended to break down shortly before the holiday period but during the holiday time itself she more or less coped, though precariously.

I will now present three successive sessions in which the patient's intense reaction to hope was at the centre of our work. Then I shall go on to conceptualise what I thought was going on, and link them with the theoretical bases of my thinking.

In a Monday session, unusually for her, Ms A spoke about the weekend not having been bad at all; she had some guests at the farm, and she mentioned her wish to be able to be friends with them. She had also gone to a dinner party where she met someone with whom she had been at boarding school. This woman, also an economist, was studying for a Ph.D., and she spoke in some detail about these events. (While she was speaking a fragment of a session from some time back came into my mind: vaguely I remembered something to do with a dream about a shattered glass, and her response to my interpretation when she had said, with intensity, 'Does this mean that I can get better?') Now I interpreted that she felt pleased with these events, and that she seemed hopeful about the analysis helping her. She responded optimistically about her plans and expectations. This soon changed. First in a patronising, sharp way she said that 'not everything was solved' for her and then added, in a bitter tone, that the woman seemed to be all sorted out, she was married, had children, looked happy and had no problems.

She seemed to have preserved a good relationship with me over the weekend, and this allowed her to think about friendship and be hopeful on her return. In other words, her life and internal world could be repaired. But these feelings also seemed to bring to the fore a sense of impatience, and mockery of the 'her' that could feel hopeful. She then split herself; the hopeful her was projected into me while she sided with the her who mocked hope (she had spoken to me as if I had gone over the top) and was rivalrous with the woman with whom she compared herself. In other words, by projecting into me the more constructive aspect of herself, she could avoid temporarily the awareness of the conflict which had been intensified by a mixture of hope and impatience. Because of these schizoid defences her arrogance increased and she felt internally impoverished. (The woman had everything, not she.) My interpretation was mainly about her conflict and her perception of me, because of the projections.

The following day she came looking agitated and was very explosive. She started the session humming to herself, and, almost shouting, she said that she had a virus: she did not like her life, she did not like her family and did not like her house. Any attempt of mine to say something was met with a barrage of scorn. I tried to speak to her about her reaction to having felt somehow hopeful the previous session but she interrupted before I could end the sentence and she mocked bitingly, by mimicking an imaginary analyst speaking about 'a typical negative therapeutic reaction'. She became very abusive, bombarding me, and I found it difficult to think. After a time, she stormed out and left before the end of the session. It was only after she left the session, when I could think more clearly, that I realised that I had missed a crucial point. This was that the virus she had was *hope*, and no sooner was hope felt than it triggered intense impatience and a wish for an instantaneous solution: house, family and life should already have changed.

The next day, Wednesday, Ms A telephoned exactly at her usual two minutes into the session to tell me that she was unwell and therefore could not come.

On Thursday she came in and sat down, looking serious and rather sad. Then with a fleeting smile she said 'I don't want you to think that I am pensive and gloomy.' After this she remained silent for sometime. I said that I thought that she did want me to know that she might be thinking about what had happened between us on Tuesday. She looked alert and expectant but said nothing. After a pause I went on to say that on Tuesday she had spoken about a virus which seemed to me to have been hope, but that the hope-virus made her ill with burning impatience, expecting everything to be changed at a stroke. I added that when I had spoken about hope she felt that *it was I* who had the hope, and that *I* had then felt very disappointed when she told me that not everything was solved; and she believed that because of my frustration I had started to accuse her, accusations to which she responded with her tirade about negative therapeutic reaction. Finally I said that I thought that she seemed not to have heard that I was not talking about her bombardment, but about her hopefulness.

After this interpretation, she mumbled something about its having been her fault. After some brief interchange, she went on to tell me what had happened since the previous session. She spoke about the amount of 'substances' she had taken which had made her ill and caused her to vomit.

She had woken from a dream in which her nanny, with a voice that was not her nanny's, was saying that she had to die, better to die or that she was going to die. (Her nanny is an important person in her life, more like a governess than a nanny, and she remains a close family friend.) After waking up, she vomited. In the morning, though she tried, she could not remain in bed, got up and kept pacing up and down. She then spoke about the rest of the morning. I asked her what voice the nanny had in the dream, and she replied 'the voice of a horse,' adding after a short pause, 'but you know that horses do not talk.'

From the beginning of this session she seemed to me to be different: thoughtful and more reachable, as if something in her had shifted. Still, she seemed to want me to start speaking, possibly as a reassurance that I was friendly to her. For whatever reasons, she seemed to come with a feeling of me as a better object, but I thought such feeling was still precarious. Once I spoke, reminding her of and clarifying to her what I thought had happened in the previous session, she became more open to my interpretations about her conflict and her projections into me. Following this she could bring further material about how difficult it was for her to hold on to good experiences: when she felt something good she also felt guilty because of what she did; she had mentioned that it was her 'fault', and this guilt seemed to be so intolerable that it made her intensify her attacks. (I will come back to this below.)

The dream seemed to indicate the kind of object I had become in her mind (represented by the nanny). It was a mixed object. It was mercilessly accusing and condemning. It was a persecuting, cruel object. It was also the voice of someone she loved (the horse, and the nanny) but it was in addition 'voiceless', that is, the object had lost its capacity to help. By becoming such a persecuting object I had lost my analytic capacity, represented by the voice.

My interpretation was directed to the facts of the previous session, which had made her feel that I had lost my understanding voice and had become totally condemning, thus leaving her hopeless. After my interpretation she went back to talk about the previous day and how frightened she had been by all the substances she had ingested. She continued describing how agitated she had been and how finally in the afternoon she had gone riding in an attempt to feel better. But this time her riding did not help and she felt terribly anxious. After a while she had started feeling 'sexed' in relation to the horse. She tried desperately to stop herself from feeling like that by trying to think about what was going on. But her attempts did not work and she ended by having sex with the animals. She was very upset while telling me this, ended by saying 'disgusting is it not?' and sounded very harsh with herself and very pained.

I now want to describe how I conceptualised this material while away from the patient during the process I have called homework. This kind of thinking is predominantly conscious, and brings together conceptualisations formed during sessions with more systematic theoretical thinking.

The experience of hope belongs to the depressive position, that is, to the experience with objects felt to be whole, for whom the patient cares and by whom he feels protected. Here Klein's ideas (1935, 1940) about the depressive position are central to my thinking, and help me to understand my patient's difficulties with hope. Hope is an affect that depends on the patient's capacity to maintain relationships with good internal objects. The patient recognises dependence on those objects and accepts the fact that they can provide mental substance for him. The more secure the relationship, the more capable of hope the person is. When the patient is well established in the depressive position, and for some reason or other this relationship is disturbed by hostile feelings which result in attacks on his good objects, the patient will tend to feel guilty. The capacity to sustain hope will depend on the degree of his destructiveness and on his capacity to tolerate guilt. It will also depend on the extent of help available from his external object. When this fails the patient feels that he has lost his good objects and may feel that he has lost hope as well. This leads to despair.

The patient I am speaking of had reached the depressive position; she could have a relationship with a whole object, but in a very precarious way, as splitting processes kept taking place which made her quickly retreat again. She was not yet able to re-establish and maintain a more integrated level of mental functioning. She had in the past managed to cope by developing a pathological organisation. Her obsessional defences (her 'routine') and her perverse masturbatory activity enclosed a more troubled part of herself, felt to be split into different parts. The trouble and anxieties caused by the feeling of being split (splitting that had been used by her to attack her object and her own perceptions) increased her anxieties, making her resort to further splitting, this time of a more fragmentative nature, to defend herself from the consequences of her previous splitting activities. The organisation confined the fragmentation and permitted her to split herself into more whole aspects of herself and thus to protect a more capable and functioning self. But her functioning was very limited and she could not tolerate guilt, waiting or dependency: the impact of any of these feelings drove her to resort to massive schizoid manoeuvres which left her persecuted and threatened the precarious functioning of her organisation. Three years of analysis had also affected her way of reacting and had weakened her defences, but I cannot go into this here.

In the first session on the Monday it was clear that she had kept a better relationship with her internal object, which allowed her to feel hopeful. At first she was friendly in the transference, but then she became impatient, probably stimulated by my presence. Fear of being overwhelmed by impatience may have led her to project her impatience into me as her internal object who was then felt to be unrealistically impatient, and since she had projected herself into me I was in possession of everything.

How is the Tuesday session to be understood? I think her projections into me had partially failed so that she was left feeling persecuted, and her behaviour in the session aimed to evacuate these feelings. During the session I failed to take them in a more containing way, that is, to make more sense of them and transform them sufficiently so that they could make sense to her, but my thinking during the session was not clear enough (at moments I felt it difficult to think at all) and was probably affected by the intensity of her bombardment. It is possible that when I tried to talk to her, especially when I was not clear enough about what was going on, she perceived my talking as trying to push her projections back into her. I also think that she felt so powerful in her bombardment that my attempts to speak to her felt false, as if I was a pretend analyst.

The material in Thursday's session permits speculation about what had happened on Wednesday when Ms A missed her session and acted out. The pressure in her mind must have felt unbearable. She wakened from a nightmare, the content of which greatly upset and frightened her, and she felt compelled to expel whatever she had in her mind (concretely she vomited). This did not seem to relieve her sufficiently and she remained agitated. She tried to use her habitual obsessional defence, the routine riding. She also tried to regain some contact with a thinking object (we had been familiar in the analysis with her feeling that she experienced me as thinking and wanting her to think, and her often declaring that she would not do so). This defence also failed. The masturbatory activity probably served partly as a discharge, and partly as a means of encapsulating her sense of disintegration. This seemed to have been more effective.

The object that appeared in the dream was a very complex one. Its most immediate characteristic is of someone that threatens her with death, or recommends death to her. In the first instance it is a hostile condemning object, because guilt about her behaviour has turned into horrible persecution. Despite this persecution she managed to keep contact with feelings of guilt, as seen in the Thursday session when she responded to my interpretation by saying 'So it was my fault.' This object is also a loved object: she loves the nanny, and she loves her horses, and she remembered in the session that she sometimes had complained that her nanny was not very effective. The horses too are often elements in her masturbation. So possibly the object in the dream is also a perverse object, since it invites her to a false solution – death or mindlessness – which she acts out instead of coming to the session. I think it is possible that when I could not get through to her on Tuesday she might also have felt me to be pretending.

On Wednesday, when her riding did not help her, she tried to think, but could not. In desperation she turned to a perverted masturbation, in a final attempt to arrest the fragmentation which she felt to be so threatening. The masturbatory activity brings to mind Freud's (1911–37) descriptions of delusions as an attempt at cure. For this patient masturbation was felt to be the only thing she could do at that moment. In the session on Thursday she was more accessible and I think this was partly due to the success of her masturbatory activity. She could then tell me what had happened, and could work with me to try to understand the meaning of the masturbation which always distressed her so much.

It is difficult to demonstrate the unconscious process of conceptualisations bit-by-bit, as part of it happens unconsciously. I think that it occurs at the point where a meaning starts to emerge in the analyst's mind from many disparate elements. For instance, pieces of observation, aspects of the patient's history, and the emotional responses of the analyst, the thoughts that come into his mind, be they directly connected with what the patient is saying or apparently unconnected to his actual discourse but referring to it: an example of this latter element was the memory I suddenly had in that Monday session of her having said some time back 'so I can get better', an aspect of her analytic history which at that moment emerged in my mind. Eventually these elements cohere into a configuration which derives from and is made sense of by one's theory. At times, of course, we simply sense something which our intuition, informed by theory, tells us is important; but it may take a long time before we can achieve some understanding of it.

Summary

In this paper I have described and illustrated the theory which helps me to decide what is a clinical fact and to conceptualise it. It is through our theory that we perceive and understand in analysis, and through our conceptualising that we can contribute further to our theories.

Notes

CHAPTER 2

1 Sandler and Sandler (1984: 384) address themselves to the problem of at which level the conflict should be interpreted. They say:

> This problem disappears if we direct our interpretations of conflict to the here-and-now, guided by what we assess to be the predominant affect as shown in the material (and also often in one way or another in the countertransference). Because the patient's conflicts are always related to the present, it is the current form that is important; their origin in the past unconscious is of secondary concern, a matter to be dealt with for reconstruction accumulates.

As can be seen, I am very much in agreement with their viewpoint, though I think I would place more importance on the role of the internal objects in the conflict and in its expression.

2 Because of the need to condense the presentation, the interpretations tend to appear to be longer than they really were.

3 Reconstruction and its place in analytical work has been a recurrent theme in analytic literature; for example, Sandler *et al.* (1973), Blum (1980), Brenman (1980).

CHAPTER 4

1 It would appear that his psychoses had prevented the establishment of a barrier that could act through repression rather than the continuous mad state. Repression in this case would have permitted an awareness of present past and future.

CHAPTER 5

1 This paper first appeared before John Steiner's (1993) book *Psychic Retreats*. The problems I address here are in the same area as Steiner's more encompassing and systematic study of pathological organisations.

2 In my paper 'The Mirror: a perverse sexual fantasy in a woman seen as a defence against psychotic breakdown' (Chapter 1 of this book), I describe in detail a perversion that protected the patient from breaking down. There are similarities between some aspects of both patients, though the problems addressed by each of them are different.

3 During the exposition of Mr K's analysis and of the problems that arose in it, I mentioned many examples of counter-transference reactions, feelings, or acting out. In explaining the difficulties in terminating such an analysis, I expanded on some specific counter-transference responses. I want to conclude the subject of counter-transference by mentioning what I think was my greatest block in perception. This was not Mr K's sado-masochistic behaviour, but the fact just mentioned, namely that most early contacts were perceived as painful, and this pain was immediately turned into sexual experience. When finally I could see this, my first reaction was a mixture of dismay and disgust. A colleague from another country, whom I supervised in the treatment of a similar patient, also went through the same difficulties and reactions. I wonder if this could express such a twist in the relation to the object that the predominance of destructive impulses, be they reactional or primary, is so intense that it becomes almost indigestible for the analyst. While I realise that my comments on this last point are not sufficiently illustrated in the material I have presented, they are very difficult to describe in an account of sessions. However speculative, they are worth consideration.

CHAPTER 9

1 It is interesting to note that he was only partially right in his quotation from the *Symposium*. In the dialogue between Socrates and Aristophanes there is a mention of complete beings that are separated and a relationship is spoken about, but the 'sorrow' in this context was added by the patient.

Bibliography

Abraham, K. (1924) 'A short study of the development of the libido, viewed in the light of mental disorders', in *Selected Papers of Karl Abraham* (1927) London: Hogarth Press, 418–501.
Bion, W. R. (1957) 'Differentiation of the psychotic from the non-psychotic personalities', *International Journal of Psycho-Analysis*, 38: 266–75; reprinted in *Second Thoughts* (1967), London: Heinemann; and also in E. B. Spillius (ed.) (1988) *Melanie Klein Today*, vol. 1, London: Routledge.
——(1962) *Learning from Experience*, London: Heinemann.
——(1963) *Elements of Psycho-Analysis*, London: Heinemann.
——(1965) *Transformations*, London: Heinemann.
Blum, H. (1980) 'The value of reconstruction in adult psychoanalysis', *International Journal of Psycho-Analysis*, 61: 39–52.
Brenman, E. (1980) 'The value of reconstruction in adult psychoanalysis', *International Journal of Psycho-Analysis*, 61: 53–60.
——(1985) 'Hysteria', *International Journal of Psycho-Analysis*, 66: 423–32.
Britton, R. (1998) *Belief and Imagination: Explorations in Psychoanalysis*, London: Routledge.
Britton, R. and Steiner, J. (1994) 'The selected fact or an overvalued idea', *International Journal of Psycho-Analysis*, 75: 1069–79.
Deutsch, H. (1942) 'Some forms of emotional disturbance and their relationship to schizophrenia', *Psychoanalytic Quarterly*, 11: 301–21.
Eissler, K. R. (1953) 'The effect of the structure of the ego on psychoanalytic technique', *Journal of the American Psychoanalytic Association*, 1: 4–143.
Freud, S. (1911) *Psycho-Analytic Notes on an Autobiographical Account of a Case of Paranoia (Dementia Paranoides)*, in the Standard Edition (SE) of *The Complete Psychological Works of Sigmund Freud*, London: Hogarth Press (1950–74) 2.
——(1893–5) *Studies on Hysteria*, SE 2.
——(1915) 'Instincts and their vicissitudes', SE 14: 109–40.
——(1917) 'Mourning and melancholia', SE 14: 237–58.
——(1920) *Beyond the Pleasure Principle*, SE 18: 7–64.

Bibliography

——(1923) *The Ego and the Id*, SE 19: 12–66.
——(1926) *Inhibitions, Symptoms and Anxiety*, SE 20: 87–175.
——(1930) *Civilization and its Discontents*, SE 21: 59–145.
——(1937) 'Constructions in analysis', SE 23: 255–69.
Gill, M. (1982) *Analysis of Transference*, vol. 1, NewYork: International Universities Press.
Glover, E. (1933) 'The relation of perversion formation to the development of reality sense', *International Journal of Psycho-Analysis*, 14: 486–504.
Isaacs, S. (1939) 'Criteria for interpretation', *International Journal of Psycho-Analysis*, 20: 148–60.
Joseph, B. (1985) 'Transference: the total situation', *International Journal of Psycho-Analysis*, 66: 447–54.
——(1989) *Psychic Equilibrium and Psychic Change: Selected Papers of Betty Joseph*, M. Feldman and E. B. Spillius (eds), London: Routledge.
Klein, M. (1935) 'A contribution to the psycho-genesis of manic-depressive states', in *Contributions to Psycho-Analysis*, London: Hogarth Press, 282–310.
——(1940) 'Mourning and its relation to manic-depressive states', in *Contributions to Psycho-Analysis*, London: Hogarth Press, 311–38.
——(1946) 'Notes on some schizoid mechanisms', in M. Klein, P. Heimann, S. Isaacs and J. Riviere (1952) *Developments in Psycho-Analysis*, London: Hogarth Press, 292–30; also in *The Writings of Melanie Klein*, vol. 3 (1975) London: Hogarth Press, 1–24.
——(1952) 'The origin of transference', in *The Writings of Melanie Klein*, vol. 3 (1975) London: Hogarth Press, 48–56.
——(1954) 'Envy and gratitude', in *Envy and Gratitude and Other Works* (1957) London: Hogarth Press, 176–235.
——(1958) 'On the development of mental functioning', in *The Writings of Melanie Klein*, vol. 3 (1975) London: Hogarth Press, 236–46.
Laplanche, J. and Pontalis, J. B. (1973) *The Language of Psycho-Analysis*, London: Hogarth Press.
Plato, 'Symposium', in *The Collected Dialogues*, Bellinger Series LXXI (1961) Princeton NJ: Princeton University Press.
Riesenberg-Malcolm, R. (1973) 'Das Werk von Melanie Klein', in *Die Psychologie des 20 Jahrhunderts* (1974) Zurich: Kindler Verlag.
Riviere, J. (1936) 'A contribution to the analysis of the negative therapeutic reaction', *International Journal of Psycho-Analysis*, 17: 304–20.
Rosenfeld, H. (1965) *Psychotic States: A Psycho-Analytic Approach*, London: Hogarth Press and the Institute of Psycho-Analysis.
Ross, N. (1972) 'The as-if concept', *Journal of the American Psychoanalytic Association*, 15: 59–81.
Sandler, J. (1983) 'Reflections on some relations between psychoanalytic concepts and psychoanalytic practice', *International Journal of Psycho-Analysis*, 64: 35–45.
Sandler, J., Dare, C. and Holder, A. (1973) *The Patient and the Analyst*, London: Maresfield Reprints.
Sandler, J. and Sandler, A. M. (1984) 'The past unconscious, the present unconscious and analysis of the transference', *Psychoanalytical Inquiry*, 4: 367–99.

Segal, H. (1957) 'Notes on symbol formation', in *The Work of Hanna Segal* (1981) New York and London: Jason Aronson.

——(1967a) 'The curative factors of psycho-analysis', *International Journal of Psycho-Analysis*, 43: 212–17.

——(1967b) 'Melanie Klein's technique', in *The Work of Hanna Segal* (1981) New York and London: Jason Aronson.

——(1973) *An Introduction to the Work of Melanie Klein*, London: Hogarth Press and the Institute of Psycho-Analysis.

Spillius, E. B.(ed.) (1988) *Melanie Klein Today*, vols 1 and 2, London: Routledge.

Steiner, J. (1984) 'Some reflections on the analysis of transference: a Kleinian view', *Psychoanalytical Inquiry*, 4: 443–63.

——(1987) 'The interplay between pathological organizations and the paranoid-schizoid position', *International Journal of Psycho-Analysis*, 68: 69–80.

——(1993) *Psychic Retreats*, London: Routledge.

Strachey, J.(1934) 'The nature of the therapeutic action of psychoanalysis', *International Journal of Psycho-Analysis*, 15: 127–59.

Wallerstein, R. (1984) 'The analysis of the transference: a matter of emphasis or of theory reformulation?', *Psychoanalytical Inquiry*, 4: 325–54.

Winnicott, D. W. (1960) 'Ego distortion in terms of true and false self', in *The Maturational Processes and the Facilitating Environment* (1965) London: Hogarth Press.

Yeats, W. B. (1927) *The Tower*, in *Collected Poems* (1965) London: Macmillan.

Index

Abraham, K. 2
acting self 146–7
agoraphobia 81–2
ambivalent feelings 63, 64, 73, 173, 177
analyst-mother object 26–7, 28–9, 35, 40, 42–3, 107
anxiety, origin of 54–5
archaic object-relation pattern 39, 51, 54, 72, 181
as-if personality 125–7, 132–6; behaviour in analysis 125, 131, 133; case studies 126, 127–32, 135
audience 147–8

Bion, Wilfred 4, 15, 59, 64, 101, 126; containment 1, 12, 33, 62, 73, 161, 177; 'minus K' 133; 'reversible perspective' 93, 94, 127, 129, 132–4; 'selected fact' 179–80; 'transformation in hyperbole' 137, 138–9, 148
'borderline phenomenon' 150
breast 28, 33–4, 35, 133
Britton, R. 4; and Steiner, J. 179
bulimia 170, 171

clinical facts 181–3; case studies 183–93
communication: projective identification as 39–40; transference as 38, 39, 43
construction: case studies 74–6, 77–9, 79–82; and interpretation 71, 72–3; and reconstruction 71–2
containment 1, 12, 62, 73, 161, 177; and containing 33

'contaminated object' 173
counter-transference 40, 73, 88, 89, 90, 165, 176–7; case study illustration 77–9

defences: against dependency 114, 122, 123–4; against envy 135; against guilt 87–8; against psychosis *see* sexual perversion; past and present 40, 52; projective identification as 42, 43; splitting as 55–6
dependency, defences against 114, 122, 123–4
depressive position 5–6, 63, 64, 65, 73–4, 131; hope 191; shifts 169, 177, 178, 187; sorrow 154
Deutsch, Helene 125
dream interpretation: as-if personality 129, 130–1, 132, 134; construction 80–1; hysterical personality 142–3, 144; internal object conflict 46–50, 184, 186; perverse sexual fantasy 19–20, 22–3, 24–31; projective identification 175–6; pseudo-compliance 115, 119–20, 121, 122; resolution 159–60; self-punishment 96, 107–9

ego 54–61; destruction of 29, 32; divided 65; preservation of 32, 36; reconstruction of 17, 32; strengthening of 63
Eissler, K.R. 111

Index

emotional responses to patient 43, 168, 182 *see also* counter-transference
encopresis 74, 82
envy 35, 49, 50, 133, 134–5, 170, 178, 179
eroticisation *see* sexual perversion
excitement 34–5
extreme control 98–102
eyes in projective identification 20–1

false self 126
falsely idealised object *see* idealisation
fragmentation: of internal object (mother-analyst) 26–7; of the object (analyst) 24–6; secondary 27–9
fragmentive-evacuative processes 114
Freud, Sigmund 2, 6, 32, 137, 153, 193; on construction 72; on ego and superego 53–4, 56–7, 57–8, 59, 60; on hysteria 139–40; on separation anxiety 150–1

Gills, M. 39
Glover, E. 94
guilt 64, 65–6, 67–8, 73, 87–8, 190, 191; and hyperbole 139, 140; *see also* self-punishment

'here-and-now' of analytic situation 38, 41, 169–70
hope 191
hostility 55, 56, 57, 61–2, 100–1, 170, 173
hyperbole *see* hysteria
hypochondriacal symptoms *see* somatization
hysteria 137–8, 139–40, 145–9; case studies 139, 140, 141–5, 147

idealisation 89, 106–7, 114–15, 117, 118, 126, 175; of self 119
infant development theory: Bion 132–3; Klein 2–4, 6–7, 54–6, 72, 73–4, 131; Winnicott 126
inner world 2–3, 57
insomnia 116, 117–18
integration 63
intelligence 35
internal objects 2–3; conflicts 44; and superego 54, 57, 59–60, 70; unresponsive 42–3, 148
interpretation: and construction 71; descriptive summaries 103; neutralised 127–9, 131; 'slicing' 129, 133–5; 'too deep' 44, 51; unsuccessful 115–17; *see also* dream interpretation; transference, interpretation of
introjection 55, 56, 57, 58, 60
Isaacs, S. 39

jealousy 19–20
Joseph, Betty 6, 92, 150, 153, 177, 187; on transference 39

Klein, Melanie: infant development theory 2–4, 6–7, 54–6, 72, 73–4, 131; 'memories in feeling' 72; superego 54–5, 57, 58–9, 60; theory of mind 54–5, 176–7, 187; transference 39

Laplanche, J. and Pontalis, J.B. 56–7
love and sadism 32, 33, 48

masochism *see* self-punishment
maternal pathology 133, 134–5
maternal relationship 49–50, 57, 63–4, 106–7; containment 1, 12, 33, 62, 73, 161, 177; transference in analysis 26–7, 28–9, 35, 40, 42–3, 107
maternal 'reverie' 40, 73, 133
'memories in feeling' 72
'minus K' 133
Mirror fantasy: acting out in transference 21–3; and fragmentation 24–9; interpretation 29–37; and promiscuity 17–18; and work situation 18–19
misunderstanding object 172

observing self 146
Oedipus Complex 35, 63, 115, 122, 171; resolution 53, 60
'overvalued idea' 179

pain, case study 151–4, 158, 161–2
panic attacks 49, 50
'parameters' 111–12
paranoid-schizoid position 3–4, 63, 73, 131; pain 151, 158, 161–2; shifts 169, 177, 178, 187; in transference 5, 6
parental relationship *see* Oedipus Complex
pathological organisation 93, 131; case studies 87–9, 191
Pontalis, J.B. *see* Laplanche, J. and Pontalis, J.B.

200

Index

pre-verbal experiences 72, 76
'present unconscious' 169, 181–2
projective identification 4–5; and attack 73, 104–5; as communication 39–40, 42, 43, 62, 177; as defence 42, 43, 56, 175; and introjection 55, 56, 58; Mirror fantasy 35–6; psychotic 75, 76; role of eyes 20–1; in sexual promiscuity 17–18
pseudo-compliance: case study 113–22; discussion 122–4
psychosis 59; case study 74–6; defences against *see* sexual perversion
psychotic transference 96–8

re-introjection 101
'reconstruction' 52, 71–2
repetitive themes 98–9, 102, 103
resolution, case study 158–61, 162
'reversible perspective' 93, 94, 127, 129, 132–4
Riviere, J. 110
Rosenfeld, H. 4, 177
Ross, N. 135

sadism 17, 122; and love 32, 33, 48
sado-masochism 88, 114
Sandler, J. 39, 169, 181–2
Segal, H. 4, 6, 92, 147
'selected fact' 179–80
self-punishment 93–5; case study 95–110; discussion 110–12
separation anxiety 119–20, 150–1, 154–5, 158–60, 161
sexual perversion 94, 111, 188, 190, 192–3; fantasies 188, 190, 193; *see also* Mirror fantasy; sadism; sado-masochism
sexual promiscuity 17–18
sexuality of object 24–6
'slicing' 129, 133–5
somatization 27, 78, 131–2; pain, case study 151–4, 158, 161–2
sorrow 154–5; case study 155–8, 162

split-off parts *see* projective identification
splitting 55–6, 73, 118, 122, 172–3, 191; and 'slicing' 129, 133–5
stagnation 102–10
Steiner, J. 6, 92, 131, 161, 162, 178; and Britton, R. 179
Strachey, J. 39, 54, 59, 60, 65, 70
superego 53–61; case studies 61–2, 64, 65–9, 70; development and fluctuations 62–9; and internal objects 54, 57, 59–60, 70; representations in fantasy 34
'symbolic equation' 147
'symbolic language' 51

terminating analysis 105–6, 109–10
theory of mind 170, 182–3; Kleinian 176–7, 187
'total transference' 6
transference 5, 6–7; acting out in 21–3, 122–3; as communication 38, 39, 43, 50; interpretation of 40–1, 44, 47, 48, 168–9, 176–80, case study 170–6, 179–80; mother-analyst 26–7, 28–9, 35, 40, 42–3, 107; phases 114–15; psychotic 96–8; *see also* construction; counter-transference
'transformation in hyperbole' 137, 138–9, 148

unconscious phantasies 2–3, 6, 43–4; talking about vs experiencing 51
unresponsive objects 42–3, 148

verbal mannerisms 41–2, 50
violence 100–1

weekend separation 47, 97, 141–2, 143, 172, 173, 177–8
Winnicott, D.W. 126
work situation and fantasy 18–19